George Eliot and the Visual Arts

George Eliot and the Visual Arts

HUGH WITEMEYER

New Haven and London
Yale University Press
1979

Designed by Sally Harris
and set in IBM Press Roman type.
Printed in the United States of America by
The Murray Printing Company, Westford, Mass.

Published in Great Britain, Europe, Africa, and
Asia (except Japan) by Yale University Press,
Ltd., London. Distributed in Australia and
New Zealand by Book & Film Services, Artarmon,
N.S.W., Australia; and in Japan by Harper & Row,
Publishers, Tokyo Office.

Library of Congress Cataloging in Publication Data
Witemeyer, Hugh.
  George Eliot and the visual arts.

  Includes bibliographical references and index.
  1. Eliot, George, pseud., i.e. Marian Evans,
afterwards Cross, 1819–1880–Knowledge–Art. I. Title.
PR4692.A66W5   823.'8   78–15580
ISBN 0–300–02281–6

For Sharon

As it is, you are a bright picture in my memory, like Raphael's St. Catherine, and I assure you I give you a high place among influences when I range you with pictures.

—*George Eliot to Martha Jackson*

George Eliot's mind is like the National Gallery; for every canvas on display there are two stored away in the basement.

—*W. J. Harvey*

Contents

Illustrations

Acknowledgments

This book has incurred many obligations in the making. E. D. H. Johnson planted the first seed in his graduate seminar on Victorian fiction at Princeton University and subsequently nurtured the project with his generous advice and support. Professor L. D. Ettlinger of the University of California at Berkeley initiated me into the study of art history and has continued to provide the warm personal counsel which distinguishes all of his teaching. I am deeply grateful to Professor Ettlinger and his wife Helen for their friendship, their hospitality, and the use of their personal library. I am no less indebted to Professor Gordon S. Haight, the founder of modern George Eliot studies. Without Professor Haight's scholarship, the research for this book could not have been undertaken; without his interest and patience in answering inquiries, it could not have been completed.

From other scholars I have also received much valuable assistance. I wish especially to thank David Bindman, Ralph Bogardus, Anthony Burton, Lawrence Evans, Barbara Hardy, Francis Haskell, Ingeborg Krueger, George Landow, John Duncan Macmillan, John Murdoch, Leonée and Richard Ormond, John Pratt, Bernard Richards, Howard Rodee, Christopher Salvesen, Norma Jean Davis Saunders, Richard Stein, and William Vaughan for offering me their perspectives on my subject and their suggestions for research. For their encouragement and material assistance I am likewise grateful to Jerome Beaty, Layeh Bock, George Bornstein, Douglas Gray, Madeline Jay, U. C. Knoepflmacher, Jacob and Cynthia Korg, A. W. Litz, Jr., Ruth

Mateer, John Norton-Smith, Morton Paley, Thomas Parkinson, Lois Potter, Michael Steig, and Alexander Welsh. Among my friends and colleagues at the University of New Mexico, I owe a great deal to Bill and Linda Dowling, Morris Eaves, David and Susan Jones, Jim and Connie Thorson, Hoyt and Margery Trowbridge, Carole Yee, and Joe Zavadil. All of these counselors have helped this book come into being, but none of them is responsible for its errors and omissions.

Two generous fellowships—one from the American Council of Learned Societies and one from the National Endowment of the Humanities—have facilitated the research for this study. I am grateful to the personnel of both agencies and to the staffs of the following libraries, who have extended an unfailing courtesy: the British Library, Reference Division; the National Art Library, Victoria and Albert Museum; the Senate House Library, University of London; the Witt Library, Courtauld Institute; the Royal Academy Library, Burlington House; Westfield College Library, University of London; the Bodleian Library, Oxford University; the University of Washington Library; Stanford University Library; and the Beinecke Rare Book and Manuscript Library, Yale University. The Beinecke Library has allowed me to quote from four unpublished journals of George Eliot housed in its collection.

The editors of two journals have granted me permission to reprint essays that originally appeared in their pages: "George Eliot, Naumann, and the Nazarenes," *Victorian Studies,* 18 (1974), 145–58; and "English and Italian Portraiture in *Daniel Deronda,*" *Nineteenth-Century Fiction,* 30 (1976), 477–94. And I am particularly obliged to F. H. M. FitzRoy Newdegate of Arbury Hall for providing photographs of Lely's portraits of Sir John Skeffington and Mary Bagot, for identifying the sitters, and for permitting the photographs to be reproduced here.

Abbreviations

In the following study the six sources most often cited are identified by abbreviations, many of them incorporated directly into the text. All quotations of George Eliot's novels come from the Cabinet Edition (Edinburgh and London: William Blackwood and Sons, 1877–80), which remains the most useful collected edition until the completion of the Oxford University Press edition now in preparation under the supervision of Gordon S. Haight. Citations comprise chapter and page numbers; thus (16:270) refers the reader to chapter 16, page 270 in the Cabinet Edition of the novel under discussion. The standard editions of George Eliot's letters, essays, and principal biographies are designated by the following abbreviations:

Letters *The George Eliot Letters,* ed. Gordon S. Haight, 7 vols. (New Haven and London: Yale University Press, 1954–55)

Essays *Essays of George Eliot,* ed. Thomas Pinney (London: Routledge and Kegan Paul, 1963)

Cross John Walter Cross, *George Eliot's Life as Related in Her Letters and Journals,* Cabinet Edition, 3 vols. (Edinburgh and London: William Blackwood and Sons, 1885),

Haight Gordon S. Haight, *George Eliot: A Biography* (New York and Oxford: Oxford University Press, 1968)

In the citations of these sources, volume numbers are identified by Roman numerals; thus (*Letters,* III, 128) refers the reader to page 128 in the third volume of Haight's edition of the letters. All quotations of Ruskin come from *The Works of John Ruskin,* ed. E. T. Cook and Alexander Wedderburn, Library Edition, 39 vols. (London: George Allen, 1903–12), identified here simply as *Works.*

1 Introduction

"'Vermilion, saffron, white' is a brilliant stroke (that is a lie, so to speak, of Lessing's that pictures ought not to be painted in verse, a damned lie—so to speak)."[1] The critic is Gerard Manley Hopkins, expressing his admiration not only for a line of R. W. Dixon's but also for literary pictorialism in general. "Wordpainting is, in the verbal arts, the great success of our day," Hopkins told Robert Bridges; ". . . wordpainting is in our age a real mastery and the second rate men of this age often beat at it the first rate of past ages."[2] Hopkins was celebrating an assimilation between the Victorian arts of literature and painting which other contemporary observers also noted with approval. Henry James remarked that "we have invented, side by side, the arts of picturesque writing and erudite painting," and Aubrey Beardsley spoke with clever paradox of "story painters and picture writers."[3] James and Beardsley were alluding to the reciprocity of influence which impelled authors toward the picturesque as it drew painters toward the narrative and literary.[4] Baudelaire concisely summarized the working sisterhood which he saw everywhere among the contemporary arts in 1863: "one of the diagnoses of the spiritual condition of our century is that the arts aspire, if not to substitute for one another, at least to lend each other new strengths."[5]

We know from the popularity of literary illustration that the Victorian audience liked to "see" its fiction, and novelists catered to the same taste by providing abundant visual description. Conrad was only reiterating a commonplace of Victorian aesthetics when he said that the "task which I am trying to achieve is, by the power of the written word, to make you hear, to make you feel—it is, before all, to make you *see.*"[6]

No writer supplied the demand for word-painting more successfully than George Eliot, whose early work capitalized brilliantly upon the popular fancy for Dutch, Flemish, and English genre pictures. The identification of her novels with such painting, which she herself encouraged in chapter 17 of *Adam Bede,* persisted in the public mind long after her pictorialism had extended its scope and diversified its effects. "The popular notion about the excellence and brilliancy of the style of George Eliot's novels is that it is simply the excellence of a painter like Teniers," observed the *Saturday Review* in 1866; and as late as 1876 a reviewer of *Daniel Deronda* was still parroting the old praises of "the exquisite cabinet pictures to which George Eliot has accustomed us."[7] The stereotype was inappropriate, not because Eliot had ceased to present cabinet pictures in *Daniel Deronda,* but because the novel contains so many other pictures that are more important: literary portraits arranged in sophisticated thematic patterns, landscapes and architectural paintings representing a natural and historical order with which the characters have lost touch, ironic conversation pieces where the apparent happiness of the family group is belied by the absence of the unlawful father. In her later work George Eliot's pictorialism moves well beyond what the *Saturday Review* described as the "photographic reproduction of the life of midland dairies and farm-houses and apple-orchards."[8] The complexity of her pictorial effects anticipates the art of Henry James.

Eliot herself considered word-painting to be one of the two main branches of the novelist's art. The other she called dramatic presentation, while G. H. Lewes called it dramatic ventriloquism.[9] Description is indispensable to the novel precisely because fiction is not drama seen in a theater. According to Lewes, "the fact that in the novel the persons are *described* instead of being *seen,* renders it necessary that the author should supplement as far as possible this inferior vividness of presentation by a more minute detail, both physical and moral."[10] Description, then, supplies the visual dimension of the drama which is otherwise missing to the reader in his closet. Thus Lewes praised Mrs. Gaskell because her *Life of Charlotte Brontë* "paints for us at once the psychological drama and the scenic accessories with so much vividness" (*Letters*, II, 315).

It follows that failure to describe is a fault in a novelist, as Lewes argued in a little-known passage of his essay on "The Novels of Jane Austen" that has important implications for George Eliot's art. Austen, Lewes charged, skimps on visual detail:

> So entirely dramatic and so little descriptive is the genius of Miss Austen, that she seems to rely upon what her people say and do for the whole effect they are to produce on our imaginations. She no more thinks of describing the physical appearance of her people than the dramatist does who knows that his persons arc to be represented by living actors. This is a defect and a mistake in art: a defect, because, although every reader must necessarily conjure up to himself a vivid image of people whose characters are so vividly presented; yet each reader has to do this for himself without aid from the author, thereby missing many of the subtle connections between physical and mental organisation.

This last phrase betrays Lewes's bias toward a physiognomical reading of human appearance. He goes on to complain that in *Pride and Prejudice* Jane Austen does not sufficiently describe Mr. Collins.

> As far as any direct information can be derived from the authoress, we might imagine that this is a purblind world, wherein nobody ever saw anybody except in a dim vagueness which obscured all peculiarities. It is impossible that Mr. Collins should not have been endowed by nature with an appearance in some way heralding the delicious folly of the inward man. Yet *all* we hear of this fatuous curate is, that "he was a tall heavy-looking young man of five-and-twenty. His air was grave and stately, and his manners were very formal." Balzac or Dickens would not have been content without making the reader *see* this Mr. Collins. Miss Austen is content to make us *know* him, even to the very intricacies of the inward man. It was not stated whether she was shortsighted, but the absence of all sense of the outward

world—either scenery or personal appearance—is more remarkable in her than in any writer we remember.[11]

This essay appeared in the same year as *Adam Bede* (1859) and echoes chapter 17 of that novel. We may assume that George Eliot agreed with Lewes's demand for full-fledged literary portraits that include a physical description of external appearances.[12] She certainly took care to render such appearances in *Adam Bede,* as we shall see.

Modern readers are not likely to lament the paucity of physical description in Jane Austen's work. The reality that interests us in fiction is psychological, behind the eyes. In our pursuit of the psychological we tend to skip the descriptive passages in nineteenth-century novels.[13] Although modern criticism pays lip service to the idea that George Eliot balances the objective and the subjective, in practice most critics are interested in her exclusively as the great fountainhead of the modern psychological novel. "Her overriding concern," writes Barbara Smalley in a recent and representative study, "is not as with earlier novelists personality as it performs its drama in the outer world. . . . Her memorable portrayals are all studies of action that goes on inside the minds of her characters."[14]

Such a perspective is achieved only by shutting out a whole order of representation that George Eliot was careful to build into her fiction. Similarly, the recent studies of "vision" in Eliot's work tend to neglect its pictorial aspects and to stress instead a moral-psychological growth-pattern with correlations in an imagery of eyes, sight, mirrors, and windows.[15] Even the critics who recognize Eliot's pictorialism are often uncomfortable with it, and characterize its effect as either sentimental and escapist, or distancing and alienating.[16] We have, then, nearly lost sight of a dimension of George Eliot's art which she and her first readers valued highly. To recover that unseen dimension is the primary aim of this study and its illustrations.

That the Victorians liked to visualize George Eliot's fiction is suggested by the vocabulary of their reviews, a good deal of which comes from painting and art criticism.[17] To be sure, such borrowing is often a symptom of poverty, mere dead metaphor and desperate

cliché revealing only that Victorian literary criticism still lacked a
sophisticated terminology of its own. But surprisingly often the
figures of speech reflect a genuine re-viewing of the book in question. For example:

> When we have passed in review the works of that great writer
> who calls herself George Eliot, and given for a time the use of
> our sight to her portraiture of men and women, what form, as
> we move away, persists on the field of vision, and remains the
> chief centre of interest for the imagination? The form not of
> Tito, or Maggie, or Dinah, or Silas, but of one who, if not the
> real George Eliot, is that 'second self' who writes her books, and
> lives and speaks through them.[18]

So strong was Edward Dowden's habit of visualizing novels that he
could even "see" George Eliot's narrator. It is a habit we no longer
cultivate, partly because we distrust its subjectivity and partly because we have come to rely upon the cinema to picture our novels
for us. Although vestiges of the old painterly vocabulary linger in
our criticism,[19] it is probably impossible for us fully to recapture the
Victorian sense of the literary text as a visual field.

A shift in modern taste is, however, taking place. Criticism today is
more receptive to the nineteenth-century interchange among the arts
than it has been at any time since the modernist revolution of 1908–
14. The sensibility which has brought representational art back into
fashion has also prompted a renewal of interest in mainstream
nineteenth-century painting. Art historians are resurrecting Victorian
pictures from the neglect into which they sank in the first half of the
twentieth century, and we are finally learning to look at the salon
work of the bourgeois romanticists and realists with something more
than amused contempt. For its part, literary criticism is far more
willing to entertain connections between the arts than it was only
ten or twelve years ago, when formalistic explication of the text was
the dominant method of literary interpretation. The trend in recent
criticism has been to put literature back into touch with other
intellectual disciplines—without, however, losing sight of what
formalism taught us about the integrity of individual works of art.

But there is still no general agreement about what constitutes a valid method in studies of literature and the visual arts. When is it legitimate to assert that a passage or an entire work of literature resembles a picture or a school of painting? The approaches used in recent studies range from the suggestive intuition of a common style among the arts of a given period (the method of Mario Praz and Wylie Sypher) to the detailed analysis of literary rhetoric that is carefully arranged to evoke the reader's pictorial experience (the method of Jean Hagstrum).[20] Given the variety of procedures available, any new study of the sister arts is obliged to declare its method at the outset.

This study starts from the premise that correspondences based only on what Mario Praz has called the *"air de famille* . . . between the expressions of the arts in any given epoch of the past" are seldom to be trusted.[21] Although the calligraphy of the *Zeitgeist* is doubtless visible everywhere in the artistic productions of a given era, the comparison of specific works from different media is likely to seem arbitrary and capricious unless the critic can provide some historical evidence of a connection between them. As Bernard Richards has said,

> Once the critic has abandoned the guidelines of what poets and painters actually saw and read, he is in a wide-open and chaotic country, and there comes a point at which he is resorting to the 'soul adventuring among the masterpieces' approach. . . . A study of inter-relations in the arts looks slightly more valid when one follows the lines laid down by the artists themselves and pursues 'influences' from the other arts or the pervasive spirit of the times which they acknowledged and believed in.[22]

This is sensible advice. The present study attempts to associate George Eliot's work primarily with pictures and pictorial traditions which she knew. At a few points, most prominently, perhaps, in the discussion of typological symbolism, the parallels that are asserted depend more upon an intuition of the spirit of the age than upon any documentary evidence. But for the most part I have tried to verify influences before asserting them. For this reason, the first two chapters of the study seek to establish just what George Eliot did know and like among the visual arts.

A distrust of intuitive methods also makes me hesitate to transfer terms derived from the stylistic history of art to the analysis of literary style or structure. To say that a literary work is written in a Mannerist or Biedermeier or Impressionist style almost always obscures more than it clarifies. The media of the two arts are so different that terms which are useful in the analysis of one usually apply to the other only by a courtesy of metaphor.[23] Often such terms are used to denote similarities of subject matter or sensibility rather than style. For example, when Praz applies the term *Biedermeier* to the work of a number of nineteenth-century English writers, he generally means either bourgeois domestic subjects or a pious-sentimental-humorous mode of regard. He is seldom referring to any specifically pictorial qualities in the literature he cites.[24]

Claims of pictorial influence should be reserved for circumscribed literary passages whose language demonstrably evokes the reader's experience of the visual arts. "In order to be called 'pictorial,'" Jean Hagstrum writes, "a description or an image must be, in its essentials, capable of translation into painting or some other visual art . . . its leading details and their manner and order of presentation must be imaginable as a painting or sculpture."[25] In other words, the pictorial consists of visual imagery ordered in certain ways. Not all visual imagery is pictorial, and not all passages which mime the processes of visual perception are pictorial.[26] To be connected with the visual arts, a passage must overtly recall (1) an identifiable work of art, (2) a tradition of graphic or plastic representation, or (3) an established convention of pictorialist rhetoric such as the formal character-portrait. The critic renders better service by explicating the local pictorial meanings of an author's language than by flying off in search of grand stylistic equations.

Literary pictorialism in the finite sense just outlined has a venerable history. As Hagstrum has shown, it came over into written literature from the oral traditions of rhetoric, and appears in the earliest surviving Greek poetry and prose fiction.[27] Pictorialism was a prominent feature of the English novel from its inception, and was especially well established in the Fieldingesque branch of the tradition which came to George Eliot through Scott.[28] Eliot transformed that inherited pictorialism, as she transformed traditional characterization, by raising it to an unprecedented level of complexity and sophistication. No novelist in English before her used pictorial devices so extensively, so diversely, or so subtly; and no major novelist after her was unaffected by her achievement. Henry James learned as much from her in this regard as he did in others, and his techniques in turn influenced those of many twentieth-century novelists.

This study of George Eliot's pictorialism will begin with a biographical chapter surveying her knowledge of art, artists, and the literature of art. The next two chapters will characterize her taste in painting and sculpture and discuss the role of painting in her theory of the novel—her version of the traditional doctrine of *ut pictura poesis*. These backgrounds having been fixed, the remaining chapters will focus upon the actual uses of painting in her fiction, examining the four principal genres that she loved to re-create: portraiture, sacred and heroic history painting, genre painting, and landscape. These chapters will find their unifying theme in George Eliot's Ruskinian emphasis upon accurate naturalistic representation as a medium of moral and spiritual vision. Particular novels or stories will be discussed in conjunction with the genres of painting that have colored them most distinctively. The penultimate chapter presents an interpretation of Frederic Leighton's illustrations of *Romola*, the only novel of George Eliot's to be illustrated in its first edition.

This book aims to challenge, on George Eliot's behalf, a claim made for Thomas Hardy by Alastair Smart: "It is questionable whether any other English novelist, with the possible exception of George Moore, possessed so intimate a knowledge of the visual arts; certainly no other writer of fiction has ever used such knowledge with equal skill or imagination."[29] Without denying Hardy's knowledge or skill, we may affirm that in neither capacity did he surpass George Eliot, his mentor in pictorialism no less than in pastoralism. To support Eliot's claims, we turn first to the question of her knowledge.

2 George Eliot's Knowledge of the Visual Arts

"George Eliot's mind is like the National Gallery; for every canvas on display there are two stored away in the basement."[1] W. J. Harvey's simile for the contents of George Eliot's mind in general aptly summarizes her knowledge of painting in particular. She had a wide acquaintance with pictures and artists. From the time she received her first illustrated book and painted her first water colors of floral arrangements, she had an abiding interest in the visual arts.[2] The record of that interest is unusually full, thanks to the many surviving letters and journals which describe her experience of painting and sculpture. Only in the cases of Thackeray and Henry James are we as well informed about the pictorial knowledge and tastes of a major Victorian novelist.[3]

There are gaps in the record, of course. We can never know the names of all the pictures, statues, and exhibitions that Eliot saw. To begin with, the record of the early years in London was partially destroyed by J. W. Cross, who removed from George Eliot's journal forty-six pages covering the years 1849–54 (Haight, p. 71). Cross's folly sadly restricts our view of an especially formative period in Eliot's life. Furthermore, although her travel journals for the period 1854–65 have survived, the journals for subsequent trips, such as the visit to the Prado during a tour of Madrid in 1867, are sketchy or missing altogether. Then, too, Eliot did not regularly record her reactions to the paintings she saw at home in London. For our knowledge of her London experience, we must depend upon chance references in her letters. Finally, she had no cause to note down all the prints, engravings, and book illustrations that enriched her daily life.[4]

Yet despite these omissions a substantial amount of information remains. We can reconstruct in surprising detail the novelist's attendance of galleries and exhibitions in London, her visits to museums on the Continent, her personal contacts with painters, and her reading in the literature of art.

In his account of George Eliot's last years, Cross reports that "she was in the habit of going with me very frequently to the National Gallery, and to other exhibitions of pictures, to the British Museum sculptures, and to South Kensington" (Cross, III, 343). This habit was of long standing; in fact, George Eliot had frequented the museums, galleries, and exhibitions of London from the time she first settled there in 1851 (Haight, p. 103). Each spring she liked to attend the exhibitions of the Royal Academy and the Society of Painters in Water-Colours.[5] She also enjoyed the annual Exhibition of Pictures by Modern Artists of the French School, instituted in 1854 by Ernest Gambart at the French Gallery.[6] She visited the National Portrait Gallery and, in 1867, attended the enormous National Portrait Exhibition at the South Kensington Museum, now the Victoria and Albert (*Letters*, IV, 37, 362–64). She saw the memorial exhibitions of William Mulready's collected works at South Kensington in 1864 and of Frederick Walker's at the Deschamps Gallery in 1876.[7] Naturally she attended the one-man shows of her friends Barbara Leigh Smith Bodichon at the French Gallery in 1859 (*Letters*, III, 124, 128) and Edward Burne-Jones at the Grosvenor Gallery in 1877 (*Letters*, VI, 365). Among the smaller London museums, George Eliot visited the Dulwich Gallery in 1859 and the newly opened Bethnal Green Museum in 1872.[8] And in 1868 she and George Henry Lewes made a trip to Leeds to see the great National Art-Exhibition, held for the benefit of the new Leeds Infirmary.[9]

In addition to these public displays, George Eliot was invited to a number of artists' studios and private collections. She saw the studios of Frederic Leighton, William Holman Hunt, G. F. Watts, Dante Gabriel Rossetti, Edward Burne-Jones, and Mrs. William

Allingham.[10] Of the notable private collections in London, Eliot knew at least two: B. G. Windus's famous collection of Turners in Tottenham, which she saw in 1850, and Alfred Morrison's collection at Carlton House Terrace, which she saw in 1872 and again in 1874.[11]

From this record we may infer that George Eliot was a devoted student of pictures during her thirty years in London. She was familiar with the city's major permanent public collections and several of its most important private ones. She kept abreast of new work by attending the annual spring exhibitions and by visiting the studios of working artists. She took a serious and continuing interest in painting, finding in it a perennial source of pleasure and intellectual stimulation. Rarely did she feel uninspired "after seeing pictures" (*Letters,* II, 155).

In *Daniel Deronda* George Eliot's narrator speaks with authority of "the galleries of Europe" (38:298). The novelist knew them well from a series of holidays and working visits to the Continent between 1854 and 1867. During most of these trips she wrote detailed accounts of the cities, museums, and individual works of art she saw. After she returned to familiar surroundings, her journals served to refresh her memory of visual experiences that she cherished and wished to retain. In later years she turned to these records for material to use in her novels. Five visits to the Continent are particularly well documented: 1854-55, 1858, 1860, 1864, and 1865.

The first of these trips was the elopement with G. H. Lewes. The lovers traveled through Antwerp, Frankfurt, and Düsseldorf to Weimar in the autumn of 1854. In Antwerp they saw Rubens's *Elevation of the Cross* and *Descent from the Cross* in the Cathedral, and they visited the art museum (Cross, I, 269-70). In Düsseldorf they toured the Städel Museum (Haight, p. 151). From Weimar they went to Berlin, where during the winter months they visited the Old and New Museums and three private collections: Graf Raczinsky's, Consul Wagner's, and the Ravené Collection. They met Wilhelm von Schadow, the famous Nazarene painter and director of the Düsseldorf Academy, and Gustav Friedrich Waagen, the great art historian. They saw two private studios as well: those of Edward Magnus, the portrait painter, and Christian Daniel Rauch, the sculptor. George

Eliot recorded these first experiences of modern German art in a notebook entitled "Recollections of Berlin" and drew upon them many years later when describing Dorothea Brooke's honeymoon in *Middlemarch.*[12]

The Leweses returned to Germany in the spring and summer of 1858. During this working vacation George Eliot was completing *Adam Bede.* She and Lewes stayed mainly in Munich and Dresden, with shorter visits to Nüremberg, Prague, Leipzig, and Vienna. George Eliot was a conscientious tourist in each city, visiting most of the best-known churches and art collections. Thus in Munich she came to know both the Old Pinakothek and the New, the Glyptothek, and the other public buildings of King Ludwig's Bavarian renaissance. She also made the acquaintance of the famous art patron, Baron Schack, and visited the studios of Wilhelm von Kaulbach and Buonaventura Genelli (Cross, II, 15-37, and *Letters,* II, 450-55). In Dresden the Leweses spent many hours in the new Gemäldegalerie, which had opened in 1855.[13] The paintings they saw there affected them powerfully, and are mentioned throughout their subsequent writings.[14] The picture-gallery in Leipzig they noted chiefly for Alexandre Calame's Swiss landscapes (Cross, II, 51). In Vienna they saw the "magnificent collection of pictures at the Belvedere" and paid two visits to the Liechtenstein collection (Cross, II, 43), which became the setting for an important scene in "The Lifted Veil" (1:303).

After these travels in the German-speaking countries, the Leweses turned their attention to France, Italy, and Spain. George Eliot visited Paris in 1859, 1860, 1861, and 1864, acquainting herself with the Louvre and Luxembourg museums (Haight, pp. 293, 322, 343, 376). Three of these Parisian holidays broke journeys to Italy. The *italienische Reise* of 1860 was a grand affair. From Paris she and Lewes proceeded southward to Turin, Milan, Pisa, Rome, and Naples. Returning northward, they stopped at Florence and Siena. Florence especially interested them "from its relation to the history of modern art" (*Letters,* III, 299). After two weeks there, they went on to Bologna, Padua, and Venice. Then they came home via Verona, Milan, Como, and Geneva. It was, George Eliot told John Blackwood, her "first journey to the greatest centres of art."[15] During this tour of Italy, Eliot conceived *Romola* and gathered some of the material she was to use in the Rome chapters of *Middlemarch*.

Eliot returned to Florence in the spring of 1861 to do research for *Romola*. She kept no journal of this visit, but we know from her correspondence and from *Romola* itself that she was particularly concerned with paintings of late fifteenth-century faces and costumes such as Ghirlandaio's frescoes in the choir of Santa Maria Novella.[16] After finishing *Romola,* she went to Italy once more—this time accompanied not only by Lewes but also by Frederic Burton, the watercolorist who was to become director of the National Gallery (Haight, p. 376). Avoiding Florence altogether, the party traveled straight to Venice via Paris, Turin, and Milan, and stopped at Padua, Verona, and Brescia on the return. George Eliot's unpublished journal of the tour, entitled "Italy 1864," contains interesting notes on the paintings she saw in each city.[17] In Venice especially, she was an indefatigable visitor of museums, churches, and palazzi. It was probably on this trip, as Gordon S. Haight has suggested, that she saw in the Scuola di San Rocco the *Annunciation* by Titian which later inspired *The Spanish Gypsy* and *Daniel Deronda.*[18]

In the summer of 1865 the Leweses took their vacation in Normandy and Brittany. The journal of this holiday is rich in observations of regional architecture.[19] Then in 1867 the Leweses made their longest trip ever, a ten-week journey to Spain during which they visited San Sebastián, Barcelona, Granada, Córdoba, Seville, and Madrid. In Madrid they went every day to see the pictures at the Prado. Unfortunately, George Eliot's journal of the trip has been lost, so we do not know which of them impressed her most.[20] Similarly sketchy are the records of her last two visits to Italy in 1869 and 1880.

Between 1854 and 1867, then, George Eliot visited many of the most important "galleries of Europe," grounding her knowledge of European painting and sculpture in a firsthand acquaintance with the major collections and masterpieces. Her experience of the visual arts was at any rate not insular.

In addition to her knowledge of art works, George Eliot had many friends and acquaintances who were artists. In her early years at

Coventry, there were the sisters Cara Bray and Sara Hennell, both amateur painters of some talent.[21] George Eliot's first proposal of marriage actually came from a young Coventry picture-restorer in 1845. His suit failed because Marian Evans was not in love with him, and because his profession was not deemed "lucrative or over-honourable" by her friends and family (Haight, p. 56). This affair was probably the model for Maggie Tulliver's respectful rejection of the artist, Philip Wakem, in *The Mill on the Floss*. And the next painter whom George Eliot met also contributed to the character of Philip.

In 1849–50 George Eliot spent eight months in Geneva, recovering from the fatigue and depression caused by her father's illness and death. During five of those months, she lived in the family of Alexandre-Louis-François d'Albert-Durade (1804–86), a Swiss painter of portraits and scenes from Genevan history. D'Albert-Durade had studied with Joseph Hornung and married Julie Covelle, an accomplished painter of flowers. "She has hung my room with pictures," George Eliot wrote, "one of which is the most beautiful group of flowers conceivable thrown on an open Bible—painted by herself" (*Letters,* I, 314). Of M. d'Albert-Durade Eliot reported:

> I love him already as if he were father and brother both. You must know he is not more than four feet high with a deformed spine—the result of an accident in his boyhood—but on this little body is placed a finely formed head, full in every direction. The face is plain with small features, and rather haggard looking, but all the lines and wavy grey hair indicate the temperament of the artist. [*Letters,* I, 307]

For this verbal and phrenological portrait, d'Albert-Durade recipro-cated by painting an actual portrait of the writer (Haight, p. 77 and Plate IV). When he accompanied her back to England in the spring of 1850, George Eliot arranged for him to see the Windus collection of Turner's work (*Letters,* I, 332).

She saw d'Albert-Durade again in June of 1860, when she and G. H. Lewes stopped in Geneva on the return from their tour of Italy. By then the painter had become director of the Athénée Museum. He took the Leweses there and also to the studio of

Calame, the Swiss painter whose Alpine landscapes had impressed George Eliot at Leipzig in 1858. Although she never saw d'Albert-Durade again, George Eliot continued to correspond with his family, and d'Albert-Durade became the French translator of *Adam Bede* and *The Mill on the Floss* (Haight, pp. 330–33). One wonders what he thought of Philip Wakem.

An even closer friend of George Eliot's was the landscape painter and feminist, Barbara Leigh Smith Bodichon (1827–91). She was the illegitimate daughter of a Radical Member of Parliament whose father before him had been an M.P., an Abolitionist, and a Unitarian. In her youth she studied with William Henry Hunt, the famous painter of naturalistic watercolors, and visited the studio of Turner. She became an accomplished painter of landscapes in watercolor who often exhibited her work in public. Among her close acquaintances were Holman Hunt, Dante Gabriel Rossetti, Mrs. Anna Jameson, Corot, and d'Aubigny. Barbara Leigh Smith was introduced to George Eliot in June 1852, but the two women did not become intimate friends until July 1856, when they shared a seaside holiday at Tenby in South Wales. In the early 1860s they were neighbors, living only a few doors apart in Blandford Square. Barbara was probably the physical model for Romola, George Eliot's principal heroine of this period.[22]

Barbara Bodichon and George Eliot supported one another not only as friends but also as women artists. Barbara was among the first to intuit the true identity of the author of *Adam Bede* in 1859. "That is written by Marian Evans," she exclaimed; "there is her great big head and heart and her wise wide views" (Haight, p. 280). A few months later George Eliot returned these enthusiastic praises when Madame Bodichon had a one-woman show at Gambart's French Gallery: "Of course we shall go and see your pictures. . . . It is really a step to have your pictures hung together in a regular gallery where you have an illustrious predecessor."[23] George Eliot delighted in success by women artists of all kinds at the moment when her own reputation as a novelist was hanging in the balance. She especially relished a remark made during the Bodichon exhibition by the painter David Roberts: "If ever one sees a fine picture now, it is by a woman."[24]

Another painter also complimented Barbara Bodichon during the exhibition of her work. As George Eliot reported, "an artist friend of ours—Mr. F. W. Burton—a nice creature, expressed high admiration of your pictures—didn't care about the want of finish in some of them—they had finer qualities than finish—he felt they were done on the spot under true inspiration" (*Letters*, III, 128). The Leweses had met Frederic William Burton (1816-1900) at Munich in 1858. Born in Ireland, he had become a watercolorist of some distinction and a member of the Old Water-Colour Society. In 1864 he accompanied the Leweses to Venice, and later that year began a portrait of George Eliot.[25] Burton was named director of the National Gallery in 1874 and served twenty years in the position, receiving a knighthood in 1884. He remained a close friend and regular dinner guest of the Leweses.

It was probably Burton who introduced Mr. and Mrs. Edward Burne-Jones to the Leweses in 1868. A fast friendship quickly developed between the younger and older couples, particularly between the women. Through the Burne-Joneses, the Leweses soon met William Morris and D. G. Rossetti (Haight, pp. 408–09). These new acquaintances nearly completed the original circle of Pre-Raphaelites, since the Leweses had already met Holman Hunt in 1864 and Thomas Woolner in 1866 (Haight, pp. 388, 398). A list of the other artists George Eliot knew would include Charles Robert Leslie, whom she met in 1851, George Cruikshank (1852), Jane Benham Hay (1860), Samuel Laurence (1860), Frederic Leighton (1862), Rudolf Lehmann (1866), William Bell Scott (1868), George Howard (1869), George Smith (1870), Charles François d'Aubigny (1871), and George du Maurier (1872).[26] Through Barbara Bodichon she also knew George Scharf, the secretary of the National Portrait Gallery (*Letters*, IV, 13).

In addition to these personal contacts with artists, George Eliot also read regularly in the literature of the visual arts. By far her most important mentor was Ruskin. In 1856 she read and reviewed volumes III and IV of *Modern Painters.*[27] "What books his last two are!" she exclaimed to Barbara Leigh Smith. "I think he is the finest writer living" (*Letters*, II, 255). To Sara Hennell she wrote:

But I venerate him as one of the great Teachers of the day—his absurdities on practical points do no harm, but the grand doctrines of truth and sincerity in art, and the nobleness and simplicity of our human life, which he teaches with the inspiration of a Hebrew prophet, must be stirring up young minds in a promising way. . . . The two last volumes of Modern Painters contain, I think, some of the finest writings of this age. [*Letters,* II, 422-23]

George Eliot's own mind was stirred up in a promising way by Ruskin—not only by *Modern Painters,* but also by *The Stones of Venice* (1851), the first letter to *The Times* in defense of Holman Hunt's *The Light of the World* (1854), the Edinburgh *Lectures on Architecture and Painting* (1854), and the Manchester lectures on *The Political Economy of Art* (1857).[28] It is difficult to overestimate Ruskin's influence upon her theory of art and her way of looking at pictures. He will be a major figure in our study of George Eliot's pictorialism.

Another important interpreter of the arts to George Eliot was G. E. Lessing. During the winter of 1854–55 in Berlin, she read a great deal of Lessing: the *Laokoön, Die Hamburgische Dramaturgie, Emilia Galotti, Nathan der Weise,* and *Minna von Barnhelm.* In her journal she described the *Laokoön* as "the most un-German of all the German books that I have ever read. The style is strong, clear, and lively; the thoughts acute and pregnant. It is well adapted to rouse an interest both in the classics and in the study of art" (Cross, I, 303). She mentioned the *Laokoön* again in one of her *Westminster Review* essays; it was also a favorite book of G. H. Lewes's.[29] As we shall see, Lessing's argument was an important influence upon George Eliot's theory of *ut pictura poesis.*

Her enthusiasm for the *Laokoön* suggests that George Eliot viewed classical art largely through the medium of German culture. She first paid attention to Greek and Roman sculpture not in the British Museum but in the museums of Berlin and Munich, and she saw many neoclassical imitations of Greek sculpture at Weimar.[30] Besides Lessing, George Eliot read other German writers on classical art such as Adolf Stahr and Johannes Adolf Overbeck. She met Stahr in Berlin, and soon thereafter read his *Torso: Kunst, Künstler, und Kunstwerken der Alten* (1854-55) and *Ein Jahr in Italien* (1847-50). The former, she said, "feeds the fresh interest I am now feeling in art."[31] She read "Overbeck on Greek art" in Munich in 1858 (Cross, II, 21)—not Johann Friedrich Overbeck, the Nazarene painter, but Johannes Adolf Overbeck, author of *Geschichte der Griechischen Plastik für Künstler und Kunstfreunde* (1857-58).[32]

If the German writers on classical art occupied her during her travels in Germany, likewise George Eliot became interested in the history of Italian painting when she was traveling in Italy in 1860 and 1861. She studied Vasari's *Lives of the Painters* in 1861 and took her portrait of Piero di Cosimo in *Romola* from Vasari (Haight, p. 350). As preparation for *Romola* she also read (or reread) *The Poetry of Sacred and Legendary Art* (1848) and *Legends of the Monastic Orders* (1850) by Mrs. Anna B. Jameson, the great Victorian popularizer of early Christian art.[33] Other surveys of Italian painting known to George Eliot are John Coindet's *Histoire de la peinture en Italie,* which she read in Rome in 1860, and Franz Theodor Kugler's *A Handbook of the History of Painting,* which she read in Florence in the same year.[34] Along with Kugler's *Handbook,* she read the *Autobiography of Benvenuto Cellini* (Haight, p. 325) and made plans to read Hawthorne's *The Marble Faun* (*Letters,* III, 300). Earlier, she had reviewed a study of *Léonard de Vinci et son école* (1855) by Alexis-François Rio; and later, she became acquainted with Walter Pater and his *Studies in the History of the Renaissance* (1873).[35]

What remains of George Eliot's library contains a number of books on aesthetics and art history. The following list includes titles she does not mention elsewhere in her writings; the dates are those of the editions she possessed. It is impossible to know just when she acquired these books or when, if ever, she read them. But she at least owned Longinus's *De Sublimitate* (1820); Quatremere de Quincy's *History of the Life and Works of Raffaello* (translated by William Hazlitt, 1846); Sir Joshua Reynolds's *Discourses* (1825); Friedrich Schelling's *The Philosophy of Art* (1845); Karl Solger's *Vorlesungen über Aesthetik* (1829; acquired by G. H. Lewes in

1839); Richard Duppa's *Life and Works of Michel Angelo* (1846); Jean Baptiste d'Agincourt Seroux's *History of Art by Its Monuments* (1847); Ralph Wornung's *The Epochs of Painting* (1864) and his *Some Account of the Life and Works of Hans Holbein* (1867); Vincenzo Marchese's *Memoire dei più insigni Pittori, Scultori, et Archetetti Domenicani* (1854); Sir John Charles Robinson's *Italian Sculpture of the Middle Ages and Period of the Revival of Art* (1862); and Hippolyte Taine's *De l'ideal dans l'art* (1867).[36]

Clearly George Eliot had a rich experience of the visual arts. As a result of her gallery-going, her friends, and her reading, she knew a good deal about the history of European painting from Giotto and the early Italians to the realists of the mid-nineteenth century. To be sure, her horizons, like those of nearly all her contemporaries, were limited to Europe and to the conventions of Greek and Renaissance art. She disliked the Moorish decorative art she saw in Spain (*Letters*, IV, 351), and she knew virtually nothing of Far Eastern or African art.[37] If she ever heard of Impressionism and the subsequent modernist movements in France, she completely ignored them. Even on her last visit to Paris in 1880, her letters are full of the realists and genre painters: "I made some pleasant new acquaintances among the painters of French peasant life. The French, I think, succeed better in giving the true aspect of their common people, than our painters succeed in the same genre. Whom have we to pair with Jules Breton?" (*Letters*, VII, 281).

Because she always assumed that European painting was evolving toward a Ruskinian naturalism, George Eliot would have had no sympathy with those who altered and finally broke the traditional Renaissance conventions of humanism and representational illusion. We do not know precisely where she stood on the famous case of Whistler vs. Ruskin, but it seems likely that she would have found Whistler's impressionistic *Nocturnes* as incomprehensible as Ruskin did. It is easy enough for the modern reader to dismiss these mid-Victorian perspectives on art as hopelessly narrow. It is more difficult sympathetically to imagine the taste that flourished within such boundaries.

3 George Eliot's Pictorial Taste

Henry James thought that George Eliot was rather obtuse about the visual arts. When he reviewed Cross's *Life* of Eliot, James commented particularly upon her responses to painting and sculpture: "She enumerates diligently all the pictures and statues she sees, and the way she does so is proof of her active, earnest intellectual habits; but it is rarely apparent that they have, as the phrase is, said much to her, or that what they have said is one of their deeper secrets."[1] Another American, Charles Eliot Norton, judged Eliot's aesthetic sensibility even more harshly after visiting the Priory in 1869: "Indeed all the works of art in the house bore witness to the want of delicate artistic feeling, or good culture on the part of the occupants, with the single exception, so far as I observed, of the common lithograph of Titian's 'Christ of the Tribute Money'" (*Letters,* V, 8). Both James and Norton underestimated George Eliot's sensitivity to painting, but their remarks do point to some limitations which should be acknowledged at the outset of any attempt to characterize her taste in the visual arts.

Certainly George Eliot did not have a Jamesian sensitivity to plastic values. Her comments on pictures usually seem a bit wooden when one comes to them from James's. Among the sister arts she responded more deeply to music than to painting or sculpture. "I agree with you as to the inherent superiority of music," she wrote to an early correspondent; ". . . painting and sculpture are but an idealizing of our actual existence. Music arches over this existence with another and a diviner" (*Letters,* I, 247). Her taste for pictures was more self-consciously acquired, and less natively sophisticated, than her taste for music.[2] It was also relatively conventional. When she writes of history, sociology, philosophy, or fiction, George Eliot seems progressive if not avant-garde; but when she writes of painting and sculpture, she seems more orthodox, a follower rather than a leader of trends.

To admit these limitations, however, is not to say that she is superficial, as James would have it, or vulgar, as Norton suggests. In a sensibility such as George Eliot's, even conventional responses are profound and distinctive. A case in point is her reaction to Raphael's *Sistine Madonna,* her favorite painting in all the world (fig. 1). To this picture she responded as the eighteenth-century traveler did to the sublime in landscape: with awe and fear, with a sense of being overwhelmed by something greater than the mind can comprehend. "I sat down on the sofa opposite the picture for an instant," she wrote in her Dresden journal, "but a sort of awe, as if I were suddenly in the living presence of some glorious being, made my heart swell too much for me to remain comfortably, and we hurried out of the room" (Cross, II, 47). Two days later, G. H. Lewes had a similar experience; he says that he "looked at the Raphael Madonna di San Sisto, till I felt quite hysterical."[3] No superlative in George Eliot's vocabulary could do justice to Raphael's painting; it was "this sublimest picture," "the *Einzige* Madonna," "the matchless Madonna di San Sisto."[4] In the face of such ecstasy, James's charge of superficiality cannot stand. George Eliot could perceive the "deeper secrets" of pictures and could respond to them with the strongest emotions. This chapter, will explore several dimensions of her passion for pictures: her affection for certain genres, styles, and schools; her criteria of critical judgment; and her iconic use of pictures in personal meditation.

The most common misconception about George Eliot's taste is that it was limited entirely to the genre painting of the seventeenth-century Dutch masters and their nineteenth-century descendants in the sentimental line of Greuze, Spitzweg, and Wilkie. The source of this notion is the famous passage in chapter 17 of *Adam Bede* in which the narrator praises a "rare, precious quality of truthfulness

. . . in many Dutch paintings" (17:268). From this passage and several like it in *Scenes of Clerical Life,* Mario Praz derived his misleading but influential thesis about George Eliot's Biedermeier taste. But the narrator of *Adam Bede* does not programmatically exclude the other genres, and George Eliot certainly liked and used them as well. Her first love was really European portraiture, of all periods and schools. More purely than other genres, portraiture posed the problem that occupied her as a novelist: how best to represent human beings. After portraiture, she admired the sacred and heroic painting of the Italian Renaissance and of Rubens. Here she found a union of the ideal with the real that she longed to recapture in her own art. Furthermore, she loved landscape painting with a passion that combined the picturesque, the Wordsworthian, and the naturalistic modes of response. These four kinds—portraiture, history painting, genre, and landscape—figure in her fiction in roughly that order of importance.

In pictorial styles, George Eliot's tastes were distinct but not exclusive. The High Renaissance style was her favorite, but she could also appreciate the mannerist and baroque styles.[5] Her early reactions to Rubens are interesting in this connection. He was the first great painter whose work, seen in the original and in quantity, entirely captivated her. She was taken by the scale and energy of his history paintings, and by the vividness of his portraits; but she felt rather guilty about her response. From Munich in 1858 she wrote:

> Rubens gives me more pleasure than any other painter, whether that is right or wrong. To be sure, I have not seen so many pictures and pictures of so high a rank, by any other great master. I feel sure that when I have seen as much of Raffaelle, I shall like him better, but at present Rubens more than any one else makes me feel that painting is a great art and that he was a great artist. His are such real, breathing men and women—men and women moved by passions, not mincing and grimacing and posing in mere apery of passion! What a grand, glowing, forceful thing life looks in his pictures—the men such grand bearded grappling beings fit to do the work of the world, the women such real mothers.[6]

These remarks show George Eliot attracted by two different styles. On the one hand, she was culturally predisposed toward Raphael and a Raphaelite norm of beauty—classical, spiritualized, and serene. On the other hand, she could also take pleasure in the style of Rubens— baroque, fleshly, and dynamic. The preference for a Renaissance style was the dominant strain in her taste, determining her great affection for Leonardo da Vinci, Bernardino Luini, and Andrea del Sarto.[7] The inclination toward the mannerist and baroque styles was a secondary strain in her taste, governing her strong but qualified admiration of Michelangelo and Tintoretto, whose work often struck her as powerful and magnificent, but sometimes seemed merely "ugly."[8] When combined, these two aspects of her taste resulted in Eliot's curious admiration of statuesque and monumental female figures, of which we shall see several striking examples in chapter 6.

As the preceding observations suggest, Eliot's view of the historical schools and masters was fairly conventional. For her, the Italian Renaissance was the greatest period; Florence, Milan, and Venice were the greatest schools; and Raphael and Titian were the greatest masters of all time. For the "early Italians," from Giotto to Perugino, she harbored a warm affection; but she resisted the Romantic tendency to rank them, for purity of spirit, above the later Renaissance masters. Following Ruskin, she admitted to an "utter dislike of the Bolognese school" (Cross, II, 196); and she detested Guido Reni (Cross, II, 49, 88), whom she burlesqued in *Middlemarch* as "the celebrated *Guydo,* the greatest painter in the world" (60:115). Among the northern European schools, she most admired the Dutch, the German, and the Flemish. She cared less for seventeenth-century Dutch landscape than one might expect; but she was an ardent student of the genre painters, and knew the work of Vermeer, the Van Ostades, Dou, Metsu, Mieris, Terborch, Maes, Ryckaert, Teniers the Younger, and Steen (Cross, II, 49; Haight, pp. 259, 264). She loved Rembrandt for the truthfulness of his portraiture, but she did not care for his history paintings and did not rank him among the supreme masters.[9] Her favorite German painters were Holbein and Dürer, whose vivid realism fascinated her. Her passion for Rubens, though early, was abiding.

Among the later schools, George Eliot's preferences were fewer but no less strong. She was devoted to the English portrait tradition that extends from Van Dyck to Lawrence. Under the tutelage of *Modern Painters,* she also loved the nineteenth-century English school of landscape painting. And she was certainly receptive to the sentimental genre painting of her Victorian contemporaries. Her views of the English Pre-Raphaelites and their German precursors, the Nazarenes, were mixed; but she followed the work of both brotherhoods with the utmost interest. The Düsseldorf school of modern German history painting attracted her, and the monumental art of Munich and Berlin interested her; but she strongly disliked German neoclassicism in the Winckelmann tradition. To French neoclassicism and French Romanticism she paid very little attention; the French painters she knew best were those promoted in England by Gambart: Paul Delaroche, Ary Scheffer, and Rosa Bonheur.

When George Eliot looked at a picture from one of her favorite schools, what did she see? Her letters and her entries in journals suggest that she judged painting by a Ruskinian combination of moral and aesthetic criteria. These include greatness of subject, truthfulness of representation, adequacy of expression, and handling of formal elements such as color and perspective. Though indivisible in practice, these standards may be separated for discussion.

Greatness of subject or conception is a criterion of neoclassical aesthetics which persists in the thought of both Ruskin and George Eliot. It rests upon a Neoplatonic hierarchy of ideas, graduated according to their inherent nobility and running from the sacred to the profane, from the aristocratic to the vulgar, from the heroic to the domestic. Treatment being equal, the painting or poem which embodies the greater subject is to be valued more highly. As Ruskin puts it, "the habitual choice of sacred subjects, such as the Nativity, Transfiguration, Crucifixion (if the choice be sincere), implies that the painter has a natural disposition to dwell on the highest thoughts of which humanity is capable; it constitutes him so far forth a painter of the highest order."[10] Their empiricism notwithstanding, the Leweses shared Ruskin's belief. As G. H. Lewes declared in 1858:

In Art, as in Life, there is high and low, great and little; and
everything that is represented is interesting in proportion to its
truth of presentation and its objective value; a well-painted table-
cover is better than an ill-painted face; but a well-painted face,
with a noble expression, is the highest reach of art, as the human
soul is the highest thing we know.[11]

The terms "high" and "low" here reflect a value-judgment that
Lewes cannot, in the end, explain on empirical or psychological
grounds. George Eliot also applied the criterion of "objective value"
to art, often to rule out certain subjects as unfit to be represented;
"for no one," she declared, "can maintain that *all* fact is a fit subject
for art" (*Essays*, p. 146). Thus she objected to Browning's *The Ring
and the Book* because "the subject is too void of fine elements to
bear the elaborate treatment he has given to it" (*Letters*, IV, 501).
Even the famous defense of Dutch painting in *Adam Bede* does not
obliterate the distinction between high and low subjects. The narrator simply argues that there is value in the faithful representation
of vulgar subjects:

> Paint us an angel, if you can, with a floating violet robe, and a
> face paled by the celestial light; paint us yet oftener a Madonna,
> turning her mild face upward and opening her arms to welcome
> the divine glory; but do not impose on us any aesthetic rules
> which shall banish from the region of Art those old women
> scraping carrots with their work-worn hands, those heavy clowns
> taking holiday in a dingy pot-house, those rounded backs and
> stupid weather-beaten faces that have bent over the spade and
> done the rough work of the world—those homes with their tin
> pans, their brown pitchers, their rough curs, and their clusters of
> onions. In this world there are so many of these common coarse
> people. . . .[12] [17:270]

It is not quite accurate to say, as Martin Price does, that George
Eliot here "effects a transference of sublimity to the low and
ugly."[13] She is pleading for catholicity of taste and sympathy, but
not for a leveling of artistic subject matter. Eliot's narrator has

strong prejudices about the limitations of the Dutch school, as does Ruskin, whose qualified defense of Dutch art in *Modern Painters* underlies chapter 17 of *Adam Bede.* [14]

Like Ruskin, however, George Eliot preferred a low subject truthfully represented to a high subject falsely represented. By truthfulness of representation she did not mean simple mimesis or photographic realism, although she could delight as much as the next spectator in *trompe-l'oeil* effects (Cross, I, 277). Rather, she meant verisimilitude of a more psychological sort—the fidelity of the artist to his vision of the world. "We *can* say a 'truthful representation' and a 'truthful exposition,'" George Eliot maintained, "but I think the strict meaning in that case is always, that the artist or expositor has no impulse to suppress or exaggerate or falsely colour the fact as apprehended by his knowing faculties" (*Letters,* III, 144). On another occasion she declared: "I only try to exhibit some things as they have been or are, seen through such a medium as my own nature gives me" (*Letters,* II, 362). Truthfulness in this sense is mature vision sincerely rendered; its antithesis is ignorant conceit masking as reality. Darrell Mansell, Jr. describes this marriage of mimetic and expressive principles quite accurately: "George Eliot wants to produce Ruskin's very special kind of 'realism'; she wants to study the real world humbly and faithfully, and then to present the real world as it has mirrored itself in her imaginative mind." [15]

We may see the criterion of truthfulness at work in George Eliot's first confrontation with the overwhelming art of Rome. At first she found herself "thrown into a state of humiliating passivity by the sight of the great things done in the far past—it seems . . . as if my own activity were so completely dwarfed by comparison that I should never have courage for more creation of my own." But the outlook was not entirely daunting. "There is only one thing that has an opposite and stimulating effect: it is, the comparative rarity even here of great and truthful art, and the abundance of wretched imitation and falsity. Every hand is wanted in the world that can do a little genuine, sincere work" (*Letters,* III, 294). By false and imitative art, George Eliot meant art predicated upon a sentimental preconception, rather than a careful observation, of its subject. The "abundance of wretched imitation and falsity" in the Roman school caused Eliot to rank it well below the schools of Florence, Milan, and Venice. In *Middlemarch,* Dorothea too is struck by the rarity of great and truthful art in Rome, though she finds the vacuum merely depressing rather than stimulating.

To no element in a picture did George Eliot apply the criterion of truthfulness more carefully than to expression. She agreed with G. H. Lewes that "a well-painted face, with a noble expression, is the highest reach of art, as the human soul is the highest thing we know."[16] To her nineteenth-century eye, expression was the gateway to the soul, the mind, the passions, the sentiments, transmitting the invisible life through a visible language of facial and corporal signs. According to Ruskin, "the expression of the thoughts of the persons represented will always be the first thing considered by the painter who worthily enters that highest school [of art]."[17] Expression was certainly the first thing considered by George Eliot in most pictures of human figures. It was her point of imaginative entry into such paintings; if it failed, so, usually, did her sympathy for the painting as a whole. But if expression succeeded, it could redeem many flaws, as we may see in her account of Titian's *The Assumption of the Virgin* (fig. 2):

> For a thoroughly rapt expression I never saw anything equal to the Virgin in this picture; and the expression is the more remarkable because it is not assisted by the usual devices to express spiritual ecstasy, such as delicacy of feature and temperament or pale meagreness. Then what cherubs and angelic heads bathed in light! The lower part of the picture has no interest; the attitudes are theatrical; and the Almighty above is as unbeseeming as painted Almighties usually are: but the middle group falls short only of the Sistine Madonna.[18] [Cross, II, 205]

The *Assumption* is one of three works by Titian that ranked second only to the *Sistine Madonna* in George Eliot's esteem; and the other two—*St. Peter Martyr* and *The Tribute Money* (fig. 22)—she valued also for their expression.[19] Conversely, nothing infuriated her more in a painting than false—that is to say, mannered, affected, or theatrical—expression. Thus she attacked Guido Reni's work at Dresden: "Guido is superlatively odious in his Christs, in agonized or ecstatic attitudes—much about the level of the accomplished London beggar" (Cross, II, 49).

Her interest in phrenology was another manifestation of her concern for expression. Although she renounced her early faith in phrenology as a science, she never entirely abandoned physiognomical premises in her descriptions of people, paintings, and fictional characters. Because they relate physical appearance to character, phrenology and expression give painting a border with the literary arts, whose special province is the representation of the inner life.

When she shifted her attention from representational to more purely aesthetic considerations, and analyzed the formal elements of a painting, George Eliot used an uncomplicated vocabulary. She mainly noticed "form," meaning composition; "color," which included lighting; "perspective"; and "finish." She was not as sensitive as Henry James was to some of these formal properties, but she was certainly not indifferent to them either. Fully to satisfy her, a painting had to excel in several respects. Rubens's *Deposition* in the Antwerp Cathedral, for example, received high marks in nearly all of the principal categories: "colour, form, and expression alike impressed me with the sense of grandeur and beauty" (Cross, I, 270). Similarly, at Munich she liked "a very striking 'Adoration of the Magi,' by Johannes van Eyck, with much merit in the colouring, perspective, and figures" (Cross, II, 27). As a rule she preferred finished pictures, which eliminate the traces of brushwork and labor, to unfinished ones, which proclaim their materials and making.

These preferences and standards of judgment were part of George Eliot's conscious culture, matters of study and carefully worded declaration. But Eliot also perceived pictures in a way that was less judicious and more intimate than any discussed so far. She liked to hold pictures in her memory, and to contemplate them as reminders of absent persons or places whom she loved intensely. In other words, she used pictures as icons in personal meditation, to focus and sustain her affections. "But I remember you very vividly," she wrote to one friend, "and if I were a painter I could make a sketch of you still, either under the bowering trees of your garden, or on your drawing room sofa with the vase of flowers before you"

(*Letters,* III, 449). In *Romola* the heroine commissions a posthumous portrait of her father "lest his image should grow dim in her mind"; the icon is to assist her in performing "the duties of memory" (28:389).[20]

This art of memory has its origins in the Christian tradition of meditation, and is a secular analogue of that religious practice. In Christian meditation, the devotee recreates and relives a scriptural or exemplary scene in his imagination, the better to grasp an underlying doctrinal truth. Icons, effigies, skulls, and the like may be used to assist the spiritual exercise; but the ultimate aim is a vivid inward seeing in which the will and the emotions are strengthened and directed toward right values. As Louis L. Martz has shown, meditative disciplines were widely practiced by Catholics and Protestants alike from the seventeenth century onward.[21] George Eliot's grasp of the tradition appears in her account of Dinah Morris's preaching, which relies upon the rhetorical equivalent of meditative picturing:

> "See!" she exclaimed, turning to the left, with her eyes fixed on a point above the heads of the people—"see where our blessed Lord stands and weeps, and stretches out his arms towards you. . . . See the print of the nails on his dear hands and feet. Ah! how worn and pale he looks! [2:40]

Savonarola's preaching in *Romola* employs the same rhetorical technique (12:191). Daniel Deronda explains the rationale of meditation to Gwendolen as follows:

> Fixed meditation may do a great deal towards defining our longing or dread. We are not always in a state of strong emotion, and when we are calm we can use our memories and gradually change the bias of our fear, as we do our tastes. . . . Try to take hold of your sensibility, and use it as if it were a faculty, like vision." [36:268]

George Eliot grew up in this Christian tradition, and retained its habits long after she rejected Christian theology. Paradoxically, religious meditation solaced her for her loss of religious faith. According to Cara Bray, when Marian Evans was translating Strauss's *The Life of Jesus, Critically Examined,* "she said she was Strauss-sick—it made her ill dissecting the beautiful story of the crucifixion, and only the sight of her Christ-image and picture made her endure it" (*Letters,* I, 206). Gordon S. Haight reports that the "Christ-image" was a small cast of Thorwaldsen's figure of the resurrected Jesus, and the "picture" was the popular Blanchard engraving (1844) of Paul Delaroche's *Savior* or *The Head of Christ.*[22] In other words, even as she was crucifying Jesus anew, "dissecting" and burying him for the last time, George Eliot found emotional solace in contemplating images of his resurrection and triumph. Her habits of meditation survived her renunciation of Christian theology, and continued in a secularized form to nourish her emotional life.

Secularized meditation substitutes friends for saints and experienced scenes for legendary ones in its affectionate imagining.[23] Traces of this transference from saints to friends sometimes linger in the similes Eliot uses to describe her remembrances: "As it is, you are a bright picture in my memory, like Raphael's St. Catherine," she wrote to an absent friend in 1845, "and I assure you I give you a high place among influences when I range you with pictures" (*Letters,* I, 188). If the original purpose of meditation was to bestow a phenomenal reality upon sacred subjects, George Eliot's meditations reverse that process and bestow a sacredness upon phenomenal experience. To Barbara Bodichon she vowed: "I will call you only Barbara, the name I must always associate with a true, large heart. Some mean, treacherous Barbara may come across me, but she will only be like a shadow of a vulgar woman flitting across my fresco of St. Barbara" (*Letters,* III, 119). This habit of imagining friends in terms of pictured saints exactly parallels, and perhaps gave rise to, George Eliot's fictional device of describing her heroines as saints and madonnas.

As for setting, the elaborate "composition of place" prescribed by most manuals of meditation yields in humanistic spiritual exercises to memories of actual places. For example, George Eliot composed a place when she wrote from London to her friends in Coventry: "I hope my imagination paints truly when it shows me all of you seated with beaming faces round the tea-table at Rosehill" (*Letters,* I, 292). So graphic was her memory of people and places that Eliot sometimes rejected the aid of actual pictures as more likely to blur than to sharpen her mental image. "My inward representation even of comparatively indifferent faces is so vivid," she wrote, "as to make portraits of them unsatisfactory to me" (*Letters,* VII, 233).

She applied her remarkable powers of visual memory to works of art as well as to people. Cross recalled her "limitless persistency in application . . . whilst looking at pictures" (Cross, III, 371). When she fell in love with a picture, a statue, or a building, she studied it with the aim of registering its details in her mind's eye, so that after leaving it she might still contemplate and cherish it, as she contemplated and cherished images of absent or dead friends. On her trip to Italy in 1860, for example, she reproached herself for inattention in this regard: "I am not enjoying the actual vision enough, and . . . when higher enjoyment comes with reproduction of the scene in my imagination I shall have lost some of the details, which impress me too feebly in the present because the faculties are not wrought up into energetic action."[24] A similar exhortation to retain "the actual vision" animates her description of the Niobe group in Berlin: "How grieved I shall be if the image of that mother in anguish sheltering her youngest child from the inevitable dart, becomes vague in my imagination."[25] George Eliot's memory for objets d'art seems to have needed more prodding than her memory for living faces; but assisted by the mnemonic entries in her journals, by prints, and by her meditative habits of imagination, she carried a rich *musée imaginaire* behind her gray eyes.

A few precious paintings suited George Eliot's taste perfectly. They satisfied all of her moral and aesthetic criteria and also became icons in her personal meditations. The *Sistine Madonna* and several works by Titian belonged to this small group of favorite masterpieces, as we have seen. So did Rubens's *Crucifixion,* of which George Eliot saw the Antwerp version in 1854 and the Munich version in 1858. Her description of the Munich version (fig. 3) illustrates much that we have said about her taste in the visual arts:

Jesus alone, hanging dead on the Cross, darkness over the whole earth. One can desire nothing in this picture: the grand, sweet calm of the dead face, calm and satisfied amidst all the traces of anguish, the real livid flesh, the thorough mastery with which the whole form is rendered, and the isolation of the supreme sufferer, make a picture that haunts one like a remembrance of a friend's deathbed. [Cross, II, 21]

Here all of George Eliot's standards function together harmoniously. Rubens's picture exemplifies greatness of conception ("the supreme sufferer"), truthfulness of execution ("the real livid flesh, the thorough mastery with which the whole form is rendered"), perfection of expression ("the grand, sweet calm of the dead face"), superb color and form ("darkness over the whole earth . . . the isolation of the supreme sufferer"), and finally an iconic stimulus to meditation ("a picture that haunts one like a remembrance of a friend's deathbed"). Her writings contain no better synopsis of what George Eliot liked in a picture.

The power of pictorial images thus to focus the viewer's attention and sympathies is a rationale for their use in fiction. The novelist can affect his readers deeply by summoning images to their minds through his descriptive language. His power so to "paint" with words is limited by the nature of his medium, as George Eliot clearly recognized; but literary pictorialism was nonetheless central to her theory of fiction.

4 George Eliot's Theory of
Ut Pictura Poesis

Ut pictura poesis, that very fiery particle of Renaissance and neo-classical aesthetic theory, was not after all snuffed out by an article.[1] Such is the conclusion suggested by several recent studies which show that the venerable Horatian dictum (*Ars poetica,* 1. 361) survived the criticism of Lessing's *Laokoön* (1766), weathered the coming of Romanticism, and led a vigorous, if significantly modified, life in nineteenth-century British thought. Ian Jack has documented the popularity of *ut pictura poesis* in the Keats circle, Roy Park has traced its permutations in the writings of Hazlitt, George P. Landow has analyzed Ruskin's version of the analogy, and Viola Hopkins Winner has studied the pictorialist elements in Henry James's theory and practice of fiction.[2] It now seems that music did not supplant painting as the dominant nineteenth-century analogue to poetry among the sister arts. And painting certainly remained the art most frequently compared to fiction. As late as 1884, James was able to say with perfect conviction that "the analogy between the art of the painter and the art of the novelist is, so far as I am able to see, complete."[3] James's opinion was a commonplace of the period, so much so that Mario Praz is quite justified in calling *ut pictura poesis* "the golden rule . . . of nineteenth-century narrative literature."[4]

To be sure, the function of the analogy had changed in several important ways since the Renaissance. One change was rhetorical. Renaissance critics usually compared painting with poetry in order to dignify the more mechanic of the two arts, and to claim for it some of the prestige traditionally associated with poetry. But later critics, as Bernard Richards has pointed out, usually compared painting with the novel in order to dignify the latter, and to claim for the new literary form some of the prestige which painting had acquired since the Renaissance.[5]

Furthermore, with the advent of Romantic poetic theory, the basis of the analogy between the arts shifted from imitation to expression. For Ruskin, painting and poetry are two forms of "language" through which the soul of the artist expresses its visions. As George P. Landow has pointed out, Ruskin "did not defend painting on the ground that, like poetry, it educates and entertains by imitating nature. In the theory of poetry which Ruskin allied with pictorial art, the expression of noble emotion had replaced the earlier concern with imitation as a center of critical attention."[6] After Ruskin, most nineteenth-century theorists grounded their conception of the sister arts in the idea of a primal inspiration that chooses between different artistic media for its embodiment.

Romantic aesthetics also placed a special emphasis upon the ideas of concreteness and particularity comprised in the traditional doctrine of *ut pictura poesis*. By imitating the specificity of painting, literature could avoid the pitfalls of abstraction and unverified generalization which Romantic critics, unfairly for the most part, identified with neoclassical aesthetics. Thus Hazlitt praised "the force and precision of individual details, transferred, as it were, to the page from the canvas."[7] The sensible reality of painting made it an attractive model for literature in the eyes of empiricist critics such as Hazlitt, Mill, Lewes, and George Eliot, who valued aesthetic experience but distrusted the abstracting and schematizing powers of language.[8]

Not even the most ardent Victorian advocates of empirical observation, however, recommended limitless description in art. Lessing's attack upon the excessively pictorial verse of the mid-eighteenth century made a mark in nineteenth-century England, where his distinction between poetry and painting was well known. G. H. Lewes, for example, criticized poetry that is merely *"an animated catalogue of things,"* and Coleridge complained of "modern poems, where all is so dutchified . . . by the most minute touches, that the reader naturally asks why words, and not painting, are used?"[9] P. G. Hamerton, a hard-line Lessingite, argued that "it is not possible to produce, with an elaborate word-picture, that single-stroke effect which makes the power of an elaborate colour-picture."[10] Clearly *ut pictura poesis,* never a simple doctrine, had acquired more ramifications than ever by the time George Eliot inherited it.

Eliot's own version of the theory unites empiricist psychology with the traditional rhetorical notion of *enargeia:* the power of verbal visual imagery to set objects, persons, or scenes before an audience.[11] Eliot and G. H. Lewes formulated an interesting psychological rationale for this power of language by combining elements from the British empiricist tradition with some of the doctrines of Ruskin. From empiricism came the concept of "images" and their function in mental processes. From Ruskin came the concept of "vision" and its role in the genesis of great art. Images and vision are central, in George Eliot's thought, to both the creation of literature and its effect upon its audience. An important corollary of her emphasis upon vision is the high value she placed upon pictorial description. But her pictorialism was qualified by an awareness derived from Lessing of the limitations of such description and the importance of supplementing it with other modes of representation.

When George Eliot spoke of "the superior mastery of images and pictures in grasping the attention," she was using the term *images* with some precison (*Essays,* p. 445). In the psychological teachings of G. H. Lewes, an image is a sense-experience mentally reproduced. Not all images are visual, but many are. From images come ideas, which result when the remembered sense-experiences lose some of their immediacy and, with the help of language, become signs or symbols. Images thus mediate between direct sensation and thought.[12] Poetry, for example, originates "when passion weds thought by finding expression in an image" (*Essays,* p. 435). Because they are closer to direct sensation than ideas are, images have a greater power than ideas to compel the emotions; "our earliest, strongest impressions, our most intimate convictions," George Eliot wrote, "are simply images added to more or less of sensation. These are the primitive instruments of thought" (*Essays,* p. 445).

Although most of our thinking is carried on with signs and symbols, the Leweses believed that some of our best thinking—especially in the arts—is done through images. "Vigorous and effective minds habitually deal with concrete images," G. H. Lewes wrote. "This is notably the case with poets and great literates. Their vision is keener than that of other men. However rapid and remote their flight of thought, it is a succession of images, not of abstractions."[13] In the same vein, George Eliot spoke of "the picture-writing of the mind, which it carries on concurrently with the more subtle symbolism of language" (*Essays,* p. 267). Imaging, because it is anchored in direct experience, helps the mind to avoid abstractions, the unreality of "verbal fallacies and meaningless phrases" to which the sign-system of language is inherently susceptible.[14] The prevalence of concrete images distinguishes the thought and language of artists from those of philosophers and scientists in G. H. Lewes's scheme of mental activities. The philosopher, Lewes argued, "aims at abstract symbols"; the poet, "at picturesque effects."[15]

Lewes used the term *vision* as a metaphor for all thinking done primarily through images. He borrowed the metaphor from the experience of the eye, which, following an ancient tradition, he considered to be "the most valued and intellectual of our senses."[16] He argued that mental vision, or "seeing with the mind's eye," is essential to perception, inference, and reasoning as well as to imagination.[17] By imagination he meant the mind's power to select, abstract, and recombine images held in the memory, sometimes forming from them new images which correspond to no external reality.

Mimetic correspondence mattered less to Lewes than expressive authenticity. From Ruskin he borrowed the principle that the artist should represent only what he has actually "seen" with his bodily or mental vision. "Some minds see things only visible to the physical eye," Lewes wrote in a review of the fourth volume of *Modern Painters;* "others see things with the mental eye. But no one should paint what he does *not* see or feel." Ruskin's principle of sincerity Lewes declared to be "as applicable to the poet (and novelist) as to the painter."[18] The greatest source of false and second-rate art is the representation of what is not truly seen but is derived at second

hand from tradition or convention. The artist must always ask himself "whether he does or does not distinctly see the cottage he is
describing, the rivulet that is gurgling through his verses, or the character he is painting . . . if he does not see these things he must wait
until he can, or he will paint them ineffectively."[19]

The clear visions of the artist penetrate the layer of habit and
"misty generality" which normally obscures our mental experience;
thus the artist causes us to see things—often very familiar things—
anew.[20] According to George Eliot, a great artist teaches "by giving
us his higher sensibility as a medium, a delicate acoustic or optical
instrument, bringing home to our coarser senses what would otherwise be unperceived by us" (*Essays,* p. 126). She quoted approvingly
some lines to the same effect from Browning's "Fra Lippo Lippi":

> For, don't you mark, we're made so that we love
> First when we see them painted, things we have passed
> Perhaps a hundred times, nor cared to see;
> And so they are better, painted—better to us,
> Which is the same thing. *Art was given for that—*
> *God uses us to help each other so,*
> *Lending our minds out.*[21]

By communicating his clear vision to an audience, the artist extends
their perceptions and sympathies. For this reason, Eliot believed that
vivid aesthetic picturing is a far more effective way of teaching than
hortatory argument.

The greatest benefit we owe to the artist, whether painter, poet,
or novelist, is the extension of our sympathies. Appeals founded
on generalizations and statistics require a sympathy ready-made,
a moral sentiment already in activity; but a picture of human life
such as a great artist can give, surprises even the trivial and the
selfish into that attention to what is apart from themselves,
which may be called the raw material of moral sentiment. When
Scott takes us into Luckie Mucklebackit's cottage, or tells the
story of 'The Two Drovers,'—when Wordsworth sings to us the
reverie of 'Poor Susan,'—when Kingsley shows us Alton Locke
gazing yearningly over the gate which leads from the highway

into the first wood he ever saw,—when Hornung paints a group
of chimney-sweepers,—more is done towards obliterating the
vulgarity of exclusiveness, than by hundreds of sermons and
philosophical dissertations. Art is the nearest thing to life; it is a
mode of amplifying experience and extending our contact with
our fellow-men beyond the bounds of our personal lot. All the
more sacred is the task of the artist when he undertakes to paint
the life of the People. [*Essays,* pp. 270-71]

What unites the sister arts of painting and literature, in this famous
passage from George Eliot's greatest essay, is their common presentation of pictures of human life seen by the moral vision of the artist
and represented so vividly as to move the sympathetic imagination
of his audience. It is worth noting that three of George Eliot's
examples are not only "pictures" in a metaphorical sense, but also
highly pictorialized in their actual forms.[22]

    To paint a picture, then, was Eliot's favorite figure of speech for
the effective realization of vision in literature. William J. Hyde
speaks of the "characteristic allusion to painting" in her *Westminster Review* essays, and certainly a pictorial vocabulary is prominent
throughout the important series of review articles in which, between
1855 and 1857, she formulated her theory of fiction.[23] The severest
criticism she could make of a novel was that it failed to "paint" its
characters or scenes. Thus she wrote of Holme Lee's *Kathie Brande*:
"Instead of vividly realizing to herself the terrible scenes, and vividly
representing them . . . the author *writes about* them, does not *paint*
them. . . . An artist would have suffered his imagination to dwell on
such scenes until, aided by his knowledge, either direct or indirect,
the principal details became so vividly present to him that he could
describe as if he saw them and we should read as if we saw them
too."[24] She considered Charles Kingsley a better painter of scenes,
but found his main fault as a novelist to be his tendency to moralize
his own pictures instead of letting them speak for themselves. In
Kingsley's *Westward Ho!,* Eliot charged, "the preacher overcomes
the painter often":

    It is as if a painter in colour were to write 'Oh, you villain!'
    under his Jesuits or murderers; or to have a strip flowing from a

hero's mouth, with 'Imitate me, my man!' on it. No doubt the
villain is to be hated, and the hero loved; but we ought to see
that sufficiently in the figures of them. We don't want a man
with a wand, going about the gallery and haranguing us. Art is
art, and tells its own story. [*Essays,* p. 123]

Such a passage suggests the elaboration and wit of which the pictorial analogy is capable in George Eliot's hands. Whatever it might
have been for other Victorian critics, it was seldom a cliché for her.

And there can be no doubt that she demanded of herself as a
novelist the same intense visualizing and vivid painting that she demanded of Holme Lee and other writers. She applied her customary
pictorial standards and vocabulary to her own work when she noted,
in a famous letter to Frederic Harrison, that aesthetic teaching becomes offensive "if it lapses anywhere from the picture to the
diagram." The letter goes on to explain how difficult it was for her
imagination 'to make art a sufficiently real back-ground, for the
desired picture, to get breathing, individual forms, and group them
in the needful relations, so that the presentation will lay hold on the
emotions as human experience—will, as you say, 'flash' conviction
on the world by means of aroused sympathy" (*Letters,* IV, 300–
01).[25] A picture can "flash" conviction because it works through
images and "our most intimate convictions are simply images added
to more or less of sensation" (*Essays,* p. 445). A diagram, by contrast, employs a more abstract symbolism.[26]

Because of their preference for concrete images in art, the Leweses
opposed the antipictorialist argument of Edmund Burke's *Philosophical Enquiry into the Origin of Our Ideas of the Sublime and Beautiful* (1757). Burke, resisting the tendency toward excessive pictorial
description in mid-eighteenth-century poetry, attacked the principle
of *enargeia* itself by denying that language can evoke visual experience. "From a pictorialist's point of view," Jean Hagstrum has
noted, "Burke's absolute disjunction between words (which create
emotional response) and images (which bring to the mental retina
the objects of nature) is nothing short of revolutionary."[27] Burke
argued for the superior efficacy of obscure, confused, and crowded
literary imagery, which makes an emotive rather than a visual im-

pact, hurrying the reader's mind beyond its usual frame of reference into an unfocused sense of grandeur and sublimity. "A clear idea," wrote Burke, "is therefore another name for a little idea."[28] G. H. Lewes devoted a three-page subsection of "The Principles of Success in Literature" to refuting Burke. It was a necessary digression if Lewes's main thesis in the essay—the highly pictorialist "principle of vision"—was to stand.

Lewes did not argue in favor of exhaustive catalogues of exclusively visual details. Nor did he contend, as the twentieth-century Imagists were sometimes to do, that language can hand over visual images intact, replete with the unmediated freshness of direct experience. He recognized that words are not things or mental images but symbols of them: "Language, after all, is only the use of symbols, and art also can only affect us through symbols."[29] The images which language evokes in a hearer's mind can never be identical with those in the speaker's mind; they can only be analogous. Lewes, then, avoided a naïve theory of verbal pictorialism. Nevertheless, he strongly favored the use of distinct and vivid imagery in literature. He argued, contra Burke, that even sublime, overwhelming impressions and confused, emotional states of mind need to be represented in clear terms if they are to be communicated effectively. All description, according to Lewes, requires "intelligible symbols (clear images)."[30]

Although they opposed Burke on the issue of clarity, the Leweses were much more sympathetic to the antipictorialist arguments of Burke's contemporary, G. E. Lessing. They admired and accepted the distinction between painting and poetry set forth in Lessing's *Laokoön, oder Über die Grenzen der Malerei und Poesie* (1766). The thesis of Lessing's essay helped George Eliot to qualify her doctrine of *ut pictura poesis,* and to articulate her sense of the limitations of literary pictorialism.

Lessing argued that painting handles forms and colors in space. It is perceived in an instant of time, and should therefore depict only an instant of time. Poetry, on the other hand, handles articulated sounds in time. It is perceived in temporal sequence and should therefore re-create processes (actions) rather than visual fields. Poetry is the more comprehensive (*weitere*) of the two arts, because it can depict what precedes and what follows the single moment to which painting is restricted. Lessing was not opposed to the principle of *ut pictura poesis* so much as to the more literal-minded applications of it in the descriptive poetry of his day.[31] There remained a sense in which he believed "der Dichter soll immer malen": not by enumerating a great many visual details that would, in a painting, be taken in at a glance, but by presenting ideas so vividly that the audience forgets that words are being used and has the illusion of direct sense-experience instead.[32]

This was close to George Eliot's view of the matter. Certainly she did not read the *Laokoön* as a purist attack upon verbal painting per se. Rather she found in Lessing a useful reminder of the limitations of such painting, and a justification of her conviction that literature is, after all, superior to the visual arts as a mode of representing human experience. "Every reader of Lessing's 'Laokoon,'" she wrote in the *Westminster Review,* "remembers his masterly distinction between the methods of presentation in poetry and the plastic arts— the acumen and aptness of illustration with which he shows how the difference in the materials wherewith the poet and painter or sculptor respectively work, and the difference in their mode of appeal to the mind, properly involve a difference in their treatment of a given subject." In particular, Eliot notes, the literary artist would be mistaken "if he adopted all the symbolism and detail of the painter and sculptor, since he has at his command the media of speech and action."[33] Literary description must, in other words, give way at some point to narrative and drama. The novelist must use "the media of speech and action" to represent the invisible and temporal aspects of human experience which painting, according to Lessing, cannot truly embody.[34]

Precisely because it can render what she once called "the truth of change," George Eliot considered fiction superior to the visual arts.[35] The novel may not only evoke a portrait in the mind's eye of the reader; it may also animate that portrait and go inside the frame. Will Ladislaw speaks for his creator when he says to Naumann in *Middlemarch:*

And what is a portrait of a woman? Your painting and Plastik are poor stuff after all. . . . Language is a finer medium. . . . Language gives a fuller image, which is all the better for being vague. After all, the true seeing is within; and painting stares at you with insistent imperfection. I feel that especially about representations of women. As if a woman were a mere coloured superficies! You must wait for movement and tone. There is a difference in their very breathing: they change from moment to moment.—This woman whom you have just seen, for example: how would you paint her voice, pray? But her voice is much diviner than anything you have seen of her. [19:291–92]

Although Naumann dismisses Ladislaw's arguments as mere symptoms of jealousy, the novel supports Will's view of the limitations of painting. That view is partly Romantic ("the true seeing is within") but it is also indebted to Lessing. Will's emphasis upon Dorothea's voice directly parallels Lessing's emphasis upon Laokoön's voice, which can be represented by Vergil but not by the sculptor.[36]

Lessing's influence upon George Eliot's theory of *ut pictura poesis* affected the structure of chapters in her fiction. As we have seen, she and Lewes commonly divided the art of the novelist into two branches: description and dramatic presentation. The characteristic George Eliot chapter begins with description, setting a scene in static, visual, often pictorial terms. Then it modulates into drama, activating the tableau with dialogue and movement, or penetrating it with psychological commentary. The picture-frame becomes a proscenium arch, and the viewer is drawn into the scene, moving from a distanced and relatively objective perception toward participation and sympathetic identification. This structure does not involve a transition from "picture" to "scene" in the Jamesian sense of the terms.[37] Rather it involves a transition from "scene" in the graphic sense to "scene" in the theatrical sense, an ambiguity nicely exploited in the title of George Eliot's first published stories. The moments of transition from one mode to the other are frequently the moments at which the narrator expresses his Lessingite reservations about literary pictorialism.

Eliot did not, then, "flout the canons of the Laocoon" in the way Ian Fletcher says many Victorian artists did.[38] Her acceptance of Lessing likewise differentiates her from many twentieth-century writers who use painting to transcend time and achieve a "spatial form" which is designed to be contemplated as a perfect, atemporal whole by the reader.[39] In many modern novels, as Jeffrey Meyers has pointed out, "evocative comparisons with works of art attempt to transcend the limitations of fiction and to transform successive moments into immediate images."[40] A familiar device in the work of the later James, Proust, Lawrence, and other writers who descend from George Eliot is the symbolic painting which subsumes the meanings of the novel at one or several crucial points in the action.[41] But Eliot herself was reluctant to place so much structural weight upon works of visual art. For example, her juxtaposition of Dorothea with the statue of "Ariadne" in the Vatican Museum scene is much less central to the meaning of *Middlemarch* than James's juxtaposition of Milly Theale with Bronzino's portrait of Lucrezia Panciatichi is to the meaning of *The Wings of the Dove*.[42] Eliot did not turn to painting because she was galled and chafed by the temporal nature of her medium. Lessing helped her to accept that limitation and even to rejoice in it.

Pictorialism, then, was a necessary but not a sufficient condition of the novelist's art as George Eliot conceived it. The writer must "paint" in the broad sense that his language must evoke vivid, concrete images rather than indistinct, abstract ideas in the reader's mind. The writer must also "paint" in the narrower sense of providing some descriptive passages to assist the reader's visualizing of the story. But word-painting of the second sort cannot adequately represent the inner, temporal aspects of human experience, and must therefore be supplemented by dramatic presentation.

Thus qualified, however, the analogy between the arts was indispensable to George Eliot's theory and practice of fiction. She chose her words carefully when, surveying her oeuvre in 1876, she said: "The principles which are at the root of my effort to paint Dinah are equally at the root of my effort to paint Mordecai" (*Letters,* VI, 318). She endeavored always to "paint" her characters, and in the next chapter we shall examine her loving yet impatient use of literary portraiture.

5 Portraiture and
Knowledge of Character

George Eliot knew from the start what her literary portraiture would *not* be. It would not, for example, be Lord Rupert Conway, the handsome young prime minister of England in *Rank and Beauty, or the Young Baroness* (1856):

> The door opened again, and Lord Rupert Conway entered. Evelyn gave one glance. It was enough; she was not disappointed. It seemed as if a picture on which she had long gazed was suddenly instinct with life, and had stepped from its frame before her. His tall figure, the distinguished simplicity of his air—it was a living Vandyke, a cavalier, one of his noble cavalier ancestors, or one to whom her fancy had always likened him, who long of yore had, with an Umfraville, fought the Paynim far beyond the sea. Was this reality?

"Very little like it," responded the author of "Silly Novels by Lady Novelists" (*Essays,* pp. 307–08). A portrait like this was to George Eliot what a portrait by Sir Sloshua was to the Pre-Raphaelite Brotherhood in 1848: lifeless convention masking as truth, hollow cliché evoking a stereotyped response. To avoid slosh, the Pre-Raphaelites maintained, one must paint from new pictorial models and from the direct observation of nature. By the same token, George Eliot wanted her literary portraits to present fresh perspectives and real knowledge of character rather than occasions for effusive sentiment.

In pursuing that aim, her portraiture passed through three major phases. In *Scenes of Clerical Life* and *Adam Bede,* she was primarily concerned to show that looks do mirror personality, that there are, as G. H. Lewes put it, "subtle connections between physical and mental organisation."[1] In these early works, phrenology helped her to create portraits that give reliable clues to temperament and behavior. With *Romola* and *Felix Holt,* however, the correlation between appearance and reality becomes more problematic. Influenced less by phrenology and more by Ruskin and Hawthorne, Eliot grew preoccupied with the portrayal of evil and with the discrepancy between innocent-looking portraits and corrupt sitters. Finally, the gap between static picture and changing person becomes normative in Eliot's portraiture, so that *Middlemarch* and *Daniel Deronda* abound with partial portraits, visual definitions of character that are qualified as soon as given. The knowledge afforded by portraiture grows more uncertain and more complex as Eliot's work progresses, and the significance of the English portrait tradition itself becomes ambiguous. Sometimes the tradition represents an admirable continuity of English history, but at other times it reflects only the vanity of an exclusive and dying aristocracy. The variety of meanings it can encompass, from the moral and psychological to the historical and sociological, makes Eliot's literary portraiture richer than that of any earlier novelist in English.

How to depict a nonentity sympathetically is the first task George Eliot set herself. The traditional rhetorical functions of the character sketch—*laus et vituperatio*—do not apply to Amos Barton.[2] He cannot be celebrated because he is not a hero, yet he cannot be caricatured because he is our fellow man. George Eliot solves the problem by turning her first literary portrait into a nonportrait:

Look at him as he winds through the little churchyard! The silver light that falls aslant on church and tomb, enables you to see his slim black figure, made all the slimmer by tight pantaloons, as it flits past the pale grave-stones . . . as Mr Barton hangs up his hat in the passage, you see that a narrow face of no particular complexion—even the small-pox that has attacked it seems to have been of a mongrel, indefinite kind—with features of no particular shape, and an eye of no particular expression, is surmounted by a slope of baldness gently rising from brow to crown. [2:23]

The model for this description is the silhouette, with its lack of internal definition and its reversal of the customary tonal values of figure and ground in portraiture. Amos Barton is defined by negation: a fleeting black shadow in a night-time setting where the chiaroscuro highlights not the protagonist but the monitory emblems of death surrounding him—the tombs and "pale gravestones" which foreshadow his loss of Milly.[3] His physiognomy is likewise that of a nonentity; it has "no particular" humor, structure, or expression. An individual without individuality, he has no hair, and his sloping forehead suggests to the phrenological eye a deficiency of intellectual faculties. Even his smallpox scars, themselves negations of the man, leave no distinctive disfigurement. His silhouette is colorless, as he is, and its form is constricted by angular, diminishing lines: a slim figure that grows slimmer below the waist, a narrow face, a sloping forehead, seen by slanting moonlight. Such a reversal of traditional portrait values would, in an eighteenth-century context, almost certainly be satiric; but here it implies no disapproval.[4] It simply introduces a nobody.

Silhouettes and physiognomy were associated in the treatises of Johann Caspar Lavater, where the standard form of illustration was the profile silhouette drawn from life.[5] If Amos's portrait descends from such sources, it is a reminder that many of George Eliot's descriptions have a rich background in the pseudo-scientific systems of expressive anatomy that influenced the arts for more than two centuries before she began to write. From the French neoclassical discourses on *l'expression des passions* to Lavater's physiognomy to the phrenology of Gall and Spurzheim, empirical observers had attempted to interpret the mind through the language of the body.[6] The common assumption of their endeavors was clearly articulated by Sir Charles Bell in 1806: "Anatomy stands related to the arts of design, as the grammar of that language in which they address us. The expression, attitudes, and movements of the human figure, are the characters of this language, which is adapted to convey the effect of historical narration, as well as to show the working of human passion, and give the most striking and lively indications of intellectual power and energy."[7] The same linguistic metaphor was used by George Eliot's favorite phrenologist, George Combe, when he spoke of "the natural language of the faculties," meaning, of course, those thirty-three faculties of the brain whose development phrenologists could interpret from the shape of the cranium.[8] Combe's treatise on *Phrenology Applied to Painting and Sculpture* (1855) taught artists how to mold heads that are phrenologically compatible with the characters and passions represented in any work of art.

George Eliot was acquainted with Combe through their mutual friend, Charles Bray, who had become an enthusiastic student of phrenology in the 1830s (Haight, p. 37). Bray took Marian Evans to London to have a phrenological cast of her head made in 1844, and he introduced her to Combe in 1851 (Haight, pp. 51, 100–01). Marian and Combe were both associated with the *Westminster Review* after she moved to London (Haight, pp. 109, 123–24), and their friendship lasted until her elopement with Lewes in 1854 (Haight, p. 166). Although she did not subscribe to every article of Combe's scientific creed, she nevertheless reiterated her belief in the general principles of phrenology in a letter to Bray of 1855: "I am not conscious of falling off from the 'physiological basis.' I never believed more profoundly than I do now that character is based on organization. I never had a higher appreciation than I have now of the services which phrenology has rendered towards the science of man" (*Letters*, II, 210).

As George Eliot's letter suggests, the basic premise of Gall's system is that mind has a physiological basis. Character is determined not by intangible, divinely implanted spirit but by the physiological organization of the brain and central nervous system. The mind is composed of more than thirty independent faculties localized in different regions or organs of the brain, developed in proportion to the growth of those organs, and mirrored in the size and shape of the cranium. The faculties fall into three general groups, each group predominating in one part of the head. The intellectual faculties center in the brow and forehead, or anterior lobe; the moral and religious faculties, in the top of the head, or coronal region; the selfish and animal faculties, in the occiput, or posterior lobe. The temperament of any individual will depend upon the balance of his propensities; thus George Eliot was a little worried that her moral aptitudes might not be strong enough to check her animal propensities (*Letters,* I, 167). Finally, phrenology postulated four major character types—the nervous, the bilious, the sanguine, and the lymphatic—which were holdovers from the older psychology of the humors.[9]

The truth and utility of this system were self-evident to many creators of literary character in the mid-nineteenth century. Poe and Whitman both drew heavily upon phrenology, as did two English writers whom George Eliot respected: Bulwer-Lytton and Charlotte Brontë.[10] In Eliot's own work, the vocabulary of phrenology is most explicit in *Scenes of Clerical Life* (1857) and *Adam Bede* (1859). Not all of the portraits in these early stories are phrenological, but a good many are. In the first chapter of "Janet's Repentance," for example, we meet Lawyer Dempster.

> Mr Dempster habitually held his chin tucked in, and his head hanging forward, weighed down, perhaps, by a preponderant occiput and a bulging forehead, between which his closely-clipped coronal surface lay like a flat and new-mown table-land. [1:41–42]

As Maurice L. Johnson observed in 1911, Dempster is described in this passage as an "animal-intellectual temperament," wanting in moral faculties.[11] His preponderant occiput indicates a massive development of the selfish faculties such as love of approbation and self-esteem, and of the animal faculties such as combativeness, destructiveness, and amativeness (sexual passion). Dempster's bulging forehead is a sign of his great intelligence, but his flat coronal surface suggests a deficiency of the moral and religious faculties such as benevolence, veneration, and conscientiousness. As Johnson points out, Dempster's character and conduct in the story "correspond strikingly with his phrenological portrait."[12] The lawyer turns out to be intelligent, unscrupulous, and sadistic.

A vivid contrast to Dempster is found in the double portrait that

opens *Adam Bede*. In Seth Bede we see a very full development of
the coronal region:

> Seth's broad shoulders have a slight stoop; his eyes are grey;
> his eyebrows have less prominence and more repose than his
> brother's; and his glance, instead of being keen, is confiding and
> benignant. He has thrown off his paper cap, and you see that his
> hair is not thick and straight, like Adam's, but thin and wavy,
> allowing you to discern the exact contour of a coronal arch that
> predominates very decidedly over the brow. [1:5]

If Dempster's coronal surface was "like a flat and new-mown table-
land," Seth's is like an "arch"; and the fact that it predominates
over his brow suggests that his moral faculties, unlike Dempster's,
are more highly developed than his intellectual capacities. Combe
could have been listing Seth Bede's virtues when he said that "to
represent strong Benevolence, Veneration, Hope, Conscientiousness,
and Firmness, the top of the head, or coronal region, must be drawn
high and arched."[13] In Seth's fully structured portrait, George
Eliot fills in the spaces that she left blank in Amos Barton's silhouette: figure, coloring, expression of the eye, and physiognomy.

Adam Bede's portrait provides another sort of contrast to Seth's.
First we hear Adam's voice singing a hymn; then we see the singer:

> Such a voice could only come from a broad chest, and the broad
> chest belonged to a large-boned muscular man nearly six feet
> high, with a back so flat and a head so well poised that when he
> drew himself up to take a more distant survey of his work, he
> had the air of a soldier standing at ease. The sleeve rolled up
> above the elbow showed an arm that was likely to win the prize
> for feats of strength; yet the long supple hand, with its broad
> finger-tips, looked ready for works of skill. In his tall stalwart-
> ness Adam Bede was a Saxon, and justified his name; but the jet-
> black hair, made the more noticeable by its contrast with the
> light paper cap, and the keen glance of the dark eyes that shone
> from under strongly marked, prominent and mobile eyebrows,
> indicated a mixture of Celtic blood. The face was large and

roughly hewn, and when in repose had no other beauty than such as belongs to an expression of good-humoured honest intelligence. [1:4-5]

A phrenologically sophisticated Victorian reader would immediately have recognized in Adam the bilious temperament, with an admixture of nervous traits. The bilious character was defined by the American phrenologist, Orson S. Fowler, as a type "in which the muscles predominate in activity, characterized by an athletic form, strong bones and sinews, black hair and eyes, dark skin, strong and steady pulse, hardness, force, and power."[14]

The bilious character is what the older humor psychology called the choleric: a temperament given to wrath and violence. In other words, Adam's shortness of temper and propensity to fisticuffs are foreshadowed in his introductory portrait. But his biliousness is balanced and held in check by his alertness and intelligence, which are qualities of the so-called nervous temperament, in whom mental activity is strong. What Adam would be without this fortunate development of his intellectual faculties may be seen in the contrast between him and his mother: "There is the same type of frame and the same keen activity of temperament in mother and son, but it was not from her that Adam got his well-filled brow and his expression of large-hearted intelligence" (4:55).

Whether Adam's intelligence came from his father we do not know, for we never see that hard-drinking carpenter in life. But the other major character who is destined to become part of the Bede family—Dinah Morris—does receive a careful phrenological portrait early in the novel, when she is preparing to preach on Hayslope Green. The portrait has more in common with Seth's than with Adam's:

> There was no keenness in the [grey] eyes; they seemed rather to be shedding love than making observations; they had the liquid look which tells that the mind is full of what it has to give out, rather than impressed by external objects. She stood with her left hand towards the descending sun, and leafy boughs screened her from its rays; but in this sober light the delicate colouring of her face seemed to gather a calm vividness, like flowers at

evening. It was a small oval face, of a uniform transparent white-ness, with an egg-like line of cheek and chin, a full but firm mouth, a delicate nostril, and a low perpendicular brow, sur-mounted by a rising arch of parting between smooth locks of pale reddish hair. The hair was drawn straight back behind the ears, and covered, except for an inch or two, above the brow, by a net Quaker cap. The eyebrows, of the same colour as the hair, were perfectly horizontal and firmly pencilled; the eye-lashes, though no darker, were long and abundant; nothing was left blurred or unfinished. [2:29–30]

Nothing, certainly, is left blurred or unfinished in this description, which Queen Victoria liked so well that she commissioned a water-color to be painted of it for her private collection (fig. 25). As with Seth, to whom Dinah is a sort of phrenological sister, the moral and religious faculties are more highly developed than the intellectual capacities. Dinah's forehead is low, and the faculties of observation, which are situated near the eyes, do not have the keenness of Adam's. But the "rising arch" above her brow implies a full growth of the coronal organs of benevolence and veneration (capacity for religious devotion). Their coronal arches, then, reveal the most characteristic propensities of the two gentle Methodists. The non-phrenological associations of Dinah with leaves and flowers comple-ment the corporal language of her portrait.

The technical vocabulary of phrenology becomes increasingly rare in George Eliot's fiction after *Adam Bede*. Felix Holt has "large veneration" and "large Ideality" (5:98), but he is alone among Eliot's later heroes and heroines in receiving so explicit a diagnosis. Although she continued to believe in the existence of what Lewes had called "subtle connections between physical and mental orga-nisation." Eliot lost faith in craniology or organology as a reliable interpreter of those connections.[15] A letter of 1870 to Dante Gabriel Rossetti articulates the diffidence of her maturity:

One is always liable to mistake prejudices for sufficient in-ductions, about types of head and face, as well as about all other things. I have some impressions—perhaps only prejudices depen-dent on the narrowness of my experience—about forms of eyebrow and their relation to passionate expression. It is possible that such a supposed relation has a real anatomical basis. But in many particulars facial expression is like the expression of handwriting; the relations are too subtle and intricate to be detected, and only shallowness is confident. [*Letters,* V, 79]

Yet the influence of her phrenological training remained with her. Even in this letter she alludes to a private theory of expressive eyebrows, and she criticizes Rossetti's illustration of a scene in *Hamlet* on Combean grounds: "admirable in conception, except in the type of the man's head. I feel sure that 'Hamlet' had a square anterior lobe."[16] So if the George Eliot of 1870 were scratched deeply enough, a phrenologist would still appear. Her literary portraits never ceased to reach, however tentatively, for physiognomical verity.

But no one with George Eliot's Puritan education could be brought entirely to trust appearances. Although most of the portraits in *Adam Bede* are reliable indicators of character, one of them involves a discrepancy between looks and true nature, and thereby anticipates the concern of *Romola* and *Felix Holt* with deceptive and corruptible character. The description of Hetty Sorrel is modeled upon formal Renaissance word-portraits of romance heroines and Petrarchan beloved ladies:

It is of little use for me to tell you that Hetty's cheek was like a rose-petal, that dimples played about her pouting lips, that her large dark eyes hid a soft roguishness under their long lashes, and that her curly hair, though all pushed back under her round cap while she was at work, stole back in dark delicate rings on her forehead, and about her white shell-like ears; it is of little use for me to say how lovely was the contour of her pink-and-white neckerchief, tucked into her low plum-coloured stuff bodice, or how the linen butter-making apron, with its bib, seemed a thing to be imitated in silk by duchesses, since it fell in such charming lines, or how her brown stockings and thick-soled buckled shoes lost all that clumsiness which they must certainly have had when empty of her foot and ankle;—of little use, unless you have seen a woman who affected you as Hetty affected her beholders, for otherwise, though you might conjure up the image of a lovely woman, she would not in the least resemble that distracting kitten-like maiden. I might mention all the divine charms of a bright spring day, but if you had never in your life utterly forgotten yourself in straining your eyes after the mounting lark, or in wandering through the still lanes when the fresh-opened blossoms fill them with a sacred silent beauty like that of fretted aisles, where would be the use of my descriptive catalogue? I could never make you know what I meant by a bright spring day. Hetty's was a spring-tide beauty: it was the beauty of young frisking things, round-limbed, gambolling, circumventing you by a false air of innocence—of a young star-browed calf, for example, that, being inclined for a promenade out of bounds, leads you a severe steeple-chase over hedge and ditch, and only comes to a stand in the middle of a bog. [7:122–23]

At first this description seems consistent with the plan, announced in chapter 17 of *Adam Bede,* to confer the dignity of Italian Renaissance art upon Dutch genre subjects. The young woman's charms are systematically catalogued from top to toe and compared with precious substances and with the most beautiful manifestations of nature, as in countless descriptions of *belle donne* from Chrétien de Troyes to Ariosto, Tasso, Spenser, Petrarch, and the Elizabethan sonneteers. Hetty's is the only portrait in all of George Eliot to follow this traditional rhetorical pattern; but the idealization is undercut, and the whole convention rendered suspect, by the tone and imagery. The narrator's self-deprecation, usually a form of hyperbole (no words of mine can do her justice), here withholds final approbation. And the nature imagery, as many commentators have noted, is less than flattering to Hetty if its developmental and moral-emblematic connotations are emphasized. The calf especially turns from a complimentary pastoral metaphor into a monitory moral parable with a letdown in the closing period that is worthy of Dr. Johnson and the eighteenth-century satirists.

Behind its alluring description of surface appearances, this Petrarchan idealization conceals the truth about Hetty's character. George Eliot implies that the convention itself involves a projection of male desire which has little to do with the real nature of women; as the passage unfolds, the voice of the male narrator takes on the clubby accents of a literate amorist recalling a particularly irresistible milkmaid. A later description of Hetty shows how even a physiognomical portrait like those of Adam, Seth, and Dinah can be falsified by male egoism: "Every man under such circumstances is conscious of being a great physiognomist. Nature, he knows, has a language of her own, which she uses with strict veracity, and he considers himself an adept in the language. Nature has written out his bride's character for him in those exquisite lines of cheek and lip and chin, in those eyelids delicate as petals, in those long lashes curled like the stamen of a flower, in the dark liquid depths of those wonderful eyes. How she will doat on her children!" (15:228). "Every man" here includes both Adam and Arthur Donnithorne, who thinks that Hetty has "the most charming phiz imaginable" (9:149). But in Hetty's case the "great physiognomist" is misled by his dream of gratification. The delicate flower-mother is actually capable of infanticide when brought to it by a man acting on a sentimental fantasy of women like this one. It takes Mrs. Poyser's "feminine eye" to detect "the moral deficiencies hidden under the 'dear deceit' of [Hetty's] beauty" (15:232).

Another pictorial deceit that pervades the courtship of Hetty and Arthur takes the form of an Ovidian mythological-pastoral motif. This favorite theme of Renaissance painters is nearly always a sign of false idealization and egoism in George Eliot's literary portraits. Arthur says that Hetty is "a perfect Hebe, and if I were an artist, I would paint her" (9:149); whereas Hetty dreams of Arthur as a Poseidon and herself as a Tyro (13:202). Allusions to the golden age and the pastoral ideal of a *locus amoenus* embellish their trysts,[17] but the motif takes an ironic turn later in the novel when Hetty, wandering lost and pregnant, is visualized as Medusa—specifically as the Medusa Rondanini at Munich.[18] Ovidian idealization in George Eliot's work is usually associated with characters who pursue a paradise of individual pleasure in a morally strenuous postlapsarian world. This pagan motif, which reappears in *Romola* and *Daniel Deronda,* is the antithesis of the Christian idealization that will be examined in the next chapter of this study.

The human potential for egoism and evil raises both philosophical and aesthetic questions for portraiture. Gall identified "Murder" as one of the basic human faculties, but his more melioristic followers dropped it from the phrenological scheme.[19] Ruskin, in the second volume of *Modern Painters* (1846), struggled to reconcile ideal portraiture with the "immediate and present operation of the Adamite curse." In order to show both good and evil, Ruskin concluded, the artist must supplement empirical physiognomy with spiritual intuition: "the pursuit of idealism in humanity . . . can be successful only when followed through the most constant, patient, and humble rendering of actual models, accompanied with that earnest mental as well as ocular study of each, which can interpret all that is written upon it, disentangle the hieroglyphics of its sacred history, rend the veil of the bodily temple and rightly measure the relations of good and evil contending within it for mastery."[20] Here Ruskin's diction moves from the dispassionate language of science to the fervent cadences of Christianity. The passage epitomizes his whole approach to nature and art, which characteristically proceeds through empirical observation to religious vision. The agency of this insight Ruskin identifies a few chapters later as the penetrative imagination, a moral and aesthetic faculty not included on most phrenological charts. Like Ruskin, George Eliot was interested in a portraiture that would reveal moral struggle and change; for although she had abandoned the Evangelical dogma of an Adamite curse, she continued to believe in the phenomenal reality of good and evil.

A new mode of portraiture came to hand in Nathaniel Hawthorne's *The Marble Faun* (1860), a seminal work in the history of literary pictorialism by virtue of its influence upon both the later Eliot and Henry James. George Eliot mentioned *The Marble Faun* in the same letter from Italy that announced the conception of *Romola* to her publisher, and she no doubt included Hawthorne's romance of contemporary Rome in the preparatory reading for her own romance of historical Florence.[21] Hawthorne taught George Eliot how to use *ecphrasis,* or the verbal imitation of works of visual art, as a technique of psychological revelation and prophecy. The characters in *The Marble Faun* pass from innocence to experience through the knowledge and commission of evil. As Donatello, Miriam, and Hilda psychically reenact the fall of Adam, they gain and lose symbolic physical resemblances to various works of art placed within the story to represent different stages of their moral transformation. The most important of these correlatives are the Faun of Praxiteles, the so-called *Portrait of Beatrice Cenci* by Guido Reni, *The Archangel Michael* by the same painter, and a bust of Donatello modeled by the sculptor, Kenyon.[22]

This technique of characterization caught George Eliot's imagination. She had created similar effects on a minor scale in her early work, but after reading *The Marble Faun* she began to amplify her *ecphrases*. In *Romola* and her later novels, she regularly juxtaposes her characters with morally significant art works located inside the story. As in Hawthorne, these art works are sometimes "real" (that is, imitated from known originals) and sometimes purely fictive.

The most important pictures in *Romola* are fictive studies of Tito Melema and the heroine by Piero di Cosimo. Piero depicts his subjects together, separately, and with third persons, often in mythological roles that bear upon their situations in the story. Knowledge of character is the primary aim of the series, which begins early in the novel when Piero and Nello the barber debate whether Tito's fair countenance is better suited for a history painting of "Sinon deceiving old Priam" or a heroic picture of Bacchus, Apollo, or St. Sebastian.[23] The question, as with Hetty Sorrel, is whether physiognomy is a reliable index of character. Nello says that he cannot "look at such an outside as that without taking it as the sign of a lovable nature" (4:66); but Piero argues that good looks may signify hypocrisy: "A perfect traitor should have a face which vice can write no marks on—lips that will lie with a dimpled smile—eyes of such agate-like brightness and depth that no infamy can dull them—cheeks that will rise from a murder and not look haggard" (4:63). Piero disavows any real knowledge of Tito's character at this first meeting, but his intuition is prophetic: Tito will betray virtually every major character in the novel.

The discussion in the barbershop establishes the frame of reference for Tito's subsequent portraiture. The young model favors Nello's vision of a Greek god, as we see when he commissions a wedding portrait of himself and Romola in the roles of Bacchus and Ariadne. In this portrait Bacchus dispels the cares of Ariadne and crowns her in a marriage ceremony attended by Cupids "shooting with roses at the points of their arrows" (18:283). The lovers are seated on a ship covered with grapevines, ivy, and flowers. Leopards and tigers surround the happy pair, while dolphins sport nearby in the waves. The entire scene is "encircled by a flowery border, like a bower of paradise" (37:56). The painting is a false pastoral fancy portrait of the sort that Arthur and Hetty like to imagine for themselves in *Adam Bede.*

Tito interprets the details of the picture to Romola as "pretty symbols of our life together—the ship on the calm sea, and the ivy that never withers, and those Loves that have left off wounding us and shower soft petals that are like our kisses; and the leopards and tigers, they are the troubles of your life that are all quelled now; and the strange sea-monsters with their merry eyes—let us see—they are the dull passages in the heavy books, which have begun to be amusing since we have sat by each other" (20:306).

This interpretation perfectly expresses Tito's hedonistic code, which seeks to achieve pleasure and power and to avoid pain. Like Hawthorne's latter-day faun, Tito-Bacchus brings pagan and epicurean values into a Christian world that has learned a deeper moral truth.[24] His mythological portrait is painted on a cabinet designed to hide and replace a crucifix which Tito finds unpleasant, and his distaste for the Christian art of Florence reflects his distaste for the Christian ideas of self-denial, sin, death, and judgment (3:49). From the same aversion, he misreads Piero di Cosimo's historical allegory of the triumph of Christianity, interpreting its central figure as a symbol of the Golden Age or "the wise philosophy of Epicurus.[25] Tito's taste in art exemplifies the worldly and sensuous response which Ruskin called "aesthesis," but shows no signs of the higher religious faculty which Ruskin called "theoria."[26]

At first Romola accepts the portrait of Bacchus and Ariadne as a true image of her marriage. Like Nello, she is highly susceptible to the physiognomy of surface appearances.[27] But later she comes to see the picture as a "pitiable mockery" (37:56). It would seem even more hollow if she knew its literary sources. The portrait conflates two Bacchic episodes from Ovid's *Metamorphoses.* The god's marriage to Ariadne occurs in Book 8, and was a favorite topos of Renaissance painters.[28] But Tito transfers the nuptials to a scene in Book 3 in which Bacchus is threatened with enslavement by the crew of a ship that is carrying him, disguised as a boy, to Ariadne on Naxos.[29] In retribution for their ill-treatment, Bacchus manifests his divinity, turns the crew into dolphins, stops the ship in mid-ocean, and covers it with vines and cats. What Tito really commissions, then, is a picture of himself triumphant over slavers at sea, with Romola inserted as the final prize of the voyage. This choice of texts is appropriate yet deeply ironic, for although Tito had the good luck to escape from pirates at sea, his fortunes in Florence are based upon his refusal to ransom his captured foster-father, Baldassarre, from Turkish slavery. Its Ovidian sources, then, hint at the dark truth which the pastoral portrait conceals.

Although the picture of Bacchus and Ariadne is painted by Piero di Cosimo, it is entirely Tito's conception. Piero's own vision of the couple is antithetical to that of his young patron. Whereas Tito appreciates an illusion of harmonious sensuous surfaces, Piero di Cosimo possesses the more disturbing faculty which Ruskin named the penetrative imagination. According to Ruskin, this power works "by intuition and intensity of gaze," and perceives "a more essential truth than is seen at the surface of things." It has insight not only into nature but also into human character: "it looks not in the eyes, it judges not by the voice, it describes not by outward features, all that it affirms, judges or describes it affirms from within . . . it is forever looking under masks and burning up mists; no fairness of form, no majesty of seeming will satisfy it."[30]

George Eliot's Piero incarnates Ruskin's conception of the penetrative imagination. Piero is a tireless seer whose sole intervention in the plot—the cutting of Baldassarre's bonds—symbolizes the artist's role as a liberator of truth.[31] Piero's aesthetic, with its combination of empirical observation and spiritual intuition, and its steady recognition of death and the grotesque, is thoroughly Ruskinian.[32] George Eliot chose Piero for her novel not only because his dates fit and his vita is one of the most colorful in Vasari, but also because his works were so little known to her audience that she could freely invent an oeuvre for him to serve her own expressive purposes.[33]

While he executes Tito's commission for the picture of Bacchus and Ariadne, Piero paints the same sitters in two portraits that express his deeper insight. He represents Romola in the role of Antigone with her blind father at Colonos, as if to suggest that Romola has not really been exalted beyond tragedy by her Bacchus. Piero also paints Tito in a scene which calls the triumph of Bacchus into question:

> Piero turned the sketch, and held it towards Tito's eyes. He saw himself with his right hand uplifted, holding a wine-cup, in the attitude of triumphant joy, but with his face turned away from the cup with an expression of such intense fear in the dilated eyes and pallid lips, that he felt a cold stream through his veins, as if he were being thrown into sympathy with his imaged self.
>
> "You are beginning to look like it already," said Piero, with a short laugh, moving the picture away again. "He's seeing a ghost—that fine young man. I shall finish it some day, when I've settled what sort of ghost is the most terrible—whether it should look solid, like a dead man come to life, or half transparent, like a mist." [18:286]

The Bacchic celebrant in this picture has been surprised by his own worst fear. He exhibits the standard facial expression prescribed for the passion of terror in physiognomical treatises, but his corporal attitude belongs to the opposite emotion of "triumphant joy." This expressive paradox may be glossed by a passage from the last volume of *Modern Painters* (1860): "Evil had been fronted by the Greek, and thrust out of his path. Once conquered, if he thought of it more, it was involuntarily, as we remember a painful dream, yet with a secret dread that the dream might return and continue for ever."[34]

Piero's portrait of Tito depicts the Greek's secret dread of the return of repressed evil. Barbara Hardy has noted that Gwendolen Harleth experiences a similar moment of obscure terror when dressed in a Greek costume for the tableau of Hermione in *Daniel Deronda*.[35] The motif of the fearful Greek also figures in *The Marble Faun*, where Donatello has a panic fear of ghosts and memento mori; and it appears earlier in *Romola*, when Tito and the heroine, immediately after viewing their Ovidian portrait, are frightened by Piero di Cosimo's allegorical procession of the triumph of time. As Ruskin reminded his readers, "Florentine art was essentially Christian, ascetic, expectant of a better world, and antagonistic, therefore, to the Greek temper."[36]

Hawthorne would have called Piero's portrait of Tito a "prophetic picture," after one of the *Twice-Told Tales* in which a young couple gradually take on the expressions of worry and madness brought out in their wedding portraits by an intuitive painter. *The Marble Faun* contains several such pictures, and Piero's portrait of Tito fits the pattern because it foretells Tito's fearful and guilty recognition of Baldassarre on the steps of the Duomo.[37] In prophetic pictures, the artist paints the reality he sees behind the veil of appearances. When that reality later manifests itself to others, nature seems to imitate his art.

Prophetic pictures therefore lend a primitive and magical quality to literary pictorialism.[38] They seem to be painted by wizards, to have souls of their own, and to exercise an occult control over their models. The convention belongs ultimately to the Gothic romance, and finds its classic Victorian avatar in Oscar Wilde's *The Picture of Dorian Gray*. Curtis Dahl has called attention to the parallels between Basil Hallward's sin-laden portrait of Dorian and Piero di Cosimo's portrait of Tito as a fear-filled phiz.[39] If *Romola* anticipates fin de siècle aestheticism, it does so in its use of prophetic pictures and its representation of Tito Melema's hedonistic temperament.[40] This is not to say, of course, that George Eliot abandoned rationalism for mysticism when she shifted from phrenological to prophetic portraiture. As the Gothic novelist may in the end provide natural explanations for apparently supernatural effects, so George Eliot attributed Piero's powers of prophecy to a secular faculty of imagination. Her interest in prevision and second sight remained firmly empirical.[41]

George Eliot did not employ prophetic pictures again until *Daniel Deronda,* but in the novel that followed *Romola* she developed the ironic portraiture she had used in Tito's picture of Bacchus and Ariadne. The discrepancy between innocent image and fallen nature is especially prominent in the representation of Mrs. Transome in *Felix Holt.* For more than thirty years, Mrs. Transome has lived with the secret that her second son, Harold, was conceived in an adulterous liaison with Matthew Jermyn, a domineering lawyer. Her un-happiness has marred her youthful beauty almost more than time itself, so that there is a touching contrast between her appearance at the time of the story (1832–33) and an earlier portrait of her that hangs in the smaller drawing-room at Transome Court: "It was a charming little room in its refurbished condition: it had two pretty inlaid cabinets, great china vases with contents that sent forth odours of paradise, groups of flowers in oval frames on the walls, and Mrs Transome's own portrait in the evening costume of 1800, with a garden in the background" (42:236).

The paradisal odors, floral groups, and garden background make it clear that this is an Edenic portrait of Mrs. Transome before her fall. The imagery recalls Tito's picture of Bacchus and Ariadne. But the sad history of the sitter is visually recapitulated by the apparition of the present Mrs. Transome: "as if by some sorcery, the brilliant smiling young woman above the mantelpiece seemed to be appearing at the doorway withered and frosted by many winters, and with lips and eyes from which the smile had departed" (42:237). This is a contrast not only between summer and winter, but also between innocence and experience. Mr. Jermyn is in the room at the time.

Another ironic portrait in *Felix Holt* is that of Harold Transome, the illegitimate son. It hangs in the same room as his mother's, "a picture of a youthful face which bore a strong resemblance to her own: a beardless but masculine face, with rich brown hair hanging low on the forehead, and undulating beside each cheek down to the loose white cravat" (1:17). Mrs. Transome contemplates this portrait at the beginning of the novel, as she awaits Harold's return after an absence of fifteen years. Although she reminds herself that he will be altered from the boy she remembers, she is emotionally unprepared to find, when he finally arrives, that "her son was a stranger to her" (1:24). Portraiture in *Felix Holt* is continually belied by the changing reality of its subjects.[42]

George Eliot suffered enough disappointment from portraits in her life to grow wary of them in her art. "Poor Marian never did like any representations of herself," according to Marghanita Laski.[43] The photograph that J. J. E. Mayall made of Eliot in 1858 so appalled her that she determined never to be photographed again.[44] Thereafter she sat for only two portraits: one by Samuel Laurence in 1860 and one by Frederic Burton in 1864–65. She expressed her most characteristic misgivings about portraiture in 1879, when the question of a commemorative effigy for G. H. Lewes arose:

> Any portrait or bust of Him that others considered good I should be glad to have placed in any public institution. But for *myself* I would rather have neither portrait nor bust. My inward representation even of comparatively indifferent faces is so vivid as to make portraits of them unsatisfactory to me. And I am bitterly repenting now that I was led into buying Mayall's enlarged copy of the photograph you mention. It is smoothed down and altered, and each time I look at it I feel its *un*likeness more. *Himself as he was* is what I see inwardly, and I am afraid of outward images lest they should corrupt the inward. [*Letters,* VII, 233].

Here George Eliot expresses her residual Puritan distrust of graven images of the Worshipped One. Portraits of those dear to her often made her feel deceived and somehow violated.

Will Ladislaw reacts in much the same way to Adolf Naumann's proposed portrait of Dorothea in *Middlemarch.* The young German artist is inspired by the sight of Dorothea standing near the statue of Ariadne in the Vatican Museum. The scene, which owes a great deal to the opening chapter of *The Marble Faun,* raises some important questions about vision and definition in portraiture. How can Dorothea be perceived and represented in her full reality? Naumann offers a number of alternative portrait schemes, but Ladislaw objects vigorously to all of them, and his resistance cannot be entirely attributed to jealousy. The next chapter will discuss his Ruskinian criticism of Naumann's religious-aesthetic idealizing; but here Will's Lessingite objections to portraiture as such must be considered, for such objections underlie and complicate many of the character-descriptions in George Eliot's last two novels.

Will's reasoning applies not so much to Naumann's work in particular as to any visual representation of a living human being. In a speech already quoted, Will argues that painting and sculpture cannot represent women because "they change from moment to moment," and the visual arts cannot capture the "movement and tone" of such change (19:292). The novel bears Will out on this point; the very next chapter emphasizes the discrepancy between what Naumann saw and what Dorothea was at the same moment experiencing: a painful change in her conceptions of her husband and her own role in marriage. Ultimately Dorothea eludes the many pictorial analogies which attempt to characterize her throughout the novel. Character, as Mr. Farebrother later says in his famous paraphrase of the *Laokoön,* "is not cut in marble—it is not something solid and unalterable. It is something living and changing . . ." (72:310). George Eliot made the same point in a letter she wrote to Sara Hennell while working on *Middlemarch:* "One must not be unreasonable about portraits. How can a thing which is always the same, be an adequate representation of a living being who is always varying?" (*Letters,* V, 97). And in *Daniel Deronda* the narrator interrupts a description of Gwendolen with the following Lessingite observation: "Sir Joshua would have been glad to take her portrait; and he would have had an easier task than the historian at least in this, that he would not have had to represent the truth of change— only to give stability to one beautiful moment" (11:170). The beautiful moment is worth capturing, but it cannot tell all that is worth knowing about a person.

Gwendolen's portraiture is elusive not only because she changes but also because she pictures herself more actively than does any previous George Eliot character. Gwendolen sees Miss Harleth in a charmingly varied sequence of paintings and *tableaux vivants.* Every time we are invited to admire her in a picturesque attitude, our response is qualified by our peripheral awareness that she has calculated the visual effect and admires it too:

> There was a general falling into ranks to give her space that she might advance conspicuously to receive the gold star from the hands of Lady Brackenshaw; and the perfect movement of her fine form was certainly a pleasant thing to behold in the clear afternoon light when the shadows were long and still. She was

the central object of that pretty picture, and every one present
must gaze at her. That was enough: she herself was determined
to see nobody in particular. . . . [10:156]

Gwendolen's continuous aesthetic consciousness of herself usurps
the narrator's. The literary portraiture is internalized by the character, and thus becomes a technique of psychological as well as of
physical representation.[45] The next chapter will examine several
of Gwendolen's self-portraits in greater detail.

If Gwendolen imagines other people as anything more than her
appreciative audience, she usually sees them as caricatures. She has a
lively satirical turn of mind which is at once engaging and slightly
heartless. Early in the novel, Rex Gascoigne, while following the
hunt at Gwendolen's instigation, falls from his father's horse, Primrose, and suffers a painfully dislocated shoulder which is reset by a
stray blacksmith. When news of the accident is brought to Gwendolen, she affects concern but soon begins to visualize the scene in
terms of a comical sporting print: "Now Rex is safe, it is so droll to
fancy the figure he and Primrose would cut—in a lane all by themselves—only a blacksmith running up. It would make a capital caricature of 'Following the hounds'" (7:110).

Gwendolen's knack for caricature extends to unknown persons,
such as the Mr. Grandcourt who is about to take up residence in the
neighborhood. "Why, what kind of man do you imagine him to be,
Gwendolen?" her mother asks. "Let me see!" replies the young
observer of men and manners:

Short—just above my shoulder—trying to make himself tall by
turning up his mustache and keeping his beard long—a glass in his
right eye to give him an air of distinction—a strong opinion
about his waistcoat, but uncertain and trimming about the
weather, on which he will try to draw me out. He will stare at
me all the while and the glass in his eye will cause him to make
horrible faces, especially when he smiles in a flattering way.
I shall cast down my eyes in consequence, and he will perceive
that I am not indifferent to his attentions. I shall dream that
night that I am looking at the extraordinary face of a magnified
insect—and the next morning he will make an offer of his hand.
[9:138–39]

This sketch is amusing, but its prophecies are shaped more by dramatic irony than by penetrative imagination. Caricature, because it wilfully distorts its subjects, tells even less about them than portraiture normally does.

When she meets Mr. Grandcourt, Gwendolen is surprised to find that he "could hardly have been more unlike all her imaginary portraits of him." George Eliot's description is at once detailed and impatient:

> He was slightly taller than herself, and their eyes seemed to be on a level; there was not the faintest smile on his face as he looked at her, not a trace of self-consciousness or anxiety in his bearing; when he raised his hat he showed an extensive baldness surrounded with a mere fringe of reddish-blond hair, but he also showed a perfect hand; the line of feature from brow to chin undisguised by beard was decidedly handsome, with only moderate departures from the perpendicular, and the slight whisker too was perpendicular. It was not possible for a human aspect to be freer from grimace or solicitous wrigglings; also it was perhaps not possible for a breathing man wide awake to look less animated. . . . His complexion had a faded fairness resembling that of an actress when bare of the artificial white and red; his long narrow grey eyes expressed nothing but indifference. Attempts at description are stupid: who can all at once describe a human being? even when he is presented to us we only begin that knowledge of his appearance which must be completed by innumerable impressions under different circumstances. We recognize the alphabet; we are not sure of the language. [11:161–62]

Attempts at description may be stupid, but the narrator of *Daniel Deronda* goes right on making them, even enlisting the venerable comparison of physiognomy with a language. In this case, the language consists of many negatives. Grandcourt has no smile, no self-consciousness, no anxiety, no hair, no beard, no grimace, no wrigglings, no animation, no expression in his neutrally colored eyes, a complexion that is no longer fair, and features that do not depart very far from a norm. These negations recall the portrait of Amos Barton, but the strategy of presentation has a different significance here. We are not meeting a nonentity. The absences in Mr. Grandcourt's portrait are dictated by the traditional definition of evil as the absence of good.

Grandcourt's soul is dead to the good. He is evil in this traditional Christian and Shakespearean sense of the term, and he is the only character so conceived in all of George Eliot. The discrepancy between appearance and reality in his case is signaled by no ironic images of a lost pastoral paradise, because, unlike Hetty or Tito or Mrs. Transome, Grandcourt has never known innocence and has no desire to regain it. He does not change, and his appearance defies physiognomical interpretation. Only a terrifying normalcy conceals the death of his soul.

George Eliot's portraiture therefore emphasizes a perfect conventionality which lacks animation, a visual effect of death-in-life. In one description, for example, we see Grandcourt by firelight, lounging in his easy-chair with an after-dinner cigar: "The chair of red-brown velvet brocade was a becoming background for his pale-tinted well-cut features and exquisite long hand: omitting the cigar, you might have imagined him a portrait by Moroni, who would have rendered wonderfully the impenetrable gaze and air of distinction; and a portrait by that great master would have been quite as lively a companion as Grandcourt was disposed to be" (28:60). Here Grandcourt has not only the inexpressiveness of a Moroni portrait but also the inhuman stasis of any portrait.[46] The limitations of painting to which Lessing called attention are, for once, perfectly suited to the subject.

In the end a true portrait of Grandcourt emerges when he becomes identified with the prophetic picture of the dead face on the concealed panel at Offendene. This melodramatic nightmare-image terrifies Gwendolen early in the novel, and haunts her later in conjunction with her last glimpse of Grandcourt drowning in the Mediterranean: "a dead face—I shall never get away from it" (56:220). The picture of the corpse is to Grandcourt precisely what Piero's picture of the frightened reveller is to Tito Melema: an accurate revelation of the character's true though hidden nature.

Many of George Eliot's character-sketches are explicitly related to the great tradition of English portraiture that lasted from the Tudor era until around 1830. Shortly after Gwendolen has married Grandcourt, for example, she is described as a "Vandyke duchess of a beauty" (45:21). The portrait thus evoked aptly symbolizes her social aspirations toward the aristocracy. Because the English portrait tradition was inseparable in George Eliot's mind from the heritage and class of those it depicts, it brings a historical and sociological dimension to her literary pictorialism.

Eliot knew the English school of portraiture well, having since childhood seen examples of it in private houses such as Arbury Hall and in public displays such as the National Portrait Gallery and the National Portrait Exhibition.[47] After attending the latter in 1867, she told Sara Hennell how worthwhile it was "to see the English of past generations in their habit as they lived—especially when Gainsborough and Sir Joshua are the painters."[48]

But Eliot's reaction to English portraiture was usually more ambivalent. On the one hand, she loved it and mourned the vanished pre-Victorian England which it represented. On the other hand, she disliked it because the social class depicted was alien to her own, and often seemed in its portraits to flaunt the vanity, affectation, and unmerited privilege of the pre-Reform aristocracy. Her mixed feelings of nostalgia and alienation are reflected in her literary pictorialism, where the English portrait tradition sometimes provides access to the past and a welcome continuity between past and present, but at other times symbolizes an inaccessible and dying elite whom the younger and less aristocratic characters cannot and should not imitate.

The characteristic strategy of George Eliot's early historical fiction, as many critics have noted, is to abolish temporal distance by converting it into aesthetic distance. The narrative composes itself into a picture, and then draws the reader through the frame as if through a time barrier. Literary portraits serve this function in "Mr Gilfil's Love-Story," the most painterly of the *Scenes of Clerical Life*. The story begins in Mr. Gilfil's old age, but soon leaves the nineteenth century and flashes back to "the evening of the 21st of June 1788" (2:149). The transition is accomplished not only by fiat of the narrator but also by means of "two miniatures in oval frames" that hang in a closed-off room of the vicar's house. These depict Mr. Gilfil himself as a young man and Caterina Sarti as a girl of about eighteen, "with small features, thin cheeks, a pale southern-looking complexion, and large dark eyes." She has "her dark hair gathered away from her face, and a little cap, with a cherry-coloured bow, set on the top of her head" (1:144). Each of these details is repeated in the description of Caterina which opens the retrospective section of the narrative in chapter 2, so that the reader seems to reach the past by watching a portrait come to life. *Ecphrasis* connects the different time levels within the story, establishing a historical continuity.

The illusion of portraits coming to life likewise governs the introductions of Sir Christopher and Lady Cheverel. They own and thoroughly resemble two portraits of themselves by Reynolds (2: 163), which are modeled upon the Newdigate portraits by Romney that George Eliot saw at Arbury Hall.[49] Lady Cheverel, for example, looks "as if she were one of Sir Joshua Reynolds's stately ladies, who had suddenly stepped from her frame to enjoy the evening cool" (2:150), while Sir Christopher "was a splendid old gentleman, as anyone may see who enters the saloon at Cheverel Manor, where his full-length portrait, taken when he was fifty, hangs side by side with that of his wife . . ." (2:153).

Both pictorially and historically, the Cheverels are in touch with the family heritage represented by the pictures that hang throughout the manor. In an upstairs gallery are "queer old family portraits—of little boys and girls, once the hope of the Cheverels, with close-shaven heads imprisoned in stiff ruffs—of faded, pink-faced ladies, with rudimentary features and highly-developed head-dresses—of gallant gentlemen, with high hips, high shoulders, and red pointed beards" (2:168). Downstairs, in the main drawing room, hangs "a portrait of Sir Anthony Cheverel, who in the reign of Charles II was the renovator of the family splendour, which had suffered some declension from the brilliancy of that early Chevreuil who came over with the Conqueror" (2:165). Opposite Sir Anthony is a handsome picture of his wife. These two portraits are modeled upon Lely's full-length portraits of Sir John Skeffington, nephew of Sir Richard Newdegate, 1st Bart. and Mary Bagot, wife of Sir Richard Newdegate, 2d Bart., which still hang in the drawing room at Arbury

Hall (figs. 4, 5).[50] They complement the pictures of Sir Christopher and his lady, and help to symbolize the continuity of the family from the Norman Conquest until the eve of the French Revolution.

But this pictorially reinforced sense of tradition and identity is in jeopardy. Sir Christopher, like Sir Hugo Mallinger in *Daniel Deronda,* has no son; and his heir, a nephew, expires of a weak heart before producing a male successor. Hence the dramatic irony of Sir Christopher's remark to his nephew early in the story: "You see, Anthony, I am leaving no good places on the walls for you and your wife. We shall turn you with your faces to the wall in the gallery, and you may take your revenge on us by-and-by" (2:162). Despite his neoclassical and sculpturesque good looks, Anthony finds no place on the wall, thereby initiating a motif that reappears in George Eliot's later fiction.[51] In *Felix Holt* and *Daniel Deronda,* the younger generation also lose contact with a venerable portrait tradition of which the older generation are the last representatives.

Caterina Sarti's relationship to the Cheverel family and its portraits reflects George Eliot's ambivalence toward the aristocratic upper class. Caterina, the orphaned daughter of an Italian music-master, loves Anthony Wybrow, the Cheverel heir, and passionately desires to marry him. They often meet secretly in the upstairs portrait gallery, a favorite haunt of Caterina's and a setting that befits her desire to become a member of the family.[52] She sometimes looks "like the ghost of some former Lady Cheverel" as she walks there (2:168). But the marriage is impossible, because Wybrow is merely toying with her affections and because no one in the family accepts her as a social equal. Although the Cheverels have reared Caterina, they have never adopted her, and they think of her more as a performing pet than as a daughter. The gulf that separates her from the family is rendered in pictorial terms as she sits in the drawing room one morning, thinking of Anthony's impending marriage to Miss Assher: "She sat with the book open on her knees, her dark eyes fixed vacantly on the portrait of that handsome Lady Cheverel, wife of the notable Sir Anthony. She gazed at the picture without thinking of it, and the fair blonde dame seemed to look down on her with that benignant unconcern, that mild wonder, with which happy self-possessed women are apt to look down on their agitated and weaker sisters" (11:252–53, fig. 5).[53] The condescension of the portrait is typical of the whole family's attitude toward Caterina.

Her jealous love eventually turns into a murderous hatred, and although this passion remains focused upon the treacherous Anthony, it is at some level a hatred of the entire family. The impulse first takes the form, appropriately enough, of an attack upon a portrait. Caterina smashes a miniature of Wybrow, cracking his face and only just suppressing an urge to "grind it under her high-heeled shoe, till every trace of those false, cruel features is gone" (12:269). She nearly murders him in effigy, just as later she nearly murders him in fact. The logic of the literary portraiture in the story makes her assault upon the miniature a symbolic assault upon all of the Cheverel family pictures. Earlier the narrative implied that Caterina's passions may be equated with the passions of the French Revolution.

Caterina's relationship to the Cheverel family pictures anticipates Hetty Sorrel's relationship to the Donnithorne family pictures in *Adam Bede*. Hetty's social aspirations are expressed in her desire to "make herself look like that picture of a lady in Miss Lydia Donnithorne's dressing-room . . . she pushed [her hair] all backward to look like the picture, and form a dark curtain, throwing into relief her round white neck. Then she put down her brush and comb, and looked at herself, folding her arms before her, still like the picture" (15:224). When Hetty later puts a rose into her hair, Adam immediately identifies her model, though he does not approve of it: "that's like the ladies in the pictures at the Chase; they've mostly got flowers or feathers or gold things i' their hair, but somehow I don't like to see 'em: they allays put me i' mind o' the painted women outside the shows at Treddles'on fair" (20:335–36). Adam rightly intuits that Hetty's ambition to become a Donnithorne lady will involve her in a form of prostitution and a fall in social rank.[54]

Like Hetty, Esther Lyon, the heroine of *Felix Holt*, has always wanted to be a fine lady. She dreams of living in the style of the Transomes of Transome Court. Her wishes seem to be coming true when she is discovered to be the true heiress to the Transome estates and is subsequently sought in marriage by Harold Transome. But Esther's initial ambition gradually changes to a recognition that the inheritance is tainted and compromising, and her moral growth is mirrored in her responses to the family portraits at Transome Court. One morning her suitor finds her in the drawing room, "looking at the full-length portrait of a certain Lady Betty Transome, who had lived a century and a half before, and had the usual charm of ladies in Sir Peter Lely's style" (40:216). Harold, who himself looks "like a handsome portrait by Sir Thomas Lawrence" (46:309), immediately associates the two women, and tells Esther that she looks as if she were standing for her own portrait. The unspoken question in the scene is whether Esther will marry Harold and thereby take a place on the wall beside Lady Betty.

But Esther senses some danger in that destiny, for she observes that "almost all the portraits are in a conscious, affected attitude. That fair Lady Betty looks as if she had been drilled into that posture, and had not will enough of her own ever to move again unless she had a little push given to her. . . . One would certainly think that she had just been unpacked from silver paper" (40:216). Here Lely's mannered style is read as a sign of precious artificiality in his aristocratic subject. The portrait is a warning to Esther, and later in the novel she comes to understand what the family pictures are trying to tell her. Shortly before receiving Harold's proposal of marriage, she contemplates the ironic image of Mrs. Transome "in the evening costume of 1800, with a garden in the background" (42:236). The discrepancy between the "youthful brilliancy" of this portrait and the "joyless embittered age" of the Mrs. Transome she has known helps to influence Esther against a loveless alliance of her own (49:332–33). Unlike Caterina, Hetty, and Gwendolen Harleth, Esther realizes in time to be saved from grief that what the English portrait tradition represents is not worth having at the price of alienation from herself and her class background.[55]

In *Daniel Deronda* the Mallinger family heritage is symbolized by the portrait collection in the Abbey, Sir Hugo Mallinger's ancestral home. The pictures descend in an unbroken line from the reign of Elizabeth to that of George IV:

Two rows of these descendants, direct and collateral, females of the male line, and males of the female, looked down in the

gallery over the cloisters on the nephew Daniel as he walked
there: men in armour with pointed beards and arched eyebrows,
pinched ladies in hoops and ruffs with no face to speak of; grave-
looking men in black velvet and stuffed hips, and fair, frightened
women holding little boys by the hand; smiling politicians in
magnificent perruques, and ladies of the prize-animal kind, with
rosebud mouths and full eyelids, according to Lely; then a generation whose faces were revised and embellished in the taste of
Kneller; and so on through refined editions of the family types
in the time of Reynolds and Romney, till the line ended with Sir
Hugo and his younger brother Henleigh. . . . In Sir Hugo's youthful portrait with rolled collar and high cravat, Sir Thomas Lawrence had done justice to the agreeable alacrity of expression
and sanguine temperament still to be seen in the original, but
had done something more than justice in slightly lengthening the
nose, which was in reality shorter than might have been expected
in a Mallinger. [16:246–47]

Sir Hugo seeks to augment the family pictures when, near the end
of the novel, he advises Hans Meyrick to give up history painting and
turn to society portraiture, beginning with a picture of Sir Hugo's
"three daughters sitting on a bank . . . in the Gainsborough style"
(52:152). This anachronistic request, which is carried out later in the
novel, places Sir Hugo's descendants in a pictorial tradition that died
with Lawrence in 1830.[56] As in "Mr Gilfil's Love-Story," the heir
of the family perishes before his picture can be added to the
collection.

Literary portraits, then, remained indispensable to George Eliot's
presentation of character. For her, the process of knowing another
person begins in pictorial first impressions. Even if those impressions
prove to be inaccurate or deceptive, they form the cognitive basis
for subsequent adjustments of comprehension. Portraiture is not, to
be sure, a satisfactory medium for the representation of living,
changing human beings; but it is a necessary starting-point for such
representation. In addition to their cognitive function, moreover,
Eliot's portraits often have an exemplary function. They depict
humanity not only as it is but also as it should be. The next chapter
will consider her pictorial idealization of character.

6 History Painting and Idealization of Character

Both in theory and in practice George Eliot's realism welcomed the idealization of character. "Paint us an angel, if you can," urges the narrator of *Adam Bede,* "paint us yet oftener a Madonna. . ." (17: 270). And as if to heed his own advice, he thrice associates Dinah Morris with the angel at Christ's sepulchre in Adam's new illustrated Bible (fig. 6).[1] By the same token, Milly Barton is "a large, fair, gentle Madonna" (2:24), and Lucy Deane in *The Mill on the Floss* has "a face breathing playful joy, like one of Correggio's cherubs" (VI, 9:267).[2] As these examples suggest, George Eliot habitually idealized her characters by associating them with sacred and heroic history painting and with classical sculpture. Her work well exemplifies what Jean Hagstrum calls "the unshakeable association that has existed between literary idealization and ideal form in the graphic arts."[3] This chapter will discuss the rationale for George Eliot's pictorial idealization of character, and relate her techniques to the revival of typological iconography in the nineteenth-century visual arts. Particular attention will be paid to Eliot's characteristic ambivalence toward such idealization as it is expressed in *Middlemarch,* and to her complex resolution of that ambivalence in the double plot of *Daniel Deronda.*

Not all Victorian novelists believed in the compatibility of the ideal and the real. Trollope, for example, assumed that the terms are antithetical. Transvaluing Reynolds's famous contrast between Italian and Dutch painting, Trollope contended that the High Renaissance art of Italy depicts what is unreal: "We are, most of us, apt to love Raphael's madonnas better than Rembrandt's matrons. But though we do so, we know that Rembrandt's matrons existed; but we have a strong belief that no such woman as Raphael painted ever did exist. In that he painted . . . for Church purposes, Raphael was justified; but had he painted so for family portraiture he would have been false."[4] This conception of realism was very different from George Eliot's. She believed that Raphael's madonnas sometimes belong in family portraiture, and she pointedly denied that the ideal is antithetical to the real. "Any real observation of life and character must be limited, and the imagination must fill in and give life to the picture," she told John Blackwood in 1861 (*Letters*, III, 427).

Eliot agreed with G. H. Lewes's argument, in his important essay on "Realism in Art" (1858), that the opposite of realism is not idealism but falsism. Lewes illustrates the compatibility of idealism with realism by citing Raphael's *Sistine Madonna* (fig. 1):

> In the figures of the Pope and St. Barbara we have a real man and woman, one of them a portrait, and the other not elevated above sweet womanhood. Below, we have the two exquisite angel children, intensely childlike, yet something *more,* something which renders their wings congruous with our conception of them. In the never-to-be-forgotten divine babe, we have at once the intensest realism of presentation, with the highest idealism of conception: the attitude is at once grand, easy, and natural; the face is that of a child, but the child is divine . . . we feel that humanity in its highest conceivable form is before us. . . . Here is a picture which from the first has enchained the hearts of men, which is assuredly in the highest sense ideal, and which is so because it is also in the highest sense real—a real man, a real woman, real angel-children, and a real Divine Child; the last a striking contrast to the ineffectual attempts of other painters to spiritualize and idealize the babe—attempts which represent no babe at all.[5]

The Leweses valued highly the ideal realism of High Renaissance painting, and George Eliot strove to create a similar effect in many parts of her own fiction.[6]

Eliot was of course no Christian, but her idealization had a rationale in the secular religion of humanity which replaced her Evangelicalism. This humanism rejected Christian theology but sought to retain the ethics, emotional culture, and social bonding of the older religion. Feuerbach, whose *Essence of Christianity* strongly influenced Eliot on these points, argued that since the Christian god is a projection of mankind, mankind itself should be worshipped in a religious spirit. Christian devotion should be transferred to secular subjects, and human experience should be venerated and sanctified.[7] George Eliot favored this redirection of emotion, and promoted it in her fiction by associating her characters with sacred and heroic visual art. Thus she attempted to hallow Romola's experience by visualizing her moral growth as a progression from "The Unseen Madonna" to "The Visible Madonna" to "the Holy Mother with the Babe, fetching water for the sick" in a plague-stricken village (43:131, 44:141, 68:406).[8] Feuerbach himself suggested a didactic and affective rationale for literary pictorialism when he defined imagination as the "type-creating [*bildliche*], emotional, and sensuous" part of the human mind, and argued that "man, as an emotional and sensuous being, is governed and made happy only by images, by sensible representations."[9]

George Eliot took something of a liberty when she rendered Feuerbach's term *bildliche* as "type-creating." But her translation points up one important element of traditional Christian thought which she sought to preserve and secularize in her religion of humanity: the concept of types. George Eliot's pictorial idealization may be viewed in the context of efforts by other nineteenth-century artists to redefine typological symbolism so that it might serve the religious and aesthetic needs of the age. Typological symbolism attracted many of the best minds of the period because it offered a way of conferring spiritual meaning upon the representation of phenomenal experience, of affirming the existence of design while yet respecting the integrity of history. Strictly speaking, a type is an Old Testament prefiguration of a New Testament truth. It is not a vehicle of allegory; a type retains its identity as a historical reality at the same time that it foreshadows the divinely ordained event which fulfills it.[10] The Victorians often used the term more loosely, however, to denote any exemplary moral or religious norm which finds successive incarnations in history.

In the visual arts the revaluation of typological symbolism was a sign of dissatisfaction with established conceptions of sacred and heroic history painting. This dissatisfaction had grown steadily since the middle of the eighteenth century.[11] In the later eighteenth century, history painters began boldly to combine the inherited motifs of Christian art with scenes of contemporary heroism.[12] By the mid-nineteenth century, a creative and nontraditional typological symbolism was widely employed in English painting. Obscure or invented incidents in the early life of Christ were made to foreshadow famous later events, and Christian types were often applied postfiguratively to secular and contemporary situations.[13] Such symbolism is a prominent feature in Pre-Raphaelite painting, where it balances the tendency of empirical realism toward fragmentation and atomism.[14] The iconography of the Deposition in Holman Hunt's *A Converted British Family Sheltering a Christian Missionary from the Persecution of the Druids* (1850), of the Pietà in Henry Wallis's *The Death of Chatterton* (1856), of the Madonna and Child in Ford Madox Brown's *The Pretty Baa-Lambs* (1852) or *Take Your Son, Sir!* (1857),[15] of the emblematic pilgrimage in Millais's *The Blind Girl* (1856),[16] suggests in each case a connection between a concrete historical moment and a recurrent type of spiritual activity.

George Eliot came to art, then, in an atmosphere congenial to "the notion that Types in their continuing cycles can be found in contemporary reality."[17] Her education had introduced her to the traditional exegesis of biblical types, which was still widespread in nineteenth-century Evangelical circles.[18] In *Scenes of Clerical Life,* Amos Barton finds it difficult to communicate "instruction through familiar types and symbols." Attempting to explain the Christian significance of unleavened bread, he carries the imagination of his audience "to the dough-tub, but unfortunately was not able to carry it upwards from that well-known object to the unknown truths which it was intended to shadow forth" (2:39). In "Janet's Repentance" the residents of Milby "had not yet heard that the schismatic ministers of Salem [the Dissenters' chapel] were obviously typified by Korah, Dathan, and Abiram" (2:60). George Eliot was obviously familiar enough with typological thinking to draw upon it for humorous effects.

The novelist often used the word *type* in connection with the representation of sublime and religious ideas in contemporary art. At Weimar she saw a portrait head of Goethe at seventy which she thought "might serve as a type of sublime old age" (*Essays*, p. 90). Also at Weimar she saw Liszt in concert, and thereafter understood why "the type of Liszt's face seems to haunt [Ary Scheffer] in so many of his compositions." She particularly recalled Scheffer's *Die drei Weisen aus dem Morgenlande* (1844), a picture "in which he expressly intended to introduce an idealization of Liszt" as one of the three Magi, "gazing in ecstasy at the guiding light above them." She herself thought Liszt looked like "a perfect model of a St. John" or "a prophet in the moment of inspiration" (*Essays*, p. 98). This kind of idealization, which ennobles without falsifying its subject, and which associates admirable human faces with established Christian exemplars, violates neither George Eliot's atheism nor her conception of realism.

She used the word *type* even more revealingly when defending her presentation of Mordecai in *Daniel Deronda*: "The effect that one strives after is an outline as strong as that of Balfour of Burley [in Scott's *Old Mortality*] for a much more complex character and a higher strain of ideas. But such an effect is just the most difficult thing in art—to give new elements—i.e. elements not already used up—in forms as vivid as those of long familiar types" (*Letters*, VI, 223). Here is a clear statement of the rationale for the pictorial idealization of character in George Eliot's fiction: she seeks to give the new elements of her religion of humanity in forms as vivid as those of the long familiar types of traditional religious culture.[19]

Eliot was well aware of the revaluation of typological symbolism in the nineteenth-century visual arts, especially within the German Nazarene and English Pre-Raphaelite movements.[20] She began to follow the work of the Pre-Raphaelites in 1852, when she commended Millais's *A Huguenot on Saint Bartholomew's Day* in May and read the famous essay on "Pre-Raphaelitism in Art and Literature" in the *British Quarterly Review* for November (*Letters*, II, 29–30, 48). This essay helped to shape her most basic beliefs about the movement: that it represented a salutary return to nature, truth, and realism in art, but that its strengths were sapped by its weakness for medieval ecclesiasticism and archaism. Thus Eliot had mixed reactions to the work of her favorite Pre-Raphaelite painter, William Holman Hunt. In 1856 she described him as "one of the greatest painters of the pre-eminently realistic school" (*Essays*, p. 268), and she remained interested in his work at least until 1864, when she sent to Sara Hennell a sympathetic critique of his *Afterglow in Egypt* (*Letters*, IV, 159). But her lack of sympathy with the theistic religious aims of Hunt's painting sometimes made her indifferent or oblivious to the workings of its figural symbolism.[21] She had no use for *The Light of the World* (1853) because "it is too mediaeval and pietistic to be rejoiced in as a product of the present age" (*Letters*, II, 156). She praised *The Hireling Shepherd* (1851) for the "marvellous truthfulness" of its landscape (*Essays*, p. 268), but quite misread the moral iconography of the shepherd and the wench, failing to see that, like *Adam Bede,* the painting is profoundly critical of false and idyllic notions of pastoral.[22] Her doctrinal antipathy probably accounts for her inability to perceive the similarity between her own mode of didactic symbolism and that of her more orthodox contemporaries.[23]

She was even less receptive to the typological history painting of the German Nazarenes, which she encountered on her trips to Berlin, Munich, and Rome in 1854–60. She was sympathetic with the early Nazarene revolt against the German neoclassical style, and once compared it (borrowing an argument from the author of "Pre-Raphaelitism in Art and Literature") with Wordsworth's rebellion against eighteenth-century poetic diction. Thus she defended "an early poem of Wordsworth's, or an early picture of Overbeck's" on the ground that "the attempt at an innovation reveals a want that has not hitherto been met" (*Essays*, pp. 99–100). But Eliot strongly disliked the monumental style of history painting which Nazarene artists and their disciples began to practice in the 1820s and perfected in the 1840s.[24] G. H. Lewes was referring to this style when he spoke of "celebrated paintings of the Modern German school . . . in which a great deal is meant and very little executed, full of symbol and historical meaning, which require a long commentary before they can be rendered intelligible, and which before and after the commentary leave the emotions untouched and the eye ungratified."[25] Because George Eliot's critique of Nazarene history painting is central both to the question of her pictorial idealization of character and to the meaning of *Middlemarch,* it is worth discussing in some detail.

It has long been recognized that Adolf Naumann, the German painter of the Rome chapters of *Middlemarch,* represents the Nazarene or revivalist tradition, which was the branch of German Romantic art best known in Victorian England.[26] Naumann is modeled upon two identifiable Nazarenes: Johann Friedrich Overbeck (1789–1869) and Josef von Führich (1800–76). Naumann's link with Overbeck is twofold. First, Naumann portrays Mr. Casaubon in a "picture in which Saint Thomas Aquinas sat among the doctors of the Church in a disputation too abstract to be represented, but listened to with more or less attention by an audience above" (22:332). Gordon S. Haight has noted the resemblance between this fictive painting and Overbeck's *The Triumph of Christianity in the Arts* (1840), a picture that George Eliot had hoped to see during her trip to Germany in 1854–55 (Haight, p. 151; fig. 7). Both of these idealized history paintings are patterned after Raphael's *Disputa* in the Vatican Stanze.[27] The second link between Naumann and Overbeck is a detail of the costume worn by Overbeck on the day George Eliot visited his Roman studio in 1860.[28] The venerable painter had on "a maroon velvet cap, and a grey scarf over his shoulders."[29] Duly recorded in the novelist's journal (Cross, II, 158), these items reappeared eleven years later as "a dove-coloured blouse and a maroon velvet cap" worn by Naumann when the Casaubons visit his studio in *Middlemarch* (22:327). Having seen the greatest of the Nazarenes in his own milieu, George Eliot knew how to dress a character partly modeled upon him.

Although Overbeck lived to be visited by George Eliot, he was nevertheless too old to be Naumann's sole original. The distinguished Nazarene was already forty in 1829, the year of Dorothea's honeymoon.[30] Chronologically, Naumann more closely resembles Josef von Führich, who was born in Bohemia in 1800 and worked under Overbeck in Rome from 1827 to 1829, helping to finish the frescoes in the Casino Massimo.[31] One of the paintings attributed to Naumann in the novel is modeled upon a painting of Führich's that George Eliot had seen during her own honeymoon trip to Berlin in 1854–55.

Ladislaw tells us that Naumann is painting "the Saints drawing the Car of the Church" (22:326). This processional allegory recalls Führich's *The Triumph of Christ,* first drawn in 1831 ("gleich nach der Rückkehr aus Rom"), engraved in 1839, and painted in 1840 (fig. 8).[32] George Eliot saw the painting in Graf Raczinsky's famous collection of modern art, and described it in her journal with a charmingly Dorothean incomprehension of the iconography, which derives from Titian's *Triumph of Faith*:[33] "Under this picture was one by a Viennese artist [Führich had become Professor of History Painting at Vienna] also shewing a great amount of misapplied power. Jesus sits in a chariot, drawn by a bullock and a lion (I think), Popes in their robes pushing along the wheels, and a saintly female figure—the Virgin, I suppose, sitting opposite him."[34] The lion and "bullock" are, of course, two of the four evangelists drawing the chariot, and the "Popes" at the wheels are the four fathers of the church, of whom only Gregory wears the papal habit. Dorothea's ignorance of Christian iconography in *Middlemarch* clearly mirrors a stage in her creator's own education. Nevertheless, George Eliot was almost certainly remembering Führich's *Triumphzug* when she attributed "the Saints drawing the Car of the Church" to Naumann.[35]

The year of Dorothea's wedding journey was a year of great change in the Nazarene movement.[36] It marked the end of the Roman phase of the movement, which had begun in 1810, when Overbeck first moved to the Eternal City to live and paint in the spirit of late medieval Christianity with his fellows in the Brotherhood of Saint Luke. After the completion of the Casino Massimo frescoes in 1829, the remaining Nazarenes disbanded to various cities in Germany, leaving Overbeck to carry on alone in Rome. By then Nazarene artists were in great demand for the decoration of public buildings and monuments, and the staffing of various academies and art institutes. Official recognition and patronage prompted a change toward a programmatic, didactic, monumental style of art suitable to the decoration of cities that had grown culturally ambitious, intensely nationalistic, and historically self-conscious. This later phase of German art, known to George Eliot chiefly through Overbeck's *Triumph of Christianity* and the fresco cycles in Berlin and Munich of Peter Cornelius and his pupil Wilhelm von Kaulbach, is clearly anticipated by Naumann's theory and practice of history painting in *Middlemarch.*[37]

George Eliot's critique of Naumann's art involves a sophisticated version of the standard Victorian charge that modern German art contains too much mind and not enough nature.[38] The Leweses thought of the Nazarenes and their followers essentially as Pre-Raphaelites who lacked the saving grace of naturalism.[39] Eliot's principal objection to German monumental art was that its symbolism is insufficiently grounded in an empirically observed and represented order of nature. This tendency to depict things "too abstract to be represented" is suggested by Ladislaw's introduction of Naumann as "one of the chief renovators of Christian Art, one of those who had not only revived but expanded that grand conception of supreme events as mysteries at which the successive ages were spectators, and in relation to which the great souls of all periods became as it were contemporaries" (22:332, 326). We are meant to take this vague but grandiose neotypological theory of history painting with a large grain of salt.[40] Idealization must not be confused with Teutonic mystification.

Naumann's pictures are open to the same objections that George Eliot made to Wilhelm von Kaulbach's *weltgeschichtliche Bilder* when she saw them at Berlin and Munich. Kaulbach's "allegorical-historical compositions . . . intended to represent the historical development of culture," she declared, "leave one entirely cold as all elaborate allegorical compositions must do."[41] Kaulbach's frescoes employ "a regular child's puzzle of symbolism," she complained to Sara Hennell; "instead of taking a single moment of reality and trusting to the infinite symbolism that belongs to all nature, he attempts to give at one view a succession of events, each represented by some group which may mean 'whichever you please, my dear'" (*Letters*, II, 454–55). In other words, Kaulbach's symbolism does not sufficiently incarnate the ideal in the real. It ignores what Ruskin termed the naturalist ideal, and it violates Lessing's prohibition against representing events separated by time in a single picture.[42]

First articulated in the 1850s, George Eliot's reaction to Nazarene art remained relatively unchanged. Reappearing in *Middlemarch,* her critique of the indeterminacy and arbitrariness of German typological symbolism amusingly unites Mr. Brooke's fuzzy response to the "Dispute" with Will Ladislaw's parody of the "Saints." Brooke, echoing Browning's Duke of Ferrara, says to Casaubon: "And we'll go down and look at the picture. There you are to the life: a deep subtle sort of thinker with his forefinger on the page, while Saint Bonaventure or somebody else, rather fat and florid, is looking up at the Trinity. Everything is symbolical, you know—the higher style of art: I like that up to a certain point, but not too far—it's rather straining to keep up with, you know" (34:86). As interpreted by Mr. Brooke, the "symbolical" style of Naumann's "Dispute" affords more delight than instruction.

Ladislaw's parody of the "Saints" likewise stresses the indeterminacy and arbitrariness of its symbolism, but does so more instructively:

> "I have been making a sketch of Marlow's Tamburlaine Driving the Conquered Kings in his Chariot. I am not so ecclesiastical as Naumann, and I sometimes twit him with his excess of meaning. But this time I mean to outdo him in breadth of intention. I take Tamburlaine in his chariot for the tremendous course of the world's physical history lashing on the harnessed dynasties. In my opinion that is a good mythical interpretation." Will here looked at Mr. Casaubon, who received this offhand treatment of symbolism very uneasily, and bowed with a neutral air. [22:326–27]

Will's statement is not, as Richard Ellmann and others have assumed, a description of an actual project.[43] Rather, it describes a purely imaginary allegory of secular history concocted by Will to parody the symbolic pretensions of Nazarene allegories of church history. Will's fantastic "Tamburlaine" belongs to the same genre as Kaulbach's "allegorical-historical compositions . . . intended to represent the historical development of culture." The point of the parody is essentially the same point that Will makes when he accuses Naumann of thinking "that all the universe is straining towards the obscure significance of your pictures" (19:290).

What weakens Naumann's history painting is precisely what vitiates Mr. Casaubon's key to all mythologies. Proceeding from dogmatic Christian preconceptions, both men approach history deductively and categorically rather than inductively and empirically. As a follower of Jacob Bryant's *A New System, or an Analysis of Ancient Mythology* (1774–76), Casaubon finds his key to all mythologies in the revealed truth of Holy Scripture, and seeks to interpret the pagan mythologies as corruptions of the one true myth.[44] Both he and Naumann read the past as a symbolic record of Christian certitudes. Their agreement on the Christian interpretation of myth and history is signified by Casaubon's decision to appear in the "Dispute" and to buy the finished painting. In *Scenes of Clerical Life*, George Eliot noted the bond between Nazarene art and Anglican sensibilities when she described a clergyman's study in which "a refined Anglican taste is indicated by a German print from Overbeck" (11:170). One wonders whether she knew that Charles Pusey visited Overbeck in Rome in 1829.[45]

To associate Naumann with Casaubon in this context is to see how Naumann's career fits the historical pattern of aspiration and failure established by the careers of the major characters in *Middlemarch*. Naumann's ambition to renovate Christian art is comparable to Casaubon's ambition to find the key to all mythologies. But like the mythographer, the painter is working along lines that future generations will judge to have been misguided and retrogressive. In George Eliot's view, Naumann's achievement belongs to a reactionary eddy in the mainstream progression of nineteenth-century painting toward a Ruskinian naturalism. She had little sympathy with the deliberate imitation of archaic pictorial styles, and less with the attempt to revive medieval Catholicism; thus she once criticized Overbeck for evoking "all the barbarisms of the Pre-Raphaelite period."[46] The Nazarene program ran dead against George Eliot's belief in humanistic empiricism and evolutionary development.

Tempering this judgment with a characteristic admixture of sym-

pathy, however, Eliot perceived many virtues in the Nazarene movement. She certainly admired the learning, energy, and commitment
of its adherents. What she said of Overbeck in 1860 might well be
applied to Naumann: "The man himself is more interesting than his
pictures" (Cross, II, 158). Eliot agreed with Lewes's observation that
German revivalist art had not only "a retrograde purpose which was
bad" but also a "critical purpose which was good."[47] The critical
purpose to which Lewes referred was the recovery of lost traditions
of Christian art, an educational endeavor which helped to overcome
precisely the kind of ignorance displayed by George Eliot's description of Führich's *Triumphzug*. According to Lewes, Overbeck and
Cornelius "lent real genius to the attempt to revive the dead forms
of early Christian art."[48] They did so not only in their own works
but also by inspiring an important body of research into the history
and iconography of European Pre-Raphaelite painting.[49] Such
studies were no doubt in Lewes's mind when he spoke in 1855 of
"the services rendered by Romanticism in making the Middle Ages
more thoroughly understood."[50] By Romanticism in this context,
he and George Eliot meant a German, Catholic, neomedieval movement whose "main feature . . . was the exaltation of the Medieval
above the Classic, of art animated by Christian spiritualism above the
art animated by Greek humanism."[51]

Largely published between 1835 and 1855, the scholarship inspired by Romanticism divided Dorothea's England of the first
Reform Bill from George Eliot's of the second. Readers of *Middlemarch* are reminded that in Dorothea's day travelers to Rome

> did not often carry full information on Christian art either in
> their heads or their pockets; and even the most brilliant English
> critic of the day mistook the flower-flushed tomb of the ascended
> Virgin for an ornamental vase due to the painter's fancy. Ro-
> manticism, which has helped to fill some dull blanks with love
> and knowledge, had not yet penetrated the times with its leaven
> and entered into everybody's food; it was fermenting still as a
> distinguishable vigorous enthusiasm in certain long-haired Ger-
> man artists at Rome. . . . [19:287]

George Eliot's example of English ignorance is accurate and well-chosen. In *Notes of a Journey through France and Italy* (1826), a book Dorothea might well have carried to Rome, William Hazlitt grossly misreads the iconography of Raphael's *The Coronation of the Virgin* in the Vatican Museum (fig. 9).[52] Referring indeed to a "vase of flowers," Hazlitt fails to recognize the Marian resurrection symbolism of the lilies and roses that spring from the Virgin's sarcophagus. And he describes the twelve apostles as a "crowd."[53] Readers of *Middlemarch* would almost certainly have possessed better "information on Christian art" than Hazlitt's. For example, Mrs. Jameson's popular *Legends of the Madonna as Represented in the Fine Arts* (1852) mentions five versions of the Coronation in which "the miraculous flowers" appear. Of Raphael's treatment Mrs. Jameson says: "Here we have the tomb below, filled with flowers; and around it the twelve apostles."[54] For such gains in precision George Eliot thanked the "long-haired German artists" of the early nineteenth century.[55]

In *Middlemarch* Naumann dramatizes the educational function of Romanticism when he plays the kindly didact to Dorothea. Her pre-Romantic ignorance of the conventions of Christian art prevents her from appreciating the "walls . . . covered with frescoes, or with rare pictures" that she sees in Rome (21:315). Although Dorothea's conscience is troubled by aesthetic apprehension per se, part of her difficulty is that often she simply does not know what the pictures represent. By explicating the iconography of his own neomedieval works, Naumann comes nearer than anyone else in the novel to teaching Dorothea how to look at traditional paintings which are not simple portraits or landscapes:

> The painter in his confident English gave little dissertations on his finished and unfinished subjects . . . and Dorothea felt that she was getting quite new notions as to the significance of madonnas seated under inexplicable canopied thrones with the simple country as a background, and of saints with architectural models in their hands, or knives accidentally wedged in their skulls. Some things which had seemed monstrous to her were gathering intelligibility and even a natural meaning. [22:327-28]

Although the narrator's dry tone suggests considerable sympathy with Dorothea's distaste for such subjects, the last sentence affirms a positive and welcome enlightenment. Here Naumann does in small what Romanticism will soon do for Europe at large: he gives "intelligibility and even a natural meaning" to symbols of Christian art that had come to seem unintelligible and unnatural.

Whether the conventions of medieval Christian art should determine the direction of nineteenth-century painting was, however, a different question in George Eliot's mind. On balance she felt they should not, because they distort more than they clarify. To teach Dorothea how to look at Madonnas is one thing; to paint her as one is another. Both Naumann and the narrator of *Middlemarch* present idealizing portraits of Dorothea as a Christian heroine, but the novel calls all such portraiture into doubt. One side of George Eliot's mind remained skeptical toward the pictorial idealization of character even as she was practicing it.

When Naumann first encounters Dorothea in the Vatican Museum, her "Quakerish" costume and meditative expression inspire him to paint her as a personification of the Christian spirit, "dressed," since Naumann is Catholic, "as a nun" (19:289). Then he sees Dorothea as a "perfect young Madonna," and eventually he settles for painting her as Santa Clara (19:290, 22:331). But Dorothea's figure and attitude resemble those of the statue of Ariadne near which she stands (fig. 10), so there are pagan elements in the scene which prompt Naumann to a more comprehensive definition. He envisions Dorothea as "antique form animated by Christian sentiment—a sort of Christian Antigone—sensuous force controlled by spiritual passion" (19:290). This formulation unites the classical and the medieval, reconciling the great antitheses of German aesthetic debate in a higher synthesis.

Though suggestive, Naumann's exalted and schematic vision is only partly valid. Will Ladislaw immediately warns his friend not to confuse a symbolic conception of Dorothea with her human reality. Actually Naumann's allegorizing distorts his subjects, much as the fantasies of the male egoists in *Adam Bede* distort Hetty. Ladislaw alludes to Naumann's egoism when he accuses the painter of "looking at the world entirely from the studio point of view" (21:317), of thinking that art perfects life, and of believing that his picture of

Dorothea would be "the chief outcome of her existence—the divinity passing into higher completeness and all but exhausted in the act of covering [a] bit of canvas" (19:290). This is a critique of the solipsistic tendency inherent in Romantic aestheticism. It no doubt reflects the many charges of spiritual pride which Ruskin laid against the Nazarenes,[56] and it may also entail a more contemporary reference to the Victorian philosophy of art-for-art's-sake that had begun to spin off from Pre-Raphaelitism by the later 1860s.[57] The critique also aligns Naumann with one of the grand themes of the novel: the inescapable corruption of aspiration by egoism.

Naumann's Christianizing aestheticism, then, is one of the many modes of human intellection tested and found wanting in *Middlemarch*. Idealizing portraiture provides no coherent vision in this novel of incomplete insights. Ultimately Dorothea eludes all of the analogies that attempt to characterize her as Santa Clara, Santa Teresa, Santa Barbara (fig. 11),[58] the Madonna, and a Christian Antigone, just as Mr. Casaubon more obviously eludes Naumann's vision of him as Saint Thomas Aquinas or Dorothea's comparison of him with "the portrait of Locke" (2:21; see fig. 12).[59] W. J. Harvey has argued that in *Middlemarch* such comparisons border upon the mock-heroic.[60]

George Eliot sometimes wished passionately to affirm the persistence of ideal types in everyday life (G. H. Lewes often called her "Madonna"), but at other times she was skeptical and satirical about just such affirmations; and her skepticism is by no means confined to *Middlemarch*. In *Felix Holt,* for example, she gently satirizes her own response to religious art in a scene between Felix and Esther Lyon: "He was looking up at her quite calmly, very much as a reverential Protestant might look at a picture of the Virgin, with a devoutness suggested by the type rather than by the image" (27:39).

Usually, of course, George Eliot tried to be as attentive to the image as to the type, and this attention often complicated her responses. She was, for instance, no indiscriminate admirer of Raphael's madonnas. Although she worshipped the *Sistine Madonna,* she disliked some of its earlier "sisters" for "their sheep-like look" (Cross, II, 189). In *The Mill on the Floss* she draws an unflattering analogy between these images and Mrs. Tulliver: "I have often wondered whether those early Madonnas of Raphael, with the blond faces and somewhat stupid expression, kept their placidity undisturbed when their strong-limbed, strong-willed boys got a little too old to do without clothing" (I, 2:15).

Eliot's ambivalent vision sometimes issued in contradictory treatments of the same picture. Raphael's *Saint Catherine,* for example, was an early favorite of hers (fig. 13). At the age of twenty-five she told a friend that "you are a bright spot in my memory, like Raphael's Saint Catherine" (*Letters,* I, 188); and she may well have had the same painting in mind when Arthur Donnithorne refers to Dinah Morris as "St. Catherine in a Quaker dress" (5:91), and when one of the characters in *Romola* says that the heroine is "fit to be a model for a wise Saint Catherine of Egypt" (49:200).[61] But Raphael's famous picture is treated much less reverently in *Middlemarch* when Dorothea, recuperating from her bereavement, begins to grow restless: "After three months Freshitt had become rather oppressive: to sit like a model for Saint Catherine looking rapturously at Celia's baby would not do for many hours in the day: (54:3-4). Viewed from this perspective, Raphael's saint seems posed and a bit silly.

George Eliot's ambivalence toward idealization also complicates her attitude toward sculpture. Her visit to Weimar in 1854 convinced her that she did not care for "classical idealising in portrait sculpture." She saw there several distasteful examples of the technique, including a "colossal statue of Goethe, executed after Bettina's design," which represents him "as a naked Apollo with a Psyche at his knee!" (*Essays,* p. 86). Any work in which the "artist tells us that the ideal of a Greek god divides his attention with his immediate subject" must be taken, Eliot warned, with a grain of salt. She declared herself particularly "irritated with idealization in portrait when, as in Dannecker's bust of Schiller, one has been misled into supposing that Schiller's brow was square and massive, while, in fact, it was receding" (*Essays,* p. 88). In other words, idealization must not exceed the bounds of phrenological realism.

Yet in other moods Eliot was not at all averse to classical idealizing in portrait sculpture. She was particularly fond of heroic and monumental images of women, such as the cockle-woman she once saw at Swansea: "the grandest woman I ever saw—six feet high, carrying herself like a Greek Warrior, and treading the earth with unconscious majesty" (*Letters,* II, 251). This taste for massive, Amazonian figures also manifests itself in Eliot's admiration of several pieces of contemporary sculpture: August Kiss's *Mounted Amazon Attacked by a Tiger* (*Essays,* p. 126) and Ludwig Schwanthaler's *Bavaria* (Cross, II, 21–22).

Given her predilection for grand, statuesque female forms, she naturally visualized her own heroines as imposing creatures. Dorothea, for example, resembles the reclining Ariadne in the Vatican Museum, and the similarity is of amplitude as well as attitude (fig. 10). The full-grown Maggie Tulliver is a tall, queenly figure whose arm resembles either one of the Parthenon sculptures or a classical sculpture that George Eliot saw in Berlin.[62] In "Janet's Repentance" we pause with the heroine's mother to admire Janet's "tall rich figure, looking all the grander for the plainness of the deep mourning dress, and the noble face with its massy folds of black hair, made matronly by a simple white cap. Janet had that enduring beauty which belongs to pure majestic outline and depth of tint" (4:195). In a word, Janet's beauty, like that of Isola Churchill, the heroine of G. H. Lewes's *Ranthorpe,* is "more sculpturesque than picturesque."[63] In *Daniel Deronda* the heroine is visualized in terms of Roman colored sculpture: "Dressed in black, without a single ornament, and with the warm whiteness of her skin set off between her light-brown coronet of hair and her square-cut bodice, she might have tempted an artist to try again the Roman trick of a statue in black, white, and tawny marble. Seeing her image slowly advancing, she thought, 'I *am* beautiful'" (23:377). As usual, Gwendolen is the first to admire her own aesthetic effects. Herein she differs from Mirah Cohen, who is all unconsciously transformed from "immovable, statue-like despair" to "a coloured statue of serenity" (17:280, 52:159).[64] Roman sculpture figures, too, in the presentation of Felix Holt: "Felix might have come from the hands of a sculptor in the later Roman period, when the plastic impulse was stirred by the grandeur of barbaric forms" (46:309). Although pagan sculptural idealization obviously does not involve the renewal of biblical types, it nevertheless serves much the same function as George Eliot's Christian pictorialism. Both modes of literary portraiture hallow character by associating it with venerated traditional norms.

Eliot also elicited exemplary values from her literary portraits by grouping them in contrasting pairs. For example, the description just quoted of Felix Holt as a late-Roman statue occurs in combination with a description of Harold Transome as "a handsome portrait by Sir Thomas Lawrence." The two Radicals, we are told, "certainly made a striking contrast" (46:309). A similar pairing takes place in *Daniel Deronda*: "Deronda, turning to look straight at Grandcourt who was on his left hand, might have made a subject for those old painters who liked contrasts of temperament" (15:240). Or again, in *Adam Bede*: "The family likeness between [Mrs. Poyser] and her niece Dinah Morris, with the contrast between her keenness and Dinah's seraphic gentleness of expression, might have served a painter as an excellent suggestion for a Martha and Mary" (6:107).

In George Eliot's work such contrasts are usually moral as well as visual, and sometimes they border on the emblematic in their clear-cut, monitory juxtaposition of virtue and vice, altruism and egoism. In "Amos Barton," for example, Milly is compared in physiognomy and moral temperament with the Countess Czerlaski: "Look at the two women on the sofa together! The large, fair, mild-eyed Milly is timid even in friendship: it is not easy to her to speak of the affection of which her heart is full. The lithe, dark, thin-lipped countess is racking her small brain for caressing words and charming exaggerations" (3:48). Exemplary pairings of women may be found among George Eliot's earliest published writings (*Essays*, pp. 21–22), and they are an important device for unifying parallel plots in her mature fiction.[65]

Perhaps the best-known of Eliot's double portraits is the "Two Bed-Chambers" scene in chapter 15 of *Adam Bede*. Here Hetty Sorrel and Dinah Morris are contrasted in great visual and moral detail. Their surroundings, their appearances, and their physical and mental activities are set forth with a painstaking realism that emulates the spirit of Dutch painting. Yet these concrete descriptive details compose themselves into coherent symbolic patterns as well, so that Hetty's portrait incorporates many traditional symbols of vanity, whereas Dinah's abounds with familiar signs of contemplation, charity, and spiritual rebirth. After describing the two women separately, George Eliot brings them together, as if joining two wings of a diptych.

> What a strange contrast the two figures made! Visible enough in that mingled twilight and moonlight. Hetty, her cheeks flushed and her eyes glistening from her imaginary drama, her beautiful neck and arms bare, her hair hanging in a curly tangle down her back, and the baubles in her ears. Dinah, covered with her long white dress, her pale face full of subdued emotion, almost like a lovely corpse into which the soul has returned charged with sublimer secrets and a sublimer love. [15:238]

The uncharacteristic absence of predication in Eliot's syntax here reinforces the impression of static, juxtaposed icons. Although *vanitas* symbolism is common enough in seventeenth-century Dutch genre painting, this sort of stark moral contrast is not common.[66] Eliot's description is so emblematic that one critic has actually proposed a direct iconographic parallel with Francis Quarles's emblem III, 14.[67] This is not a convincing analogy, however. R. T. Jones is closer to the mark when he compares the scene to a hypothetical nineteenth-century painting: "It might be called 'Sacred and Profane Love,' and it might have been painted by, say, Holman Hunt."[68] This is a perceptive suggestion, especially if Jones is thinking of Hunt's famous pair of moral pictures, *The Light of the World* and *The Awakening Conscience*.

Yet Hunt never depicted two women together in quite the way that Eliot does here. A better pictorial analogy for "The Two Bed-Chambers" scene, if one need be sought, is Wilhelm von Schadow's *Pietas und Vanitas: Parabel der klugen und törichten Jungfrauen* (1842), a painting displayed at the great Munich exhibition of 1858 within two months of George Eliot's visit to the Bavarian capital (fig. 14).[69] Schadow's wise and foolish virgins are juxtaposed as if in a diptych, equipped with contrasting symbolic accoutrements and differentiated by the directions of their gazes. Although the painting does not resemble George Eliot's text in every detail, the correspondences are nonetheless suggestive.[70]

This sort of contrast attains massive proportions in the structure of *Daniel Deronda*, where the English and Jewish parts of the novel incorporate two distinctive and antithetical modes of literary portraiture. Both modes involve the idealization of character and the reincarnation of sacred types, but the novel treats one mode as false and the other as true. Throughout *Deronda*, George Eliot regularly visualizes Gwendolen and the other English characters in terms of the English portrait tradition, and especially of the "fancy" portraits that were fashionable among the upper classes in the seventeenth and eighteenth centuries. Conversely, Eliot visualizes Daniel and other Jewish characters in terms of Italian Renaissance painting, especially that of Titian and the Venetian school. The contrasts between these two schools of painting reflect moral contrasts between the two races and cultures represented. George Eliot's characteristic ambivalence toward the pictorial idealization of character finds a complex resolution in the double plot of *Daniel Deronda*: her ironic portraiture has full play in the English half of the novel, while her ennobling portraiture finds a more ardent and affirmative expression in the Jewish part than anywhere else in her fiction.

Gwendolen, as we have seen, likes to imagine herself as the central subject of attractive pictures. Her favorite attitudes in these imaginary self-portraits are borrowed from the allegorical society portraiture of the Van Dyck tradition. In the seventeenth and eighteenth centuries it was fashionable to idealize sitters by depicting them in costumes, poses, and settings that recall heroic, mythical, or religious figures from earlier works of art.[71] Van Dyck popularized this technique of pictorial quotation in England when he transferred the baroque style of his Genoese religious work into his society portraiture. Thus he painted *Lady Venetia Digby as Prudence, Rachel, Countess of Southampton, as Fortuna,* and *Mary, Duchess of Lenox, as Saint Agnes.*[72] Continuing the fashion, "Sir Peter Lely drew the Duchess of Cleveland as Juno, Mrs. Middleton as Pomona, Jane Kelleway as Diana, the Duchess of Rutland as Saint Agnes. Godfrey Kneller drew Anne, Lady Middleton, and Mrs. Voss and her daughter as Arcadian shepherdesses bearing staffs in their hands, and, on another occasion, the same Mrs. Voss as St. Agnes holding a prayer book in her hand and cuddling a lamb."[73] Reynolds, in his turn, portrayed *Mrs. Quarrington as St. Agnes, Mrs.*

Crewe as St. Genevieve, The Daughters of Sir William Montgomery as the Graces Adorning a Term of Hymen, The Duchess of Manchester as Diana, Mrs. Blake as Juno, and the famous courtesan *Kitty Fisher as Cleopatra.*[74] Because they allude to the subjects of historical or "fancy" painting, these pictures are often referred to as "fancy portraits."[75]

It is with fancy portraits that Gwendolen is most prominently associated in *Daniel Deronda.* At the Archery Meeting in Brackenshaw Park, for example,

> it was the fashion to dance in the archery dress, throwing off the jacket; and the simplicity of [Gwendolen's] white cashmere with its border of pale green set off her form to the utmost. A thin line of gold round her neck, and the gold star on her breast, were her only ornaments. Her smooth soft hair piled up into a grand crown made a clear line about her brow. Sir Joshua would have been glad to take her portrait. . . . [11:170]

Clearly Sir Joshua would have entitled the portrait *Miss Harleth as Diana.* Earlier in the same scene, a comparable portrait is evoked when we are told that "Gwendolen seemed a Calypso among her nymphs. It was in her attitudes and movements that every one was obliged to admit her surpassing charm" (10:147). We are dealing once more with Ovidian mythological fantasies of the sort that were treated so ironically in *Adam Bede* and *Romola.* The self-indulgence of the fantasies is underlined by the fact that Gwendolen is critical of other women who might figure in the same sort of painting. After observing that Charlotte Arrowpoint "would make quite a fine picture in that gold-coloured dress," Gwendolen decides that the picture would be "perhaps a little too symbolical—too much like the figure of Wealth in an allegory" (10:151). Too many allegorical figures might crowd Gwendolen's canvas.

Gwendolen's most memorable borrowed attitudes are Hermione and Saint Cecilia. The famous tableau of Hermione in *Daniel Deronda* is indebted to a similar scene in Goethe's *Die Wahlverwandtschaften,* which was in turn inspired by the drawing-room attitudes of Lady Emma Hamilton.[76] In her tableau Gwendolen chooses to imitate the attitude in which Mrs. Siddons and other eighteenth-century actresses regularly played the statue scene in *The Winter's Tale*: "Hermione, her arm resting on a pillar, was elevated by about six inches, which she counted on as a means of showing her pretty foot and instep, when at the given signal she should advance and descend" (6:85). Edgar Wind, in his classic essay on English heroic portraiture in the eighteenth century, reproduces engravings of Mrs. Siddons and Miss Farren in the role of Hermione, holding precisely this pose (figs. 15, 16). He shows that the attitude descends from classical representations of the Muses, and that it was "an established formula" for all actresses who played the statue scene in the eighteenth century.[77] Gwendolen, then, is imitating pictures of Mrs. Siddons as Hermione. As Wind notes, in society masquerades the ladies "often learned the attitudes which they assumed from actresses on the stage."[78]

Gwendolen's Hermione is designed primarily to allow her to display "a statuesque pose" in her Greek dress (6:82). The planned effect perfectly exemplifies Ruskin's assertion that "the modern 'ideal' of high art is a curious mingling of the gracefulness and reserve of the drawing-room with a certain measure of classical sensuality."[79] But it is Gwendolen's expression, not her attitude, that is affected by the sudden apparition of the prophetic picture of the dead face and fleeing figure. Instead of assuming the radiant face of comedy appropriate to the end of *The Winter's Tale*, Gwendolen unwittingly dons the mask of tragedy:

> Gwendolen . . . stood without change of attitude, but with a change of expression that was terrifying in its terror. She looked like a statue into which a soul of Fear had entered: her pallid lips were parted; her eyes, usually narrowed under their long lashes, were dilated and fixed. [6:86]

The complacent beauty has now become a study in physiognomical expression, a sculpturesque representation of Terror, one of the two passions appropriate to Aristotelian tragedy. Instead of *Miss Harleth as Hermione,* we have, still in the Reynolds tradition, *Miss Harleth as the Tragic Muse.* The picture distinctly recalls Piero di Cosimo's picture of Tito as a terror-stricken reveller in *Romola.*

More to Gwendolen's taste is the attitude of Saint Cecilia:

"Here is an organ. I will be Saint Cecilia: some one shall paint me as Saint Cecilia. Jocosa (this was her name for Miss Merry), let down my hair. See, mamma!"

She had thrown off her hat and gloves, and seated herself before the organ in an admirable pose, looking upward; while the submissive and sad Jocosa took out the one comb which fastened the coil of hair, and then shook out the mass till it fell in a smooth light-brown stream far below its owner's slim waist.

Mrs Davilow smiled and said, "A charming picture, my dear!" not indifferent to the display of her pet, even in the presence of a housekeeper. Gwendolen rose and laughed with delight. All this seemed quite to the purpose on entering a new house which was so excellent a background. [3:33–34]

Here the imaginary portrait is in the style of Kneller's *Lady Elizabeth Cromwell as Saint Cecilia* (1703, fig. 17), Reynolds's *Mrs. Sheridan as Saint Cecilia* (1775, fig. 18), or Reynolds's *Mrs. Billington as Saint Cecilia* (1790).[80] The aristocratic life to which Gwendolen aspires is again presented as an eighteenth-century affair. The attitude of Saint Cecilia in society portraiture was familiar enough by 1735 to be an object of Pope's satire in *Moral Essay II*, "On the Characters of Women":

> How many pictures of one Nymph we view,
> All how unlike each other, all how true!
>
> . . . .
>
> Let then the Fair one beautifully cry,
> In Magdalen's loose hair and lifted eye,
> Or drest in smiles of sweet Cecilia shine,
> With simp'ring Angels, Palms, and Harps divine;
> Whether the Charmer sinner it or saint it,
> If folly grows romantic, I must paint it.[81]

Edgar Wind argues that English allegorical portraiture reflects a heroic conception of mankind. But Pope and George Eliot see in such portraiture mainly the affectation and folly of the social class depicted. Indeed, for the middle-class Victorian intellectual, fancy portraits must have epitomized all that was Dandy about the fashionable classes under George III and George IV. Ruskin strikes the characteristic Victorian tone when he speaks of paintings which

> introduce pretty children as cherubs, and handsome women as Magdalens and Maries of Egypt, or portraits of patrons in the character of the more decorous saints; but more frequently, for direct flatteries of this kind, recurring to pagan mythology, and painting frail ladies as goddesses or graces, and foolish kings in radiant apotheosis.[82]

The portraits in which Gwendolen loves to see herself do not in George Eliot's view truly idealize their subjects; they falsify in order to please the vanity of their subjects. Hans Meyrick temporarily resists Sir Hugo Mallinger's advice to take up portraiture because the sort of painter Sir Hugo has in mind "has a little truth, and a great facility in falsehood—[his] idealism will never do for gods and goddesses and heroic story, but it may fetch a high price as flattery" (52:152). That Hans has higher standards of truthfulness in portraiture is perhaps suggested by the fact that he is "christened after Holbein" and that "only to look at his pinched features and blond hair dangling over his collar reminded one of pale quaint heads by early German painters" (16:270).

Early German is not the only school to be contrasted with the English in *Daniel Deronda*. Before discussing George Eliot's Italian sources, we should glance briefly at her use of the Dutch school in the presentation of Mordecai. Eliot's idealization of Mordecai is pictorial and overtly typological. Daniel's first impression of the consumptive scholar is that "such a physiognomy as that might possibly have been seen in a prophet of the Exile, or in some New Hebrew poet of the medieval time" (33:165). Later Daniel sees Mordecai as "an illuminated type of bodily emaciation and spiritual eagerness" (40:327). For Hebrew portraiture Eliot turned naturally to Rembrandt's pictures of rabbis. G. H. Lewes spoke of "a Rembrandtish background to her dramatic presentation" of the Jews in *Daniel Deronda* (*Letters*, VI, 196), and certainly a Rembrandtish chiaroscuro is suggested by the first glimpse of Mordecai's face, "with its dark, far-off gaze, and yellow pallor in relief on the gloom of the backward shop" (33:165).[83] Later Hans Meyrick, who is painting the picturesque figure, says: "Our prophet is an uncommonly interesting sitter—a better model than Rembrandt had for his Rabbi" (52:147). It is difficult to know which of Rembrandt's so-called rabbis Hans has in mind, but perhaps he is referring to the only one in the collection of the National Gallery, purchased under the title *A Jewish Rabbi* in 1844 (fig. 19).[84] The picturesque caps of Rembrandt's sitters were probably in George Eliot's memory when she wrote of Mordecai: "he commonly wore a cloth cap with black fur round it, which no painter would have asked him to take off" (38: 298). Mordecai himself may be thinking of Rembrandt when he envisions his messiah "from his memory of faces seen among the Jews of Holland and Bohemia, and from the pictures which revived that memory" (38:300).

Nevertheless, Dutch art does not dominate the Jewish part of *Daniel Deronda* as completely as might be expected. It is an exaggeration to say, as Harold Fisch does, that "the Jewish portraiture of Rembrandt" is "the true prototype" of George Eliot's treatment of the Jews.[85] Except for Mordecai, no important character in the novel is associated with Rembrandt's portraiture. Eliot's use of Dutch painting is highly selective, no doubt because the idealization she wished to confer upon her Jewish characters was incompatible with her audience's preconceptions about the limitations of the Dutch school. No one did more than Eliot herself had done in *Adam Bede* to foster the notion that the province of Dutch art is "the faithful rendering of commonplace things," and that it depicts "few prophets . . . few sublimely beautiful women; few heroes" (17: 270). In *Adam Bede* Dutch models sufficed for the mundane range of experience she wised to present. But in *Daniel Deronda* she ventures into precisely those extraordinary reaches of experience which she chose to avoid in *Adam Bede*. She could not make an extensive use of Dutch models because she shared with a substantial part of her audience the venerable prejudice that Dutch painting rarely achieves the sublime.[86]

Instead she relies heavily upon Italian, especially Venetian, models. So persistently does she associate Jews with Italians that the Anglo-

Saxon reader of *Daniel Deronda* is induced almost subliminally to grant the Jews whatever tolerance and respect he is accustomed to grant the Italians. It is as though George Eliot were saying to her Protestant English audience: you have learned to appreciate the Italians despite their ethnic, religious, and cultural foreignness; you can learn to appreciate the Jews in the same way: both peoples are of Mediterranean origin, both have distinguished non-Protestant religious traditions, and the Italian Renaissance painting you admire realizes many motifs of the Hebrew scriptures.[87] Eliot's pictorialism, in other words, here becomes a sophisticated rhetorical device employed in the service of a liberal social vision.

The Italian connection affects major and minor characters alike. An elderly man at the synagogue in Frankfurt, for example, has an "ample white beard and felt hat framing a profile of that fine contour which may as easily be Italian as Hebrew" (32:136). Of Klesmer, the Jewish pianist, the narrator says: "draped in a loose garment with a Florentine *berretta* on his head, he would have been fit to stand by the side of Leonardo da Vinci" (10:149).[88] Even Mirah Cohen is associated with Italians in Hans Meyrick's Titus and Berenice series; she is to be the model for the Jewish mistress of the prospective emperor of Rome. The series was originally suggested, as Hans explains, by "a splendid woman in the Trastevere—the grandest women there are half Jewesses—and she set me hunting for a fine situation of a Jewess at Rome" (37:276). The fusion of Jewish and Roman identities here is threefold: in Berenice, in the Trasteverina, and by association in Mirah.[89]

Finally, Daniel Deronda himself, who learns *in Genoa* that he is a Jew, has "a face not more distinctively oriental than many a type seen among what we call the Latin races" (40:332). Gwendolen's mother says the same thing more concisely: "he puts me in mind of Italian paintings" (29:83). That Deronda does not belong pictorially to the English school is made clear when Gwendolen notices that "hardly any face could be less like Deronda's than that represented as Sir Hugo's in a crayon portrait at Diplow" (29:84).

Of the regional schools of Italian painting evoked in *Daniel Deronda*, the most prominent is the Venetian. Venetian painting regained its prestige in England in the 1860s and 1870s after the rage for Pre-Raphaelite styles had run its course. Ruskin's revaluation of the Venetian school in the last volume of *Modern Painters* (1860) concludes that "the Venetian mind . . . and Titian's especially, as the central type of it, was wholly realist, universal, and manly. . . . In all its roots of power, and modes of work . . . I find the Venetian mind perfect."[90] Earlier in the same work Ruskin contrasted Venetian Renaissance portraiture to modern English portraiture in terms that parallel George Eliot's handling of the two schools in *Daniel Deronda*:

> the first step towards the ennobling of any face is the ridding it of its vanity; to which aim there cannot be anything more contrary than that principle of portraiture which prevails with us in these days, whose end seems to be the expression of vanity throughout, in face and in all circumstances of accompaniment; tending constantly to insolence of attitude, and levity and haughtiness of expression, and worked out farther in mean accompaniments of worldly splendour and possession . . . whence has arisen such a school of portraiture as must make the people of the nineteenth century the shame of their descendants, and the butt of all time. To which practices are to be opposed both the glorious severity of Holbein, and the mighty and simple modesty of Raffaelle, Titian, Giorgione, and Tintoret, with whom armour does not constitute the warrior, neither silk the dame. And from what feeling the dignity of that portraiture arose is best traceable at Venice. . . .[91]

According to Ruskin, painting done before 1600 embodies a greater purity of religious spirit than painting done since, and the Venetians "were the *last believing* school of Italy."[92] Hence the Venetian school is appropriate to the Jewish characters in *Daniel Deronda*, who have preserved a vital contact with their ancient religion; whereas the modern school is appropriate to the English characters, who are vain and worldly. In characterizing modern portraiture as an art of vanity, Ruskin anticipates George Eliot's pictures of Gwendolen.

Among the Victorians the chief technical excellence of the Venetian painters was generally held to be their color. In *The Stones of Venice* Ruskin spoke of "that mighty spirit of Venetian colour, which was to be consummated in Titian," and argued that there is always a "connexion of pure colour with profound and noble thought."[93] In *Deronda* George Eliot draws upon the pure color values of Venetian painting when she describes Daniel's visit to the family of Ezra Cohen:

> When she showed him into the room behind the shop he was sur-
> prised at the prettiness of the scene. . . . The ceiling and walls
> were smoky, and all the surroundings were dark enough to throw
> into relief the human figures, which had a Venetian glow of
> colouring. The grandmother was arrayed in yellowish brown
> with a large gold chain in lieu of the necklace, and by this light
> her yellow face with its darkly-marked eyebrows and framing
> roll of grey hair looked as handsome as was necessary for pic-
> turesque effect. Young Mrs Cohen was clad in red and black,
> with a string of large artificial pearls wound round and round
> her neck: the baby lay asleep in the cradle under a scarlet
> counterpane; Adelaide Rebekah was in braided amber; and Jacob
> Alexander was in black velveteen with scarlet stockings. As the
> four pairs of black eyes all glistened a welcome at Deronda, he
> was almost ashamed of the supercilious dislike these happy-
> looking creatures had raised in him by daylight. [34:178–79]

Here the Venetian aura of color in the group portrait dignifies the London Jewish family in Deronda's eyes and is meant to have the same effect upon the reader.[94] Once again we see "Hebrew dyed Italian" (55:213). No doubt the coloristic style of Venetian painting seemed to George Eliot more exotic, more "oriental," and therefore more appropriate to her Jewish characters than did the linear styles of other Italian schools.

If Reynolds dominates the English portraiture in *Daniel Deronda,* then Titian dominates the Jewish. "One can," says Jean Hagstrum, "almost always count on a literary Englishman's admiration of Titian."[95] In a sense, the entire novel was inspired by a Titian painting—the *Annunciation* at the Scuola di San Rocco in Venice, which gave George Eliot the theme she developed first in *The Span-ish Gypsy* and later in *Deronda* (fig. 20). In "this small picture of

Titian's," she found "a great dramatic motive": a young person "chosen to fulfil a great destiny . . . chosen, not by any momentary arbitrariness, but as a result of foregoing hereditary conditions . . . I came home with this in my mind, meaning to give the motive a clothing in some suitable set of historical and local conditions" (Cross, III, 34–35). Here is an excellent example of the typological thinking that underlies so much of Eliot's art. Titian's handling of a traditional biblical type inspires Eliot to reincarnate the same type in a more contemporary setting.

Small wonder, then, that the literary portraiture of George Eliot's hero derives principally from two of Titian's paintings. In the early part of the novel, before he has accepted his Zionist mission, Daniel is associated with a secular portrait in the Louvre—*The Young Man with a Glove*. In the later part of the novel, after his destiny has been revealed, Daniel is associated with a religious painting at Dresden— *The Tribute Money*. The change of portraits symbolizes Daniel's progression from a life of aimless upper-class ease to a life of religious commitment. Deronda comes to exemplify G. H. Lewes's belief that "a well-painted face, with a noble expression, is the highest reach of art."[96]

The Young Man with a Glove (fig. 21) is evoked in chapter 17 as Deronda rows on the Thames:

> Look at his hands: they are not small and dimpled, with tapering fingers that seem to have only a deprecating touch: they are long, flexible, firmly-grasping hands, such as Titian has painted in a picture where he wished to show the combination of refinement with force. And there is something of a likeness, too, between the faces belonging to the hands—in both the uniform pale-brown skin, the perpendicular brow, the calmly-penetrating eyes. [17:277–78]

George Eliot might have seen this portrait during visits to the Louvre in 1859 and again in 1864.[97] Here is Deronda as handsome young gentleman, idle perhaps but potentially energetic and less affected than he might be if he belonged to the English school.

The young man's potential is fully realized in the painting that represents Deronda's later, more spiritual aspect. Titian's *The*

Tribute Money (fig. 22) is evoked immediately after Deronda is recognized by Mordecai as the incarnation of his messianic vision:

> In ten minutes the two men, with as intense a consciousness as if they had been two undeclared lovers, felt themselves alone in the small gas-lit book-shop and turned face to face, each baring his head from an instinctive feeling that they wished to see each other fully. . . . I wish I could perpetuate those two faces, as Titian's "Tribute Money" has perpetuated another type of contrast. Imagine—we all of us can—the pathetic stamp of consumption with its brilliancy of glance to which the sharply-defined structure of features reminding one of a forsaken temple, give already a far-off look as of one getting unwillingly out of reach; and imagine it on a Jewish face naturally accentuated for the expression of an eager mind—the face of a man little above thirty, but with that age upon it which belongs to time lengthened by suffering, the hair and beard still black throwing out the yellow pallor of the skin, the difficult breathing giving more decided marking to the mobile nostril, the wasted yellow hands conspicuous on the folded arms. . . . Seeing such a portrait you would see Mordecai. And opposite to him was a face not more oriental than many a type seen among what we call the Latin races: rich in youthful health, and with a forcible masculine gravity in its repose, that gave the value of judgment to the reverence with which he met the gaze of this mysterious son of poverty who claimed him as a long-expected friend. [40: 331–32]

The scene in the bookshop is analogous, not identical, to the scene in *The Tribute Money*. In particular, Mordecai does not resemble the tax-collecting Pharisee through whom Jesus renders unto Caesar what is Caesar's. Yet Titian's Christ looks enough like *The Young Man with a Glove* to resemble Deronda as well, and Deronda is bearded. Probably we *are* meant to visualize Deronda in terms of Titian's Christ.[98] "In this way," to borrow a remark made by Albert R. Cirillo in another context, "Eliot fleshes out Daniel's portrait as a paragon, as a symbol, or personal savior."[99]

That Daniel's portrait involves a form of typological incarnation is strongly suggested by the language of the novel. Deronda is "the antitype of [the] visionary image in Mordecai's mind" (41:352). An antitype is not the opposite of a type but its fulfillment. As soon as he meets Daniel, Mordecai is struck by "a face and frame which seemed to him to realise the long-conceived type . . . Deronda had that sort of resemblance to the preconceived type which a finely individual bust or portrait has to the more generalised copy left in our minds after a long interval" (38:307–08).[100] The type in question reveals its virtues through its expression; it has "a face at once young, grand, and beautiful, where, if there is any melancholy, it is no feeble passivity, but enters into the foreshadowed capability of heroism" (38:298). This face, at once contemplative and active, belongs both to Mordecai's messiah and to Titian's Christ in *The Tribute Money*. In effect, Eliot seeks to make Deronda a convincing postfiguration of Christ in her secular religion of humanity by contrasting his unconscious pictorial fulfillment of the role with Gwendolen's self-conscious fulfillment of the pictorial roles of saints and goddesses in fashionable society portraiture.

Deronda's literary portrait associates him with one of George Eliot's favorite paintings in all the world. During her extended stay at Dresden in the summer of 1858, she and G. H. Lewes visited the Gemäldegalerie "three mornings in the week" and "looked at the Zinsgroschen (Titian's), too, every day" (Cross, II, 47). In an essay written that summer, Lewes explained their reasons for admiring the picture. He cites *The Tribute Money* to illustrate the compatibility of idealism with realism in art:

> Titian's unsurpassable head of Christ, in the famous "Christo del Moneta," if compared with all other heads by other painters, will likewise be found to have its profound significance and idealism in the wonderful reality of the presentation: the head is more intensely human than that of any other representation of Christ, but the humanity is such as accords with our higher conceptions.[101]

In other words, *The Tribute Money* is a supreme example of the ideal in the real. It successfully achieves the idealization which fancy portraits fail to achieve when they depict their sitters as saints or mythological divinities. And it realizes a higher conception of humanity than does *The Young Man with a Glove,* as Lewes made clear when he ranked the two paintings on a Ruskinian scale of "greatness":

> Titian's portrait of "The Young Man with a Glove" is a great work of art, though not of great art. It is infinitely higher than a portrait of Cromwell, by a painter unable to see into the great soul of Cromwell, and to make us see it; but it is infinitely lower than Titian's "Tribute Money," "Peter the Martyr," or the "Assumption."[102]

During the story, Deronda traverses the spiritual distance that separates *The Young Man with a Glove* from *The Tribute Money* on Lewes's scale. Deronda moves from a secular to a religious life, from a poised sitter in a portrait to a dramatic actor in a sacred history painting.

With this bold pictorial affirmation George Eliot's career as a novelist ends. The techniques we have observed call into doubt Henry James's influential description of George Eliot's idealization. "We feel in her, always," wrote James, "that she proceeds from the abstract to the concrete: that her figures and situations are evolved, as the phrase is, from her moral consciousness, and are only indirectly the products of observations. They are deeply studied and elaborately justified, but they are not *seen* in the irresponsible plastic way."[103] James's metaphors do not provide an altogether accurate account of the process which produced such characters as Dinah Morris, Romola, Mordecai, and Daniel Deronda. To be sure, these figures were evolved from Eliot's moral consciousness; but they were also seen in a plastic way virtually from the moment of their conception. They are not abstract or indirectly observed in any visual sense of the terms; on the contrary, they are highly particularized and often modeled upon specific, identifiable pictures.[104] If we judge the characters to be failures, our verdict may be based upon our distaste for exemplary typological characterization rather than upon George Eliot's failure to achieve presentational concreteness.

7 Genre Painting and
Common Life

George Scharf, a friend of George Eliot's and an important figure in
the Victorian art world, once contrasted "the historical, heroic, or
idealised style of figure-painting" with genre painting, which he defined as the "representation of life in its unheroic forms." It was
into genre, Scharf believed, that "all the imaginative art of this
country seems in progress of being absorbed."[1] Scharf was acknowl-
edging an important trend. Throughout the eighteenth century,
Dutch and Flemish genre painting had gained in popularity among
British collectors.[2] Genre conventions were successfully adapted to
British scenes by painters such as George Morland and David Wilkie,
and they in turn were imitated by many Victorian followers.

Genre painting and the novel arose together as middle-class art
forms and retained close connections until the end of the nineteenth century. According to Richard Stang, it was a French treatise
of 1846 on Dutch and Flemish painting that first popularized the
application of the term *réalisme* to fiction.[3] And certainly it is with
Dutch, Flemish, and English genre painting that George Eliot's
realism is most often compared. She herself invites the comparison
in chapter 17 of *Adam Bede,* and Mario Praz applies it to all of her
work in his study of *The Hero in Eclipse in Victorian Fiction.*

Genre painting suited both George Eliot's experience and her artistic goals. The domestic reality depicted in seventeenth-century
Netherlandish pictures was of a piece with the domestic reality
surrounding her in the preindustrial English countryside of the

1820s and 1830s. The photographs of her environs that have been
published by C. S. Olcott and Marghanita Laski suggest how readily
the scenes and customs Eliot knew as a girl could be perceived in
terms of genre painting.[4] Many of the descriptions in her early fiction are at once literal accounts of identifiable places and pictorial
arrangements imitating a well-established visual style. Metaphors
derived from genre painting served to describe even the intellectually
oppressive aspects of her early world: "mine is too often a world
such as Wilkie can so well paint, a *walled-in* world, furnished with all
the details which he remembers so accurately, and the least interesting part thereof is often what I suppose must be designated the
intelligent" (*Letters*, I, 71). She must often, before moving to
Coventry, have felt herself to be living in the world painted by
Wilkie and his Dutch and Flemish predecessors.

Furthermore, the spirit in which ordinary domestic life is treated
in the best Netherlandish genre pictures harmonizes perfectly with
the spirit in which George Eliot wished to write. Often the painter
appears to value quotidian existence so much that he invests profane
subjects with a numinous, radiant, almost sacred aura that evokes
memories of the religious art from which secular painting originally
derived. As Walter Pater put it, the "ideal of home" in genre painting "was not without a kind of natural religiousness."[5] To hallow
everyday communal life with a sense of "natural religiousness" was
a primary goal of George Eliot's fiction, as we have seen. Her genre
pictorialism therefore emphasizes the values of harmony, order, and
love in the visual tradition which she inherited.

Yet it is possible to exaggerate the importance of genre painting
to Eliot. Because she drew upon many other kinds of painting, an
indiscriminate application of the genre-painting analogy can distort
her achievement. Praz's crude and unilluminating characterization of
Eliot's art as "Biedermeier" perfectly illustrates the danger of taking
the remarks on Dutch painting in chapter 17 of *Adam Bede* as the
key to her entire oeuvre.[6] Those remarks, as Darrell Mansell, Jr.,
has shown, do not invest supreme value in Dutch genre, and do not
offer it as a complete prototype of the narrator's own art.[7] To be
sure, *Adam Bede* contains many word-pictures in the Dutch manner;
but chapter 17 is primarily a plea against prescriptive generic crit-

icism, echoing Ruskin's defense of Dutch painting against the categorical strictures of Reynolds. It is an argument for the importance of truthfulness and sympathy as critical criteria, not a manifesto for the inherent superiority of genre to history painting.

To avoid a simplistic view of Eliot's depictions of common life, we should distinguish some of the different schools and sorts of genre painting which she imitated. This chapter will outline the principal visual traditions that inform her genre pictorialism, and discuss her literary use of those traditions.

William Bell Scott was mindful of the diversity of nonheroic subjects when in 1873 he named "genre, familiar subjects illustrative of real life, *tableaux de société*, or 'conversation pieces'" as a single branch of painting.[8] George Eliot employed each sort of picture listed by Scott and several that he did not list. In chapter 17 of *Adam Bede* she mainly evokes seventeenth-century Dutch and Flemish scenes of humble bourgeois or peasant life, some of them comical or satirical in emphasis, some of them realistic and intimist. This Netherlandish tradition descends from Pieter Brueghel the Elder to Adriaen Brouwer and David Teniers II in Belgium, and passes thence to Gerhard Dou and the Leyden School in Holland.[9] The heritage includes Mieris, Metsu, Maes, Steen, the Ostades, De Hooch, Terborch, and Vermeer. The pleasure these painters gave nineteenth-century viewers may be gauged from a remark of Henry James's: "We never fail to derive a deep satisfaction from these delectable realists—the satisfaction produced by the sight of a perfect accord between the aim and the result."[10]

An important offshoot of the Dutch tradition was the conversation piece, a mixture of genre and portrait in which a group of friends or relatives is depicted in an intimate and informal setting.[11] The Dutch bourgeois conversation piece had an aristocratic Flemish counterpart which often located the portrait group in a ballroom or garden. The Flemish conversation piece is closely allied to the French *tableau de société* and, through Watteau, to the *fete galante*.[12] Both the Dutch and the Flemish styles helped to shape the English conversation piece, which flourished in the eighteenth century. This type of picture appealed greatly to George Eliot and proved especially useful to her fiction because the element of portraiture could readily be adapted to her habitual techniques of characterization.

Eliot also admired nineteenth-century genre painting and was sensitive to many of the innovations which her contemporaries made in the genre tradition. These included the introduction of contemporary themes, the use of genre motifs for historical subjects, an increased emphasis upon narrative techniques, and the invention of the problem picture. These Romantic and Victorian tendencies found their way into George Eliot's pictorialism and exerted no less influence upon her descriptive style than did the earlier phases in the history of genre painting.

If we examine Eliot's actual practice, we shall see that she evokes seventeenth-century Netherlandish art most often in her earliest work. The Dutch tradition appears at least once, for instance, in each of the *Scenes of Clerical Life,* helping to define the tea-preparations at Mrs. Patten's in the opening pages of "Amos Barton," the kitchen at Cheverel Manor in the fourth chapter of "Mr Gilfil's Love-Story," and Mrs. Jerome at her tea-table in the eighth chapter of "Janet's Repentance." But it was not until Eliot visited the galleries of Munich and Dresden while working on *Adam Bede* in the summer of 1858 that Teniers and Dou and their compatriots made their deepest impression upon her art. "I did not half satisfy my appetite for the rich collection of Flemish and Dutch pictures here," she wrote in her Dresden journal, "for Teniers, Ryckart, Gerard Dow, Terburg, Mieris and the rest" (Cross, II, 48–49). It was a great pleasure, after a visit to the Alte Pinakothek at Munich, "to call up in your imagination a little Gerard Dow that you have seen hanging in a corner of one of the cabinets" (*Letters,* II, 454).

One such Dou reappears in chapter 17 of *Adam Bede*; for, as Norma Jean Davis and Bernard Richards have shown, the *Betende Spinnerin* at Munich is clearly the model for Eliot's "old woman . . . eating her solitary dinner, while the noonday light, softened perhaps by a screen of leaves, falls on her mob-cap, and just touches the rim of her spinning-wheel, and her stone jug" (17:268).[13] The details of this description correspond exactly with those of the painting, and show how attentively Eliot could look at a picture that interested her (fig. 23).[14]

Both Davis and John Goode have demonstrated that *Adam Bede* contains a great many motifs and light effects that are commonplace in seventeenth-century Netherlandish pictures: the woman on the doorstep, framed by the domestic architecture behind her; the interior furnished with household objects and illuminated by sunlight through a window; the interior glimpsed through a window and lit by a candle or lamp within.[15] The first of these arrangements governs the initial description of Adam's home and mother:

> It was a low house, with smooth grey thatch and buff walls, looking pleasant and mellow in the evening light. The leaded windows were bright and speckless, and the door-stone was as clean as a white boulder at ebb tide. On the door-stone stood a clean old woman, in a dark-striped linen gown, a red kerchief, and a linen cap, talking to some speckled fowls which appeared to have been drawn towards her by an illusory expectation of cold potatoes or barley. [1:14]

The same composition reappears in a later account of Lisbeth (4:54) and in the closing glimpse of Dinah Morris (Epilogue: 374). Dutch interiors are given to the Hall Farm (6:106-07, 14:215, 22:374) and Bartle Massey's house (21:348-49). The Hall Farm dairy is unmistakably a Dutch scene:

> The dairy was certainly worth looking at: it was a scene to sicken for with a sort of calenture in hot and dusty streets—such coolness, such purity, such fresh fragrance of new-pressed cheese, of firm butter, of wooden vessels perpetually bathed in pure water; such soft colouring of red earthenware and creamy surfaces, brown wood and polished tin, grey limestone and rich orange-red rust on the iron weights and hooks and hinges. But one gets only a confused notion of these details when they surround a distractingly pretty girl of seventeen, standing on little pattens and rounding her dimpled arm to lift a pound of butter out of the scale. [7:120]

The first illustrator of this scene had no doubt about what pictorial style the author intended. In *Hetty and Captain Donnithorne in Mrs. Poyser's Dairy* (1861), E. H. Corbould imitates precisely the kind of seventeenth-century setting that Eliot's text is designed to recall (fig. 24). This faithful and highly successful illustration shows how at least one attentive Victorian reader visualized the genre descriptions in *Adam Bede*.

After *Adam Bede,* however, Eliot never again used Dutch and Flemish painting on so large a scale. *The Mill on the Floss* and *Silas Marner,* as we shall see in the next chapter, do not depend heavily upon pictorial techniques; and even the famous scene at the Rainbow Inn, which has often been compared to a genre picture, is almost entirely aural and dramatic, controlled by the remembered rhythms of country dialogue rather than the visual precedents of Teniers or Steen. Any resemblance to Netherlandish painting is in the subject, not in the treatment. Eliot evoked Dutch still-life painting in one vivid passage of "Brother Jacob" in 1864 (2:368), but not until she described the Garths in *Middlemarch* did she return to the descriptive mode of *Adam Bede.* She visualizes Mary Garth in terms of a Rembrandt portrait (12:169), and her parents in terms of a genre picture:

> On entering the quarried parlour, which had no carpet, but was well hung with maps and plans, Fred saw Mrs Garth standing with her hand on her husband's shoulder. He was seated at his desk by the fire, and had just called her out of the kitchen to read a letter which he had finished. Mrs Garth was of the same curly-haired square-faced type as Mary, but handsomer, with more delicacy of feature, a pale skin, a solid matronly figure, and a remarkable firmness of glance. In her snowy frilled cap she reminded one of that delightful Frenchwoman whom we have all seen marketing, basket on arm.[16]

The first two sentences of this passage exist only in the manuscript, however, and not in the final version of the novel. Their omission reduces the effect of a "solid sort of Dutch realism" (*Essays,* p. 331). In fact, Eliot associates the Garths, as we shall see, with Victorian genre painting more often than with Dutch. Netherlandish art, then, provides a systematic pictorialist program only in George Eliot's first novel.

By contrast, the conversation piece appears throughout Eliot's oeuvre. As a social novelist she often had need to present portraits of families or groups of friends, "seen in their home surroundings or engaged in some favourite occupation."[17] The conversation piece unites portrait and genre by placing identifiable instead of anonymous figures in genre contexts. In such pictures the sitters enjoy a special harmony with their setting; they belong in it, and usually it belongs to them. The repertoire of settings varies, as Mario Praz has shown, from a table in a room, to a porch or balustrade in a courtyard or garden, to a tree in the open air, or a park with a country house in the distance, or even a boat.[18] The outdoor settings sometimes have greater affinities with landscape than with genre painting, as we shall see in the next chapter when we discuss the motif of the aristocratic family depicted against a background of park and country house.

The activities of the portrait group are also important, since the conversation piece is essentially informal, private, and casual rather than formal, public, and posed. The term *conversation* itself refers to the interplay among the members of the group, which usually centers upon some recreation or avocation: a game, a dance, a theatrical performance, a concert, a sport, a hobby, a collection. Several kinds of activity may take place within a single picture, especially if children and pets are represented. Having originated in Belgium and Holland in the seventeenth century, the conversation piece achieved its highest development in England between 1720 and 1810. Thereafter it fell from fashion, but its tradition remained well known throughout the nineteenth century.

The essential elements of the conversation piece are all present in George Eliot's description of the Garth family at the beginning of chapter 57 of *Middlemarch*. The group is not stiffly posed but engaged in informal diversions of several sorts:

[Fred Vincy] found the family group, dogs and cats included, under the great apple-tree in the orchard. It was a festival with Mrs Garth, for her eldest son, Christy, her peculiar joy and pride, had come home for a short holiday. . . . He was lying on the ground now by his mother's chair, with his straw-hat laid flat over his eyes, while Jim on the other side was reading aloud from that beloved author who has made a chief part in the happiness of many young lives. The volume was 'Ivanhoe,' and Jim was in the great archery scene at the tournament, but suffered much interruption from Ben, who had fetched his own bow and arrow, and was making himself dreadfully disagreeable, Letty thought, by begging all present to observe his random shots, which no one wished to do except Brownie, the active-minded but probably shallow mongrel, while the grizzled Newfoundland lying in the sun looked on with the dull-eyed neutrality of extreme old age. Letty herself, showing as to her mouth and pinafore some slight signs that she had been assisting at the gathering of the cherries which stood in a coral-heap on the tea-table, was now seated on the grass, listening open-eyed to the reading. [57:57–58]

The group is disposed about a large tree which symbolizes the fruitfulness and continuity of the family—a common arrangement in eighteenth-century conversation pieces, as Ronald Paulson has observed.[19] The connotations of the apple tree are repeated in the cherries and borne out by the concentration of the portraiture upon the younger generation. The theme of generation(s) extends even to the Landseerian dogs. The word-picture implies that the Garth family renews itself as nature does, accommodating diversity, spontaneity, friction, and separation within an orderly ongoing rhythm.[20] The doubts which darken the affirmative portraiture of other characters in *Middlemarch* cast no shadow upon the Garths.

Eliot's description of the Garth children and their dogs evokes a distinctly nineteenth-century pictorial idiom, with perhaps a touch of the Dutch heritage in the bourgeois boisterousness of the group. More in the eighteenth-century mode is the subdued, aristocratic conversation piece in chapter 35 of *Daniel Deronda.* Entertaining the Grandcourts for the first time since their marriage, Sir Hugo Mallinger has invited them to dine at the Abbey with a carefully assorted group of his friends. The party has assembled in the drawing-room to await the guests of honor.

The scene was really delightful—enlarged by full-length portraits with deep backgrounds, inserted in the cedar panelling—surmounted by a ceiling that glowed with the rich colours of the coats of arms ranged between the sockets—illuminated almost as much by the red fire of oak-boughs as by the pale wax-lights—stilled by the deep-piled carpet and by the high English breeding that subdues all voices; while the mixture of ages, from the white-haired Lord and Lady Pentreath to the four-year-old Edgar Raymond, gave a varied charm to the living groups. Lady Mallinger, with fair matronly roundness and mildly prominent blue eyes, moved about in her black velvet, carrying a tiny white dog on her arm as a sort of finish to her costume; the children were scattered among the ladies, while most of the gentlemen were standing rather aloof conversing with that very moderate vivacity observable during the long minutes before dinner. Deronda was a little out of the circle in a dialogue fixed upon him by Mr Vandernoodt, a man of the best Dutch blood imported at the Revolution: for the rest, one of those commodious persons in society who are nothing particular themselves, but are understood to be acquainted with the best in every department; close-clipped, pale-eyed, *nonchalant,* as good a foil as could well be found to the intense colouring and vivid gravity of Deronda. [35:194–95]

The arrangement of the group is semiformal, and its main activity is literally conversation. The portraiture is likewise semiformal, in that it emphasizes the ages, ranks, backgrounds, and social roles of the individuals who make up the party. The passage supports Ronald Paulson's thesis that the conversation piece strives above all for a precise social definition of its subjects.[21] In this connection Deronda's physical position—slightly outside the circle of English gentlemen—is as significant as the position of the ladies and children.

As these examples suggest, Eliot drew upon the conversation piece for a variety of fictional effects. The form is ideally suited to the celebration of family harmonies, but it can also be used to spotlight family problems. As we shall see, Eliot developed a highly effective kind of literary problem picture which ironically inverts the benign conventions of the conversation piece. Perhaps because it is such an adaptable pictorial form, the conversation piece appears at least once in each of her novels.

The problem picture was but one of the modifications which

British artists made in the genre tradition when they took it up in the nineteenth century. They also introduced contemporary social themes into their pictures of humble life, infused history painting with genre motifs, and extended the techniques of narrative presentation which they learned from Hogarth. Each of these innovations made a mark upon George Eliot's pictorialism. She was a keen student of contemporary genre painting as it developed from the work of David Wilkie.[22] We have already observed that she refers to Wilkie in a letter of 1840 (*Letters,* I, 71) and later praises the scene in *The Antiquary* in which Scott evokes Wilkie's cottage-pictures (*Essays,* p. 270). When she visited Berlin in 1854–55, she remarked "some clever Wilkie-like pictures by Hasenclever."[23] She also liked the work of the prolific Irish genre painter, William Mulready, and the French genre painters, Henriette Browne and Jacques Feyen (*Letters,* III, 134; IV, 144; VII, 281). The novelist's regular visits to the Royal Academy and French Gallery exhibitions no doubt kept her well informed of the latest trends in the pictorial representation of common life.

In her early stories George Eliot drew unhesitatingly upon themes that were popular in contemporary genre painting. For example, she liked to end her tales with word-pictures of deathbed and village-wedding scenes. The death of Milly Barton and the weddings of Mr. Gilfil, Adam Bede, and Eppie Marner are unabashedly conventional in their appeal to an established visual taste. But Eliot also employed less conventional genre themes, for example at the beginning of *Adam Bede:*

> With this drop of ink at the end of my pen, I will show you the roomy workshop of Mr Jonathan Burge, carpenter and builder, in the village of Hayslope, as it appeared on the eighteenth of June, in the year of our Lord 1799.
>
> The afternoon sun was warm on the five workmen there, busy upon doors and window-frames and wainscoting. A scent of pine-wood from the tent-like pile of planks outside the open door mingled itself with the scent of the elder-bushes which were spreading their summer snow close to the open window opposite; the slanting sunbeams shone through the transparent

shavings that flew before the steady plane, and lit up the fine grain of the oak panelling which stood propped against the wall. On a heap of those soft shavings a rough grey shepherd-dog had made himself a pleasant bed, and was lying with his nose between his forepaws, occasionally wrinkling his brows to cast a glance at the tallest of the five workmen, who was carving a shield in the centre of a wooden mantelpiece. It was to this workman that the strong barytone belonged which was heard above the sound of plane and hammer singing—

> "Awake, my soul, and with the sun
> Thy daily stage of duty run;
> Shake off dull sloth . . ."
> [1:3–4]

The imagery of the passage appeals to several senses, as R. T. Jones has noted.[24] But it is predominantly visual and pictorial. Like the title of a Victorian painting, the words of the hymn underline the moral meaning served by the detailed realism of the technique. The passage is George Eliot's version of a Victorian picture of duty or work. Like Ford Madox Brown's *Work* (1852–65), William Bell Scott's *Newcastle Quayside in 1861,* or James Hook's *From under the Sea* (1864), Eliot's description emphasizes the quasi-religious, Carlylean significance of socially useful endeavor and presents the worker as an impressive, almost heroic figure.[25]

Adam and his fellows are not, to be sure, set in the postindustrial world of Brown's navvies, who are excavating for a sewer, or Scott's shipbuilders, or Hook's miners. But the pastoral environment of the shop enhances the biblical connotations of the carpentry. The typological resonance of the scene helps to ennoble the carpenters and to push the genre subject in the direction of sacred and heroic history painting. The workshop motif is repeated in chapters 19 and 38, with interesting variations that correspond to Adam's psychic fall from innocence to experience. It is a skillful novelistic handling of a new and important pictorial theme.

The blurring of the boundaries between genre and history painting is characteristic of Victorian art. Weary of what George Scharf called "the exclusive reign of the high historical," the Victorians carried through a pictorial revolution which had begun in the last half of the eighteenth century.[26] By incorporating genre motifs into history painting, they broke away from neoclassical restrictions upon subject and treatment. Private persons and minor domestic incidents began to displace famous persons and great public moments in history pictures. "The introduction of *genre*," according to Scharf, "has opened to our figure-painters the whole range of subjects in past and contemporary life."[27] This expansion in English painting was influenced by parallel developments in France and Germany. The works of Paul Delaroche and of the Düsseldorf school of history painting (Lessing, Hildebrandt, Hübner, Bendemann, and Sohn) were well known in England and admired by George Eliot, among others.[28]

The new taste in history painting gave rise to a popular motif of lovers placed in interesting historical situations. George Eliot was deeply affected by Millais's *A Huguenot on St. Bartholomew's Day* at the Royal Academy of 1852 and by Frederic Burton's *The Meeting on the Turret Stairs* (fig. 26) at the Old Water-Colour Exhibition of 1864 (*Letters,* II, 29–30; IV, 147). She tried her own hand at such a picture when she described Romola and Tito on the day of their betrothal:

> It was not long before Romola entered, all white and gold, more than ever like a tall lily. Her white silk garment was bound by a golden girdle, which fell with large tassels; and above that was the rippling gold of her hair, surmounted by the white mist of her long veil, which was fastened on her brow by a band of pearls, the gift of Bernardo del Nero, and was now parted off her face so that it all floated backward.
> "Regina mia!" said Tito. . . . They held each other's hands while she spoke, and both looked at their imaged selves [the picture of Bacchus and Ariadne]. But the reality was far more beautiful; she all lily-white and golden, and he with his dark glowing beauty above the purple red-bordered tunic. [20:303–05]

The rich color-imagery and the motif of the couple in this passage are somewhat reminiscent of Rossetti's watercolors of the mid-1850s but could have been inspired by any number of medievalizing Victorian pictures. The lovers are seen to be involved in a conflict of allegiances resembling that which complicates many Victorian pictures of historical romance. The symbolic attributes bestowed upon Romola and Tito suggest that theirs is a marriage of the Marian and the Bacchic, of the Christian and the pagan. The result will be either a perfect union of opposites or a disastrous mingling of incompatible cultures and temperaments.

The wars between the Puritans and the Cavaliers provided the most popular setting for dilemmas of loyalty in nineteenth-century English painting. In Millais's *The Proscribed Royalist* (1853) a sequestered cavalier kisses the hand of the young woman who has smuggled food to him. William Shakespeare Burton's *A Wounded Cavalier* (1856) complicates matters further by implying the possibility of an amorous attraction between the cavalier and the Puritan lady who is nursing him. George Eliot employs a similar motif in the dramatic reconciliation scene between Will Ladislaw and Dorothea in *Middlemarch*.

> "I don't doubt you any longer," said Dorothea, putting out her hand; a vague fear for him impelling her unutterable affection.
> He took her hand and raised it to his lips with something like a sob. But he stood with his hat and gloves in the other hand, and might have done for the portrait of a Royalist. [83:422]

The image of Will as a Royalist reminds us that Dorothea is a Puritan, and evokes not only the contrast of their temperaments but also the differences of background and allegiance that still divide them. The pictorial tension is created only to be resolved as the lovers are finally united; but in the meantime "the portrait of a Royalist" has helped to distance the sentiment of the scene by establishing a perspective beyond that of the characters, and by encouraging us to visualize the stylized gallantry of Will's attitude even under the stress of intense emotion.

Genre also invaded the realm of sacred history painting in the nineteenth century. The void left in religious art by the demise of traditional Christian iconography was filled in part by genre pictures of biblical scenes and of worship itself. Robert Rosenblum has called attention to "the new Romantic domain of spectator Chris-

tianity, where genre scenes of communal piety replace traditional
Christian subject matter." In such pictures we observe "scenes of
piety and ritual, and man-made objects of Christian art and architecture" rather than biblical events.[29] Religious feelings are evoked,
but religious belief is not solicited. Thus spectator Christianity
offends neither the faithful nor the lapsed Christian. At once empirical and nostalgic, it is a pictorial compromise well suited to an
age of waning faith.

It certainly suited the purposes of George Eliot, who remained
sympathetic to the culture of Christianity even though she had
abandoned its theology. Because she valued communal activity informed by a sense of the sacred, her descriptions of sincere be-
lievers at worship—be they Anglicans, Methodists, Catholics, or
Jews—are always sympathetic. "It was a pretty sight, that family
assembled to worship in the little chapel, where a couple of wax-
candles threw a mild faint light on the figures kneeling there." This
passage in "Mr Gilfil's Love-Story" (2:171) implies that the custom
of family worship in the private chapels of country houses, though
now largely a thing of the past, was both picturesque and beneficial
to the participants. Equally rich in human and pictorial interest was
the habit of Sunday Bible-reading, a favorite theme among French
genre painters of the eighteenth century.[30] In *Adam Bede* we are
assured that "You would have liked to see Adam reading his
Bible. . . . He held one hand thrust between his waistcoat buttons,
and the other ready to turn the pages; and in the course of the
morning you would have seen many changes in his face" (51:318).
Here the believer's state of mind matters more than the contents of
his creed. Such a focus is typical of spectator Christianity, which
appreciates the aesthetic, historical, and humanistic values of Christian occasions but does not necessarily assent to their dogma.

The same viewpoint governs George Eliot's elaborate descriptions
of Dinah's preaching and of Hayslope Church in *Adam Bede*. In the
church we notice first its antiquity, then its furnishings and decoration, and finally its parishioners and minister.

> I cannot say that the interior of Hayslope Church was remark-
> able for anything except for the grey age of its oaken pews—
> great square pews mostly, ranged on each side of a narrow aisle.

It was free, indeed, from the modern blemish of galleries. The choir had two narrow pews to themselves in the middle of the right-hand row, so that it was a short process for Joshua Rann to take his place among them as principal bass, and return to his desk after the singing was over. The pulpit and desk, grey and old as the pews, stood on one side of the arch leading into the chancel, which also had its grey square pews for Mr Donnithorne's family and servants. Yet I assure you these grey pews, with the buff-washed walls, gave a very pleasing tone to this shabby interior, and agreed extremely well with the ruddy faces and bright waistcoats. And there were liberal touches of crimson toward the chancel, for the pulpit and Mr Donnithorne's own pew had handsome crimson cloth cushions; and, to close the vista, there was a crimson altar-cloth, embroidered with golden rays by Miss Lydia's own hand.

But even without the crimson cloth, the effect must have been warm and cheering when Mr Irwine was in the desk, looking benignly round on that simple congregation—on the hardy old men, with bent knees and shoulders, perhaps, but with vigour left for much hedge-clipping and thatching; on the tall stalwart frames and roughly-cut bronzed faces of the stonecutters and carpenters; on the half-dozen well-to-do farmers, with their apple-cheeked families; and on the clean old women, mostly farm-labourers' wives, with their bit of snow-white cap-border under their black bonnets, and with their withered arms, bare from the elbow, folded passively over their chest. . . . I beseech you to imagine Mr Irwine looking round on this scene, in his ample white surplice, that became him so well, with his powdered hair thrown back, his rich brown complexion, and his finely-cut nostril and upper lip; for there was a certain virtue in that benignant yet keen countenance, as there is in all human faces from which a generous soul beams out. And over all streamed the delicious June sunshine through the old windows, with their desultory patches of yellow, red, and blue, that threw pleasant touches of colour on the opposite wall. [18:295–97]

The passage is suffused by a sentiment of nostalgia for the religious simplicities and social harmonies of a bygone era, a tone which is characteristic of Victorian spectator Christianity. The visual imagery is deliberately organized to recall the style of Victorian historical genre painting, and looks forward to the even more elaborate description of the interior of Santa Maria Annunziata in chapter 14 of *Romola*.

As genre encroached upon history painting, its narrative ambitions increased. History painting has always been literary, taking its subjects from either the Scriptures or "the poets." Modern poets and novelists were gradually added to the pantheon of classical authors eligible for illustration, so that by the nineteenth century perfectly respectable subjects for both history and historical genre painting could be found in Shakespeare, Milton, Tasso, Malory, Cervantes, Molière, Sterne, Goldsmith, Goethe, or Scott. Narrative and dramatic elements were naturally prominent in such pictures, as the artist strove not only to depict a climactic scene, but also to recall its literary context to the viewer's mind.

For nineteenth-century English artists the most important source of narrative techniques was Hogarth, whose "Progress" sequences brilliantly demonstrated the use of dramatic expression, innovative iconography, and emblematic detail in a pictorial structure that can be "read" and translated into verbal terms.[31] Because they have no immediate literary sources, Hogarth's sequences set a precedent for the application of narrative techniques to any genre scene in which moral meanings might be found. In the nineteenth century many nonheroic pictures of daily life required the viewer to imagine a temporal context of events leading to and from the moment actually represented.[32] This narrative element distinguishes Victorian from Dutch and Flemish genre painting, which only occasionally implies a rudimentary story in courtship and epistolary scenes.

If, as Peter Conrad has suggested, narrative painting aspired to the condition of the novel, it is equally true that the novel sometimes aspired to the condition of narrative painting.[33] George Eliot, for one, made good use of telltale pictorial structures to arouse suspense in her stories. Will Grandcourt propose to Gwendolen, and will Gwendolen accept him? These questions in *Daniel Deronda* are asked in pictorial terms:

A moment afterwards, when they were both of them seated on

two of the wreath-painted chairs—Gwendolen upright with downcast eyelids, Grandcourt about two yards distant, leaning one arm over the back of his chair and looking at her, while he held his hat in his left hand—any one seeing them as a picture would have concluded that they were in some stage of love-making suspense. [27:36]

"The Imminent Proposal" might be a suitable title for the narrative painting George Eliot asks us to envision here. Courtship scenes were among the first genre subjects to attract narrative treatment, and from the seventeenth century through the nineteenth they retained a lasting popularity.

The conversation piece also lends itself to narrative treatment by virtue of the dramatic activities of the group portrayed. When the pastimes of the sitters become morally significant actions, the picture no longer depicts "conversation" in the eighteenth-century sense of the term. As Sacheverell Sitwell has observed, many well-known Victorian paintings would be classifiable as conversation pieces but for the drama and strong moral sentiment of the moment represented.[34] Ford Madox Brown's *The Last of England* (1855) and R. B. Martineau's *Last Day in the Old Home* (1862) are two cases in point. In these pictures, scenes of family crisis have displaced scenes of family amusement.

This new Victorian emphasis is visible in a scene of George Eliot's *The Mill on the Floss*:

Tom drew to the corner of the table near his father when the tin box was set down and opened, and the red evening light falling on them made conspicuous the worn, sour gloom of the dark-eyed father and the suppressed joy in the face of the fair-complexioned son. The mother and Maggie sat at the other end of the table, the one in blank patience, the other in palpitating expectation. [V, 6:130]

On one level, this is an informal portrait of the family group at home. But the members of the group are occupied with the restoration of the family fortunes and honor rather than with recreation. The gamut of expressions in the scene far exceeds that of the ordinary conversation piece, and arouses sympathetic curiosity rather than admiring delight. The narrative picture shows character and situation in the making, whereas the conversation piece shows them as made.

When the situation implied by a narrative painting must be puzzled out by the viewer without the help of an external literary source, the result is a Victorian "problem picture." The term has a double reference, for such a picture both shows forth a problem and poses one for the viewer, who must make inferences from the given clues. Many problem pictures are based on the conventions of the conversation piece, since the affirmation of family prosperity and harmony can easily be inverted to underline problems of poverty and marital discord. Both Mario Praz and Ronald Paulson have called attention to a Dutch conversation piece by Julius Quinkhard, *Paulus Determeyer Weslingh and His Accountant* (1765), in which Weslingh's wife and daughter have been painted out as the result of a bitter family quarrel.[35] Two empty chairs remain, and the absence of their occupants is, as Paulson says, "the most important thing about the picture." This conversation piece, which hints mysteriously at family troubles, accidentally anticipates many nineteenth-century treatments of domestic dispute, abandonment, infidelity, or bereavement.

In George Eliot's literary problem pictures, the favorite theme is illegitimacy. Eliot liked to evoke the benign conventions of the conversation piece and then invert them ironically by leaving out a member of the family whose connection with it is unlawful. Thus an apparently innocuous pictorial passage in *Felix Holt* actually hints at Mrs. Transome's adultery and Harold Transome's illegitimacy:

She was standing on the broad gravel in the afternoon; the long shadows lay on the grass; the light seemed the more glorious because of the reddened and golden trees. The gardeners were busy at their pleasant work; the newly-turned soil gave out an agreeable fragrance; and little Harry was playing with Nimrod round old Mr Transome, who sat placidly on a low garden-chair. The scene would have made a charming picture of English domestic life, and the handsome, majestic, grey-haired woman (obviously grandmamma) would have been especially admired. But the artist would have felt it requisite to turn her face towards her husband and little grandson, and to have given her an elderly amiability of expression, which would have divided remark with his exquisite rendering of her Indian shawl. Mrs Transome's face was turned the other way, and for this reason she only heard an approaching step, and did not see whose it was; yet it startled her: it was not quick enough to be her son's step, and besides, Harold was away at Duffield. It was Mr Jermyn's. [8:168–69]

The scene is almost a perfect conversation piece. But Mrs. Transome's attitude is not the expected grandmaternal attitude, and the picture for which she is not quite posed is presented through a series of subjunctive verbs ("would have been"). In fact, two questionable members of the family are missing—Mrs. Transome's former lover and her natural son. Because they do not belong in "a charming picture of English domestic life," the picture dissolves before they enter it, depriving Mrs. Transome of the true family harmony for which she longs with averted head. In a later conversation piece which again features old Mr. Transome, Harry, and the family dogs, Harold is present but Mrs. Transome herself is not (43:254). On yet another occasion, Esther perceives Mrs. Transome "to stand apart from the family group, as if there were some cause of isolation for her both within and without" (40:212).

Mrs. Transome's plight resembles that of Mrs. Glasher in *Daniel Deronda*. As Grandcourt's former mistress, Mrs. Glasher has borne him four illegitimate children. Her establishment is introduced to the reader through a conversation piece which gradually turns into a problem picture:

Mrs Glasher was seated in the pleasant room where she habitually passed her mornings with her children round her. It had a square projecting window and looked on broad gravel and grass, sloping towards a little brook that entered the pool. The top of a low black cabinet, the old oak table, the chairs in tawny leather, were littered with the children's toys, books, and garden garments, at which a maternal lady in pastel looked down from the walls with smiling indulgence. The children were all there. The three girls, seated round their mother near the window, were miniature portraits of her—dark-eyed, delicate-featured brunettes with a rich bloom on their cheeks, their little nostrils and eyebrows singularly finished as if they were tiny women, the eldest being barely nine. The boy was seated on the carpet at some distance, bending his blond head over the animals from a Noah's ark, admonishing them separately in a voice of threatening command, and occasionally licking the spotted ones to see if the colours would hold. Josephine, the eldest, was having her French lesson; and the others, with their dolls on their laps, sat demurely enough for images of the Madonna. Mrs Glasher's toilet had been made very carefully—each day now she said to herself that Grandcourt might come in. Her head, which, spite of emaciation, had an ineffaceable beauty in the fine profile, crisp curves of hair, and clearly-marked eyebrows, rose impressively above her bronze-coloured silk and velvet, and the gold necklace which Grandcourt had first clasped round her neck years ago. [30:99–100]

Once again the absence of the father belies the apparent normalcy of the family group. Like Weslingh alone with his accountant, Mrs. Glasher dominates the scene visually, but the interpretive focus comes finally to rest upon the missing spouse. In *Silas Marner* it is a missing child—Godfrey Cass's illegitimate daughter—who haunts an otherwise benign conversation piece organized around Sunday dessert in the parlour of Red House (17:226–27).

The theme of illegitimacy was not uncommon in Victorian problem pictures; for example, both Millais's *Retribution* (1854) and Ford Madox Brown's *"Take Your Son, Sir!"* (ca. 1857) raise the issue. But George Eliot had compelling personal reasons to be interested in the question, for she was obliged to decide whether to try to bear children out of wedlock. Her determination not to try suggests that she considered illegitimacy too cruel a handicap to be imposed upon the innocent. Perhaps she was thinking of the children whom Lewes's wife had borne to Thornton Hunt. Society might always treat them as nonpersons, as it had treated Eliot herself when she first became a common-law wife. To represent the dilemma of the nonperson, she devised her characteristic technique of creating troublesome voids in innocent-looking literary conversation pieces. The technique is more subtle and more poignant than the melodramatic confrontations used in some other Victorian treatments of illegitimacy.

Eliot did, then, use genre painting in her novels with a greater confidence in its correlation to reality than she displayed in her ambivalent handling of sacred and heroic history painting. But it is important to recognize the diversity of the reality involved in this genre pictorialism. The technique is far less reductive and simplistic than Mario Praz and Peter Conrad have suggested. Eliot imitated a wide variety of schools and styles within the genre tradition, from the seventeenth-century Dutch intimists to the Georgian painters of conversation pieces to the Victorian masters of narrative and domestic-historical art. This range of effects cannot be lumped under the heading "Biedermeier" or done justice by such a statement as the following: "George Eliot cultivates a uniform greyness of tone, a concentration on the middling qualities of characters with their spots of commonness, and presents this as the whole truth about them."[36] This generalization reflects an inattention to both the human and the pictorial dimensions of George Eliot's art. Neither in her genre scenes nor, as we are about to see, in her landscapes did she cultivate a uniform grayness of tone.

8 Landscape and the Beholder

Landscape and landscape painting afforded George Eliot great visual pleasure and spiritual refreshment. Her enjoyment and careful study of natural appearances found full expression in her novels, impelled by personal feeling and summoned by a tradition of landscape description that had become established in British and American fiction in the time of Mrs. Radcliffe, Scott, and Fenimore Cooper.[1] Eliot's responsiveness to landscape views in fiction may be seen in her appreciation of Charles Kingsley's "scene-painting" in *Alton Locke, Yeast,* and *Westward Ho!* (*Essays,* pp. 129–30). Her own vision of landscape combined several important eighteenth- and nineteenth-century traditions. The cult of the picturesque and the English school of topographical painting, both of which had reached their prime in the eighteenth century, were second-nature to George Eliot in her perception and description of country scenes. But she was also profoundly influenced by three nineteenth-century developments in landscape sensibility, each of which came to her in part through the work of Ruskin: the cult of detailed naturalism, which Ruskin advocated and the Pre-Raphaelites practiced; the nature poetry of Wordsworth, which Ruskin echoed in many parts of *Modern Painters*; and the moral critique of the cult of the picturesque, which finds its classic formulation in volume IV of *Modern Painters.* To explore these five aspects of George Eliot's landscape vision is the purpose of the present chapter.

Several of the traditions just mentioned work together harmoniously in the following passage of *Middlemarch:*

> The ride to Stone Court, which Fred and Rosamond took the next morning, lay through a pretty bit of midland landscape, almost all meadows and pastures, with hedgerows still allowed to grow in bushy beauty and to spread out coral fruit for the birds. Little details gave each field a particular physiognomy, dear to the eyes that have looked on them from childhood: the pool in the corner where the grasses were dank and trees leaned whisperingly; the great oak shadowing a bare place in mid-pasture; the high bank where the ash-trees grew; the sudden slope of the old marl-pit making a red background for the burdock; the huddled roofs and ricks of the homestead without a traceable way of approach; the grey gate and fences against the depths of the bordering wood; and the stray hovel, its old, old thatch full of mossy hills and valleys with wondrous modulations of light and shadow such as we travel far to see in later life, and see larger, but not more beautiful. These are the things that make the gamut of joy in landscape to midland-bred souls— the things they toddled among, or perhaps learned by heart standing between their father's knees while he drove leisurely.
> [12:155-56]

The narrator here is in part a Gilpinesque tourist, in search of the picturesque in all its roughness, variegation, chiaroscuro, and suggestive antiquity ("old, old thatch full of mossy hills and valleys with wondrous modulations of light and shadow such as we travel far to see in later life"). But there is also an element of Ruskinian naturalistic precision in the description of individual features in the landscape, the "little details" that give "each field a particular physiognomy" such as "the great oak *shadowing a bare place* in mid-pasture." And finally there is a Wordsworthian emphasis upon the "joy" that such landscape brings in maturity to those who have grown up amidst it. All these tones are characteristic of the George Eliot landscape, which we may now examine in greater detail.

"The power of description, both of scenery and of character . . . may be very puissant in the hands of a fine writer, gifted with a

real sense of the picturesque," G. H. Lewes argued.[2] The cult of the
picturesque grew up in the late eighteenth century, making it fashionable to travel in search of landscape views that compose themselves pictorially.[3] The models for such views derived in part from
the neoclassical heroic landscapes of Claude Lorrain and the Pous-
sins, in part from the wilder, more dramatic visions of Salvator
Rosa, and in part from the leafy, aqueous, rock-strewn country
scenes of Ruisdael, Hobbema, and other seventeenth-century Dutch
painters. William Gilpin's initial definition of the picturesque in
1768 as "that peculiar kind of beauty which is agreeable in a picture"[4] was refined by a complex debate in the 1790s and early
1800s to mean a kind of aesthetic effect which is neither awe-
somely sublime nor smoothly beautiful but a blend of those two
extremes distinguished by roughness, variety, sudden contrast,
chiaroscuro, signs of age or decay, and a power to stimulate in
the viewer a piquant mixture of painful and pleasurable impressions
and associations.

The coming of Romanticism modified but did not extinguish the
cult of the picturesque. Christopher Hussey is more right than not
when he asserts that "the picturesque became the nineteenth century's mode of vision."[5] It was certainly a natural mode for George
Eliot, whose letters and journals are full of descriptions in the Gilpin
tradition. Italy in 1860 showed her "Claude-like scenes of mountains,
trees, and meadows, with picturesque accidents of building, such as
single round towers, on the heights" (Cross, II, 178). Biarritz in
1867 seemed to G. H. Lewes, and doubtless to Eliot as well, "so
picturesque that it may be called a succession of Prouts" (*Letters,*
IV, 331-32). Switzerland in 1860 was mediated through the
novelist's prior experience of Alexandre Calame's landscape painting (*Letters,* III, 79, 309; Cross, II, 51). Except for ruins, the valley
of Bercka near Weimar in 1854 had all the necessary ingredients of
the picturesque:

> The hanging woods—the soft colouring and graceful outline of
> the uplands—the village with its roofs and spire of a reddish vio-
> let hue, muffled in luxuriant trees—the white *Kurhaus* glittering
> on a grassy slope—the avenue of poplars contrasting its pretty

primness with the wild bushy outline of the wood-covered hill, which rises abruptly from the smooth, green meadows—the clear winding stream, now sparkling in the sun, now hiding itself under soft grey willows—all this makes an enchanting picture. [*Essays*, p. 121]

Returning from Germany in 1855, the ardent tourist found a charming English landscape at Dover: "As I walked up the Castle hill this afternoon, the town, with its background of softly rounded hills shrouded in sleepy haze, its little lines of water looking golden in the sun, made a charming picture" (Cross, I, 307). Jersey in 1857 offered a feast for the wandering eye (Cross, I, 360–63), and a stroll along the banks of the Trent near Newark in 1868 brought "some charming quiet pictures—Frith landscapes" (*Letters*, IV, 473).

In 1879, less than two years before her death, Eliot sought to pass on her taste for the picturesque to young Blanche Southwood Lewes, who had just celebrated her seventh birthday with a visit to an exhibition and a boatride on the Thames: "I am sure you must have liked being on the river in the steamboat for the first time. The wide river, and the bridges, and the great buildings that can be seen a long way by the waterside, are all very beautiful, are they not? It would seem to you like another and grander sort of picture, after seeing the small pictures on the wall at the Exhibition" (*Letters*, VII, 186). Eliot wanted Blanche's vision to be shaped and enriched, as hers was, by the experience of pictures.

Eliot's novels, from the start to the finish of her career, abound with picturesque descriptions in an eighteenth-century vein. She was especially fond of "pretty bits of midland landscape" like the one quoted above from *Middlemarch*. Here is another representative "bit," this time from *Felix Holt*:

The Rectory was on the other side of the river, close to the church of which it was the fitting companion: a fine old brick-and-stone house, with a great bow-window opening from the library on to the deep-turfed lawn, one fat dog sleeping on the door-stone, another fat dog waddling on the gravel, the autumn leaves duly swept away, the lingering chrysanthemums cherished, tall trees stooping or soaring in the most picturesque variety, and a Virginian creeper turning a little rustic hut into a scarlet pavilion. [23:343-44]

After reading a similar description of a parsonage and farm in "Mr Gilfil's Love-Story," John Blackwood wrote to George Eliot: "The picture reminds me strongly of the genuine English rural landscapes with which we are all familiar on canvas or in nature" (*Letters*, II, 323). Blackwood's was precisely the sort of response Eliot wanted her langue in such passages to elicit.

The convention of the Gilpinesque tourist-guide may help to account for the anonymous observer who opens so many of George Eliot's stories, mediating between author, reader, and action. The horseback traveler in *Adam Bede,* the armchair dreamer in *The Mill on the Floss,* the Florentine shade in *Romola,* and the stagecoach passenger in *Felix Holt* are visitors or revisitors on holiday, having no business in the scene except to appreciate it. They make a Gilpinesque discrimination of landscape and figures, and disappear as soon as they have drawn the reader into engagement with the prospect (though the traveler in *Adam Bede* does reappear later in the novel as the magistrate who helps Dinah gain admission to Hetty's prison cell). They are guides and tutors, demonstrating the quality of perception that the reader must learn to apply to the world within the novel.

Though it came so naturally to her, Eliot knew that the picturesque way of seeing has its dangers. For one thing, it can become facile and overgeneralized. She did not favor the Claudian technique, often imitated by Gilpin in his sketches of Wales and the Lake District, of reconstructing an actual landscape according to an ideal model.[6] She preferred a sense of unique place and abundant local detail in landscape descriptions.[7] From this preference stems her critique of Tom Tulliver's drawing lessons in *The Mill on the Floss.*

Tom found, to his disgust, that his new drawing-master gave him no dogs and donkeys to draw, but brooks and rustic bridges and ruins, all with a general softness of black-lead surface, indicating that nature, if anything, was rather satiny; and as Tom's feeling for the picturesque in landscape was at present quite latent, it is not surprising that Mr Goodrich's productions seemed to him an uninteresting form of art . . . Tom learned to make an extremely fine point to his pencil, and to represent landscape with a "broad generality," which, doubtless from a narrow tendency in his mind to details, he thought extremely dull. [II, 4:260]

A broad generality in which no characteristic details can be discerned was not George Eliot's idea of a good landscape style. The picturesque must be tempered by the naturalistic. We shall see that in *Adam Bede*, as in *Modern Painters*, Claudian ideal landscape is something of a villain.

George Eliot's taste for the representation of actual places shows itself in her imitation of eighteenth-century topographical painting, especially in her descriptions of English country houses and their grounds. John Steegman has shown how the bird's-eye perspective and diagrammatic cartography of early country-house portraits gave way in the eighteenth century to a lower viewpoint, a placing of the house itself in the middle or far distance, and a bringing forward of human and/or animal groups into the intervening space.[8] Engraved views of noblemen's and gentlemen's country seats were especially popular between 1760 and 1840.[9] J. P. Neale's six-volume set, published between 1818 and 1823, had a standard pictorial format that can be characterized in the words of John Dixon Hunt: "The typical English landscape garden as generally visualized would consist of undulating grass that leads somewhere down to an irregularly shaped piece of water over which a bridge arches, of trees grouped casually, with cattle or deer, about the slopes, and of houses and other buildings glimpsed in the middle or far distance."[10] When Phillipe Mercier, a transplanted imitator of Watteau, began around 1725 to make the figures in the foreground into portraits, he initiated a special and highly influential form of semitopographical English conversation piece which depicts "family groups in their proper setting, that is in their own park or garden, with a sight of the family home in the background."[11]

Eliot's skill at country-house portraiture may be seen in her descriptions of Hall Farm and the Chase in *Adam Bede*, of Transome Court in *Felix Holt*, and of Offendene, Brackenshaw Park, the

Abbey, Diplow, and Gadsmere in *Daniel Deronda.*[12] A favorite and recurring form of architecture in her novels is a plain red-brick structure built in the Queen Anne period, sometimes adjoining the ruins of a medieval abbey. The gables, windows, and doors are ornamented with limestone, but the contrast between the limestone and the brick is diminished by the growth of a powdery, greenish-grey lichen. A flowery lawn cut by graveled, often tree-lined walks or driveways runs from the house to a plantation of trees which nearly surround the house or screen it on the north. The plantation frequently contains Scotch firs, while one or two large firs or cedars or beeches may stand immediately adjacent to the house. If the estate is landscaped, the garden is in the picturesque style, with rolling lawns, manmade lakes, serpentine paths, clumps of trees, and perhaps an occasional glimpse of a white temple. Eliot's affection for "grounds, which are laid out with a taste worthy of a first-rate landscape gardener" was expressed in her early descriptions of the Belvedere gardens at Weimar (*Essays,* pp. 86–87, 118).

Eliot's most elaborate country-house portrait is of the neo-Gothic Cheverel Manor in "Mr Gilfil's Love-Story." Here the topographical element is very strong; for, as Marghanita Laski has said, "Cheverel Manor is photographically Arbury Hall," the Newdigate family seat in Warwickshire near which George Eliot grew up.[13] Her description is also a full-fledged conversation piece, beginning with close-up portraits of Caterina Sarti and Lady Cheverel, and then placing the sitters in their habitat:

> they sat down, making two bright patches of red and white and blue on the green background of the laurels and the lawn, which would look none the less pretty in a picture because one of the women's hearts was rather cold and the other rather sad.

> And a charming picture Cheverel Manor would have made that evening, if some English Watteau had been there to paint it: the castellated house of grey-tinted stone, with the flickering sunbeams sending dashes of golden light across the many-shaped panes in the mullioned windows, and a great beech leaning athwart one of the flanking towers, and breaking, with its dark flattened boughs, the too formal symmetry of the front; the

broad gravel-walk winding on the right, by a row of tall pines, alongside the pool—on the left branching out among swelling grassy mounds, surmounted by clumps of trees, where the red trunk of the Scotch fir glows in the descending sunlight against the bright green of limes and acacias; the great pool, where a pair of swans are swimming lazily with one leg tucked under a wing, and where the open water-lilies lie calmly accepting the kisses of the fluttering light-sparkles; the lawn, with its smooth emerald greenness, sloping down to the rougher and browner herbage of the park, from which it is invisibly fenced by a little stream that winds away from the pool, and disappears under the wooden bridge in the distant pleasure-ground; and on this lawn our two ladies, whose part in the landscape the painter, standing at a favourable point of view in the park, would represent with a few little dabs of red and white and blue. [2:150-52]

Eliot's sensitivity to color is evident here, and the reference to an "English Watteau" is entirely apt since, as we have noted, Watteau's *fetes galantes* were the immediate predecessors of Mercier's pioneering English conversation pieces.[14] Eliot even includes the artist in her scene, as Mercier did in his seminal *Viscount Tyrconnel with His Family in the Grounds of Belton House* (1725-26).[15]

When the narrator moves inside Cheverel Manor to describe the dining-room and saloon, we seem to be observing two of Joseph Nash's views of *The Mansions of England in the Olden Time* (1839-49), staffed by figures in Georgian instead of Tudor or Restoration costume.[16] What Neale had done for the exteriors of country houses, Nash did for their interiors, by publishing detailed engravings of their great halls, drawing-rooms, parlors, bay windows, galleries, bedchambers, staircases, porches, and chapels. Again, however, Eliot's description combines view-painting with portraiture, turning the picture into a conversation piece. She presents informal portraits of Sir Christopher Cheverel and Anthony Wybrow, surrounded by the architecture which is Sir Christopher's proudest domestic achievement.

George Eliot's penchant for topographical specificity in landscape also took a form that was more characteristic of the nineteenth century than of the eighteenth. Her passion for precise naturalistic detail was kindled by the teachings of Ruskin, the practice of the Pre-Raphaelite painters, and the scientific researches of G. H. Lewes. After reading the third volume of *Modern Painters* in February of 1856 and reviewing it in April, Eliot spent May and June at Ilfracombe on the north coast of Devon, where Lewes was conducting the fieldwork in marine biology that eventually led to the publication of his *Sea-Side Studies* (1858). Art and science were in perfect harmony during these happy months. The picturesque took on an ecological dimension:

> From this end of the Capstone we have an admirable bit for a picture. In the background rises old Hillsborough jutting far into the sea—rugged and rocky as it fronts the waves, green and accessible landward; in front of this stands Lantern Hill, a picturesque mass of green and grey surmounted by an old bit of building that looks *as if it were the habitation of some mollusk that had secreted its shell from the material of the rock;* and quite in the foreground, contrasting finely in colour with the rest, are some lower perpendicular rocks, of dark brown tints patched here and there with vivid green. In hilly districts, where houses and clusters of houses look so tiny against the huge limbs of Mother Earth one cannot help thinking of man *as a parasitic animal—an epizoon making his abode on the skin of the planetary organism.* [*Letters,* II, 241–42; emphasis added]

It is difficult to know whether these words came originally from George Eliot or from Lewes, since they appear almost verbatim in *Sea-Side Studies.*[17] But the ideas were in any case shared. Man, the figure in the landscape, becomes a mollusc or epizoon when viewed from a biological perspective.

Ruskin's mixture of science and aesthetics was very much in Eliot's mind at Ilfracombe, as a letter sent from there to Barbara Leigh Smith suggests: "What books his last two are! I think he is the finest writer living" (*Letters,* II, 255; Haight, p. 197). She must have been thinking in part of Ruskin's defense of the naturalistic landscapes of the Pre-Raphaelite painters:

I have talked of the Ilfracombe lanes without describing them, for to describe them one ought to know the names of all the lovely wild flowers that cluster on their banks. Almost every yard of these banks is a "Hunt" picture—a delicious crowding of mosses and delicate trefoil, and wild strawberries, and ferns great and small. But the crowning beauty of the lanes is the springs, that gush out in little recesses by the side of the road—recesses glossy with liverwort and feathery with fern . . . I never before longed so much to know names of things as during this visit to Ilfracombe. The desire is part of the tendency that is now constantly growing in me to escape from all vagueness and inaccuracy into the daylight of distinct, vivid ideas. The mere fact of naming an object tends to give definiteness to our conception of it—we have then a sign that at once calls up in our minds the distinctive qualities which mark out for us that particular object from all others.[18] [*Letters,* II, 250–51]

The "Hunt" mentioned here could be either William Henry ("Bird's-Nest") Hunt, who had tutored Barbara Leigh Smith, or William Holman Hunt, whose landscape in *The Hireling Shepherd* (1851) Eliot had already praised for its "marvelous truthfulness" (*Essays,* p. 268). Both Hunts practiced a painstaking realism, and their treatment of vegetation made a lasting impression upon the novelist, who sought an equivalent precision in her own medium. She had been accustomed to think of "attention to vegetation as one of the most remarkable characteristics of the Pre-Raphaelite painters" by the essay on "Pre-Raphaelitism in Art and Literature" which she read and praised in 1852.[19]

Lewes once defined "the ideal of a pre-Raphaelite landscape" as "isolating one part of the landscape, and thus concentrating attention on it alone."[20] This formulation was prompted by an experience he and George Eliot had in the Belvedere gardens at Weimar. Walking through the park, they came upon a set of "large glass globes of different colours" placed upon an artificial rock. "It is wonderful to see with what minute perfection the scenery around is painted in these globes," Eliot wrote. "Each is like a pre-Rafaelite

picture, with every little detail of gravelly walk, mossy bank, and
delicately-leaved, interlacing boughs, presented in accurate miniature" (*Essays*, p. 119). The eighteenth-century connoisseur of the
picturesque had composed his landscapes in a special mirror known
as a Claude glass. But George Eliot's equivalent of the Claude glass
isolated "every little detail" for special attention, heightening what
Mario Praz has called the "microscopic structure" of represented
reality.[21]

Pre-Raphaelite attention to natural detail helped to shape George
Eliot's technique of landscape description. The Huntian treatment of
vegetation especially influenced her rendering of the hedgerows that
she considered the most distinctive feature of the English midlands
landscape.[22] In the following passage from *Felix Holt,* the precise
botanical naming imitates the Hunts' leaf-by-leaf drawing:

> But everywhere the bushy hedgerows wasted the land with their
> straggling beauty, shrouded the grassy borders of the pastures
> with catkined hazels, and tossed their long blackberry branches
> on the corn-fields. Perhaps they were white with May, or starred
> with pale-pink dog-roses; perhaps the urchins were already
> nutting amongst them, or gathering the plenteous crabs. It was
> worth the journey only to see those hedgerows, the liberal
> homes of unmarketable beauty—of the purple-blossomed ruby-
> berried nightshade, of the wild convolvulus climbing and spread-
> ing in tendrilled strength till it made a great curtain of pale-green
> hearts and white trumpets, of the many-tubed honeysuckle
> which, in its most delicate fragrance, hid a charm more subtle
> and penetrating than beauty. Even if it were winter the hedge-
> rows showed their coral, the scarlet haws, the deep-crimsoned
> hips, with lingering brown leaves to make a resting-place for the
> jewels of the hoar-frost. ["Introduction": 3–4]

These hedgerows reappear in *Adam Bede* (18:283) and *Middlemarch*
(12:155), where George Eliot's prose again follows the principle laid
down at Ilfracombe: "to describe them one ought to know the names
of all the lovely wild flowers that cluster on their banks." Passages
like these inspired Ruskinian praises from at least one of George
Eliot's contemporaries: "Marian Evans does really good landscape-
sketching, of an intensely truthful character."[23]

Yet Eliot's strong local attachment to her native midlands scenery is due neither to the cult of the picturesque nor to the cult of outdoor naturalism. Rather it shows the Wordsworthian side of her landscape sensibility. "I am afraid you despise landscape painting," she wrote to an early correspondent, "but to me even the works of our own Stanfield and Roberts and Creswick bring a whole world of thought and bliss—'a sense of something far more deeply interfused.' The ocean and the sky and the everlasting hills are spirit to me, and they will never be robbed of their sublimity" (*Letters,* I, 248). This is the voice of a young person who has been reading the early volumes of *Modern Painters* in conjunction with "Tintern Abbey," and mediating her Wordsworthian responses to landscape through the vision of the landscape painter. The enthusiasm was by no means temporary, for in her maturity George Eliot continued to pair Ruskin with Wordsworth and to draw inspiration from the association.[24] "The two last volumes of Modern Painters," she wrote in 1858, "contain, I think, some of the finest writing of this age. He is strongly akin to the sublimest part of Wordsworth, whom, by the bye, we are reading now with fresh admiration for his beauties and tolerance for his faults" (*Letters,* II, 422–23).

Eliot read Wordsworth often from 1839 till the end of her life.[25] She felt a considerable affinity of temperament with the great poet: "And I often smile at my consciousness that certain conservative prepossessions have mingled themselves for me with the influences of our midland scenery, from the tops of the elms down to the buttercups and the little wayside vetches."[26] This vocabulary of influences, mingling, and prepossessions reflects the change Wordsworth had wrought in the literary representation of landscape. Wordsworth "began in the picturesque," as J. R. Watson has noted.[27] The early poem, "An Evening Walk," continues a tradition of loco-descriptive poetry that descends from John Denham and James Thomson. But as early as "Descriptive Sketches" (1793), Wordsworth began to grow restless with the picturesque apprehension of nature, and to evolve a new sense of landscape which placed greater emphasis upon the affective and experiential interchange between the observer and the scene. The Wordsworthian observer is in the landscape and part of it, rather than separated from it by an aesthetic distance. He is more concerned to render the emotional impact of the outdoor setting, the sense of its total presence, than to distinguish and analyze its constituent parts. The landscape affects him in a diffuse but profound and permanent manner, creating in his memory an "obscure sense/Of possible sublimity" which is a source of both joy and moral strength in later years.[28] This complex sense of an environment that functions in many ways as a deity was immensely congenial to George Eliot. "I never before met with so many of my own feelings, expressed just as I could like them," she declared shortly after reading Wordsworth in 1839 (*Letters,* I, 34).

Having originated in a reaction against the picturesque tradition, the mature Wordsworthian mode is essentially nonpictorial. As Christopher Salvesen has noted, "Wordsworth is always much more aware of the *presence* of landscape, of its surrounding influence, than of any pictorial qualities it might have . . . the fundamental landscape of his best poetry is not at all detailed: the unifying force of nature is what creates it and holds it together, and this force is conveyed by Wordsworth's emotion rather than by his observation. He responds to a landscape rather than observes it: he feels it, almost, rather than sees."[29] The distinction Salvesen is making could be illustrated by the well-known comparison between "I Wandered Lonely as a Cloud" and Dorothy Wordsworth's far more particularized journal description of the same field of daffodils.[30] The distinction may also be illustrated by two passages from George Eliot:

> Janet's way thither lay for a little while along the highroad, and then led her into a deep-rutted lane, which wound through a flat tract of meadow and pasture, while in front lay smoky Paddiford, and away to the left the mother-town of Milby. There was no line of silvery willows marking the course of a stream—no group of Scotch firs with their trunks reddening in the level sunbeams—nothing to break the flowerless monotony of grass and hedgerow but an occasional oak or elm, and a few cows sprinkled here and there. A very commonplace scene, indeed. But what scene was ever commonplace in the descending sunlight, when colour has awakened from its noonday sleep, and the long shadows awe us like a disclosed presence? Above all, what

scene is commonplace to the eye that is filled with serene gladness, and brightens all things with its own joy? And Janet just
now was very happy. [26:305–06]

And the mill with its booming—the great chestnut-tree under
which they played at houses—their own little river, the Ripple,
where the banks seemed like home, and Tom was always seeing
the water-rats, while Maggie gathered the purple plumy tops
of the reeds, which she forgot and dropped afterwards—above
all, the great Floss, along which they wandered with a sense of
travel, to see the rushing spring-tide, the awful Eagre, come
up like a hungry monster, or to see the Great Ash which had
once wailed and groaned like a man—these things would always
be just the same to them. [I, 5:57]

The second of these passages is more truly Wordsworthian than
the first, yet the first is more pictorial in the strict sense of the term.
What makes it so is the addition of topographical and picturesque
details to the basically nonpictorial Wordsworthian emphasis upon
presences, awe, gladness, and joy. The second passage abounds with
visual images, but they are not arranged pictorially. Their disposition
is controlled rather by what Wordsworth might have called the
inward eye of contemplation and memory, as opposed to the outward or bodily eye.

It is not surprising, then, that Eliot's two most Wordsworthian
novels—*The Mill on the Floss* and *Silas Marner*—are her two least
pictorial. Although both are full of visually memorable scenes, the
construction of those scenes is seldom indebted to the visual arts. To
be sure, the panoramic landscape which opens *The Mill on the Floss*
is pictorial, as Reva Stump has pointed out.[31] The passage appeals to
other senses than sight in an effort to create the illusion of a total
environment, but the dominant mode of the description is picturesque. The details constitute a virtual anthology of motifs from
seventeenth-century Dutch landscape painting: a distant view of a
town and river in a flat, wide, cultivated plain; a mill and cottage
among trees by a stream; a covered wagon pulled by a team of horses
across a bridge. It is tempting to connect this word-painting with

Constable's Suffolk landscapes, especially in view of the many affinities between Constable and Wordsworth.[32] But the motifs are commonplace, and since George Eliot never mentions Constable in any of her published writings, there is no independent evidence that his work was important to her.[33] After its opening passage, the novel offers relatively little of a pictorial nature until Maggie emerges in Book 5 as a stately hamadryad among the Scotch firs in the Red Deeps.[34] Pictures are used within the story to characterize the amusingly provincial taste of St. Ogg's, and to act as Hogarthian emblematic warnings of Maggie's fate;[35] but the scenes and characters in the first four books of the novel are only rarely conceived as pictures.

Likewise in *Silas Marner,* as Norma Jean Davis has pointed out, "there is a general absence of pictorial patterns."[36] The principal exceptions to this rule are two contrasting scenes in Godfrey Cass's parlor at the Red House (3:35–36, 17:226–27); the introduction of Nancy Lammeter (11:136); and the description of the churchgoers which opens part 2 and shows the main characters after a lapse of sixteen years (16:204–05). But the climactic discovery of Eppie by Silas turns upon Silas's nearsightedness and is therefore not visualized pictorially, while the famous scene at the Rainbow Inn, as we have seen, is not visually indebted to Dutch genre painting. *Silas Marner,* too, works mainly by the Wordsworthian inner eye of memory and feeling.

In *Daniel Deronda* the English landscape has a Wordsworthian potential to heal and integrate the human personality, but that potential is largely unrealized by the English characters. Gwendolen's family has led a rootless and nomadic modern life, and therefore lacks the sense of selfhood that comes from full integration with a relatively permanent environment.[37] Although their new home at Offendene affords "a glimpse of the wider world in the lofty curves of the chalk downs, grand steadfast forms played over by the changing days" (3:27–28), the inhabitants are unable to incorporate that stability. Mrs. Davilow passes untouched through a landscape which combines picturesque and Wordsworthian elements in the most characteristic George Eliot manner.

It was a fine mid-harvest time, not too warm for a noonday ride of five miles to be delightful: the poppies glowed on the borders of the fields, there was enough breeze to move gently like a social spirit among the ears of uncut corn, and to wing the shadow of a cloud across the soft grey downs; here the sheaves were standing, there the horses were straining their muscles under the last load from a wide space of stubble, but everywhere the green pastures made a broader setting for the corn-fields, and the cattle took their rest under wide branches. The road lay through a bit of country where the dairy-farms looked much as they did in the days of our forefathers—where peace and permanence seemed to find a home away from the busy change that sent the railway train flying in the distance.

But the spirit of peace and permanence did not penetrate poor Mrs Davilow's mind. . . . [13:192–93]

Only at the very end of the novel, after suffering has burned away her alienation, does Gwendolen have "a more wakeful vision of Offendene" and its landscape, accepting them at last as her home (64:332). She is finally able to hear what George Eliot, in the "Impressions of Theophrastus Such," calls "the speech of the landscape" (2:39).

Just as the portraiture in the Jewish part of *Daniel Deronda* contrasts with the portraiture in the English part, so the landscapes of the two plots differ. The Jewish landscape belongs to Mordecai, and is not Wordsworthian but Turnerian and visionary. Its distinguishing features are a brilliant yellow sun near the horizon, a luminous hazy atmosphere, water, and indistinct shapes of boats and men.

Thus, for a long while, he habitually thought of the Being answering to his need as one distantly approaching or turning his back towards him, darkly painted against a golden sky. The reason of the golden sky lay in one of Mordecai's habits. He was keenly alive to some poetic aspects of London; and a favourite resort of his, when strength and leisure allowed, was to some one of the bridges, especially about sunrise or sunset. . . . Leaning on

the parapet of Blackfriars Bridge, and gazing meditatively, the
breadth and calm of the river, with its long vista half hazy, half
luminous, the grand dim masses or tall forms of buildings which
were the signs of world-commerce, the oncoming of boats and
barges from the still distance into sound and colour, entered into
his mood and blent themselves indistinguishably with his thinking. . . . Thus it happened that the figure representative of Mordecai's longing was mentally seen darkened by the excess of
light in the aerial background. [38:299–300]

When Daniel fulfills this vision, he is rowing downstream toward
Blackfriars Bridge at the sunset hour of half-past four. He appears
to Mordecai out of "a wide-spreading saffron clearness, which in the
sky had a monumental calm, but on the river, with its changing objects, was reflected as a luminous movement" (40:327). Eliot clearly
has the work of Turner in mind here, as Edward Dowden rightly
sensed when he referred in 1877 to "the Turneresque splendour"
of the bridge scenes.[38] The novelist had acquired a firsthand knowledge of Turner's pictures in 1851 (*Letters,* I, 347). She had spoken
of "a Turnerian haze of network" in "Janet's Repentance" (3:73)
and of "a fäery landscape in Turner's latest style" in "Brother Jacob"
(2:368). She also mentioned Turner in connection with a London
sunset in a letter of 1868 to Barbara Bodichon (*Letters,* IV, 476).
Turner's visionary painting is well suited to the visionary temperament of Mordecai, in whom George Eliot boldly asserts the Romantic possibility of second sight and prophecy.

Turner, like Wordsworth, had gone beyond the picturesque
mode;[39] and so in a different way did Ruskin. In his discussion "Of
the Turnerian Picturesque" in *Modern Painters,* Ruskin denied that
the picturesque as traditionally defined is a valid aesthetic category,
a tertium quid mediating between the sublime and the beautiful.
Ruskin's preference was all for the sublime, and he argued that the
qualities of roughness, variety, irregularity, and chiaroscuro are in
fact qualities of the sublime which connoisseurs of the picturesque
mistakenly transfer from mountains, trees, and other sublime natural
growths to cottages, ruins, and other objects that are not inherently
sublime. He thus defined conventional picturesqueness as a parasit-

ical sublimity, and since it was in his view an entirely superficial effect, he called it also the "surface-picturesque." The apprehension of the surface-picturesque involves a failure of the moral-aesthetic imagination, according to Ruskin, for the viewer not only fails to grasp the true nature of what he contemplates, but he also fails to sympathize with the human suffering which ruins and broken cottages so often imply. Ruskin declared that "the lower picturesque ideal is eminently a *heartless* one," and he characterized the lover of the lower picturesque as "kind-hearted, innocent, but not broad in thought; somewhat selfish, and incapable of acute sympathy with others."[40] The only true form of the picturesque, Ruskin argued, is one in which the objects depicted express suffering, poverty, or decay in an unselfconscious manner. This mode of representation he called the noble, or Turnerian, picturesque, and attributed above all to Turner and Prout among contemporary painters.[41]

A moral critique of the cult of the picturesque was not original with Ruskin. Gilpin was aware that *banditti,* though pictorially colorful, are morally reprehensible and socially undesirable. The moral question was also raised in the debates between Uvedale Price and Richard Payne Knight around 1800.[42] By the mid-nineteenth century such reservations about the picturesque had become almost commonplace in England and America.[43] But Ruskin's statement of the argument was classic for its eloquence, incisiveness, and passion; and it exercised a powerful influence upon contemporary readers such as George Eliot.[44]

In the same volume of *Modern Painters,* in the famous chapter on "Mountain Gloom," Ruskin applies his critique compellingly. Here he is out to quash naïve romantic notions of the beneficial effects of living close to nature. He undertakes to show that even the magnificent scenery of the Swiss Alps, created nature's nearest approximation to paradise, contains elements of suffering, poverty, and decay behind its picturesque surface. The landscape itself has a dark and ominous aspect, and its sublime influences do not protect its human inhabitants from squalor, misery, disease, ignorance, and Catholicism. Ruskin vividly describes the dismal condition of the Swiss peasantry, and then contrasts their reality with false and sentimentally picturesque representations of peasant life in contemporary opera:

nightly we give our gold, to fashion forth simulacra of peasants in gay ribands and white bodices, singing sweet songs, and bowing gracefully to the picturesque crosses: and all the while the veritable peasants are kneeling, songlessly, to veritable crosses, in another temper than the kind and fair audiences dream of, and assuredly with another kind of answer than is got out of the opera catastrophe.[45]

The chapter effectively advances the argument made throughout *Modern Painters* that the fallen world contains both good and evil, that the greatest art represents both the beauties and the imperfections of nature, and that any art which does not acknowledge the existence of evil is likely to be false and sentimental.

Ruskin's critique of the picturesque is an informing principle of George Eliot's great essay on Riehl's *Natural History of German Life*. Here the novelist-to-be transfers Ruskin's attack upon the opera to contemporary fiction and painting.

Opera peasants, whose unreality excites Mr. Ruskin's indignation, are surely too frank an idealization to be misleading; and since popular chorus is one of the most effective elements of the opera, we can hardly object to lyric rustics in elegant laced boddices and picturesque motley, unless we are prepared to advocate a chorus of colliers in their pit costume, or a ballet of char-women and stocking-weavers. But our social novels profess to represent the people as they are, and the unreality of their representation is a grave evil. [*Essays*, p. 270]

When she turns to contemporary English painting, the unreality of the peasants she finds represented there prompts Eliot to grumble about "cockney sentimentality" and to draw unfavorable comparisons between Holman Hunt and Teniers or Murillo.[46] English painters display "a total absence of acquaintance and sympathy with our peasantry," she argues. They "treat their subjects under the influence of traditions and prepossessions rather than of direct observation. . . . The painter is still under the influence of idyllic literature, which has always expressed the imagination of the cultivated, and town-bred, rather than the truth of rustic life" (*Essays*, pp. 268–69). She proceeds to contrast, in thoroughly Ruskinian manner, a sentimentalized view of haymakers seen from a safe aesthetic distance with a more realistic view from close up which does not shirk their coarseness and dependence upon drink. The artistic manifestoes of Ruskin and Eliot, both published in 1856, coincide historically with a general change in English rustic genre painting away from depictions of the countryside as a place of simple pleasures, pieties, and harmonies, toward depictions of "dreary landscapes" and scenes of rural poverty such as sickbeds, deathbeds, acts of charity, floods, evictions, redundancy, alcoholism, prostitution, workhouses, and emigration.[47]

Social and moral concerns are reflected in the presentation of landscape throughout George Eliot's fiction. *Felix Holt,* for example, opens with a dioramic view of the midlands countryside circa 1832 as it passes before a hypothetical passenger on the outside box of a stagecoach. The reader is offered a rich description of such natural beauties as meadows, watercourses, ponds, lanes, willows, elders, yews, hedgerows, wildflowers, ricks, and cattle. But the landscape, as Arnold Kettle has pointed out, is sociological as well as pictorial.[48] It offers what Eliot, in the "Impressions of Theophrastus Such," calls "a piece of our social history in pictorial writing" (2:40). The narrator of *Felix Holt* not only places a shepherd in the scene but pauses to characterize his mental horizons. She contrasts an impoverished, benighted cluster of laborers' cottages ("their little dingy windows telling, like thick-filmed eyes, of nothing but the darkness within") to a more prosperous, better-schooled village. Many of the visual details take on an emblematic moral significance, as they do so often in Ruskin's great set-piece descriptions.

Both *Adam Bede* and *Middlemarch* are deeply influenced by Ruskin's critique of the picturesque. The landscape of *Adam Bede* consistently reflects a Ruskinian awareness of the dark underside of an apparently Edenic setting. Loamshire at first seems the classic *paysage riant,* ideally fertile and perfectly suited to man's needs. But a close scrutiny of the opening prospect reveals some ominous tints. In the following passage the nameless Gilpinesque traveler begins and ends in the picturesque, but symbolic elements intervene.

On the side of the Green that led towards the church, the broken line of thatched cottages was continued nearly to the church-

yard gate; but on the opposite, northwestern side, there was
nothing to obstruct the view of gently-swelling meadow, and
wooded valley, and dark masses of distant hill. That rich undulating district of Loamshire to which Hayslope belonged, lies
close to a grim outskirt of Stonyshire, overlooked by its barren
hills as a pretty blooming sister may sometimes be linked in the
arm of a rugged, tall, swarthy brother; and in two or three hours'
ride the traveller might exchange a bleak treeless region, inter-
sected by lines of cold grey stone, for one where his road wound
under the shelter of woods, or up swelling hills, muffled with
hedgerows and long meadow-grass and thick corn; and where
at every turn he came upon some fine old country-seat nestled in
the valley or crowning the slope, some homestead with its long
length of barn and its cluster of golden ricks, some grey steeple
looking out from a pretty confusion of trees and thatch and
dark-red tiles. [2:21–22]

The distant glimpse of Stonyshire introduces a touch of mountain
gloom into the agreeable vista.[49] Bleakness and barrenness, according to Gilpin, are distinctly nonpicturesque; here they function as
emblematic reminders of an alternate and far less pleasant state of
nature.

The traveler proceeds to analyze the landscape in the approved
Claudian terms of foreground, middle distance, and background. The
prospect accommodates this conventional zoning, first by falling
away from the viewer, who occupies a middle elevation, and then by
rising in the distance to its maximum elevation in the form of large
hills. But the description emphasizes that the zoning is nature's
rather than man's; and the foreground, with its "level sunlight lying
like transparent gold among the gently curving stems of the
feathered grass and the tall red sorrel, and the white umbels of the
hemlocks lining the bushy hedgerows," is far more Pre-Raphaelite
than Claudian (2:23).

Moreover, a strong consciousness of time invests the considera-
tion of space. Although the moment is 18 June 1799, the description evokes the grand perennial cycle of nature, so that the reader
seems to glimpse the same landscape under different seasonal as-

pects. The passage of time brings renewal to nature, but has a different meaning for mortal man. The "keen and hungry winds of the north" and the "sound of the scythe being whetted [which] makes us cast more lingering looks at the flower-sprinkled tresses of the meadow" remind man of his finite term, as they often do in traditional pastoral literature. The description suggests that man will be swallowed up from view, much as the "tall mansion" and its landscaped park are swallowed up from view by the woods and meadows (2:22–23).[50]

The truly Ruskinian landscape always contains intimations of mortality as well as of immortality. The bay into which Romola's boat drifts is spectacularly beautiful and peaceful but contains a plague-stricken village. As Norma Jean Davis points out, "both Ruskin and Romola discover, in their exploration of Italian landscape, that behind the apparent picturesque beauty and green luxuriance are elements of death and decay."[51] In *Adam Bede* Eliot twice introduces overt memento mori into apparently idyllic landscapes. Early in the novel Adam and Seth carry a coffin through a scene of "Eden-like peace and loveliness," creating, as the narrator says, "a strangely-mingled picture" (4:73). A moment later they come upon their drowned father's body. This effect of moral chiaroscuro is repeated in the setting through which the pregnant Hetty sets off in search of Arthur. The early February landscape is astir with signs of spring and hope, but the narrator thinks of the wayside crucifix one might encounter in a Continental countryside on such a day:

an image of a great agony—the agony of the Cross. It has stood perhaps by the clustering apple-blossoms, or in the broad sunshine by the cornfield, or at a turning by the wood where a clear brook was gurgling below; and surely, if there came a traveller to this world who knew nothing of the story of man's life upon it, this image of agony would seem to him strangely out of place in the midst of this joyous nature. He would not know that hidden behind the apple-blossoms, or among the golden corn, or under the shrouding boughs of the wood, there might be a human heart beating heavily with anguish; perhaps a young blooming girl, not knowing where to turn for refuge from swift-advancing shame; understanding no more of this life of ours than a foolish lost lamb wandering farther and farther in the nightfall on the lonely heath; yet tasting the bitterest of life's bitterness. [35:112]

This appeal for sympathy is a virtual reprise of the third and fourth paragraphs of Ruskin's "Mountain Gloom." There, too, a naïve traveler comes upon "a cross of rough-hewn pine, iron-bound to its parapet" amidst an inspiring landscape. This cross is an emblem of the misery of the peasants who inhabit the landscape and who die contemplating images of the suffering Christ. Eliot's comparison of the incomprehending Hetty to a biblical lost lamb may have been prompted by Ruskin's comparison of the insensible Swiss peasants to the wild mountain goats which take no "passion of joy in all that fair work of God" surrounding them.[52] The cross in the landscape is a reminder of unseen moral forces in nature.[53]

The moral intrudes upon the picturesque again in the climactic recognition scene of *Adam Bede*. Adam, passing through the Fir-tree Grove, stops to contemplate a beech-tree as Gilpin himself might have done in his *Remarks on Forest Scenery*. The sensitive carpenter registers aesthetic detail as well as potential board-feet:

Adam delighted in a fine tree of all things; as the fisherman's sight is keenest on the sea, so Adam's perceptions were more at home with trees than with other objects. He kept them in his memory, as a painter does, with all the flecks and knots in their bark, all the curves and angles of their boughs; and had often calculated the height and contents of a trunk to a nicety, as he stood looking at it. No wonder that, notwithstanding his desire to get on, he could not help pausing to look at a curious large beech which he had seen standing before him at a turning in the road, and convince himself that it was not two trees wedded together, but only one. For the rest of his life he remembered that moment when he was calmly examining the beech, as a man remembers his last glimpse of the home where his youth was passed, before the road turned, and he saw it no more. The beech stood at the last turning before the Grove ended in an

archway of boughs that let in the eastern light; and as Adam
stepped away from the tree to continue his walk, his eyes fell on
two figures about twenty yards before him. [27:10]

This is the moment of Adam's psychic fall from innocence to experience. His innocent perception of the picturesque variegation of
tree-trunks and boughs gives way to a shattering recognition of Eve
with her seducer. The recognition is still pictorial, since the "archway of boughs" makes a perfect frame; but the picture now admits
the existence of treachery and evil in the idyllic scene. This episode
may have been the model for the great recognition scene in Henry
James's *The Ambassadors,* in which Lambert Strether, like Adam,
sees two trusted friends in a compromised position amidst a landscape which only moments before had been a pleasant picture.[54]

The Fir-tree Grove in *Adam Bede* is a delusory paradise for all who
enter it. It is the regular trysting-place of Hetty and Arthur, and the
scene of the seduction that has such tragic consequences. Michael
Squires has rightly related the setting to the tradition of the *locus
amoenus* in pastoral poetry, the erotic and magical pagan paradise
which changes those who enter it.[55] But George Eliot treats the
topos with a Protestant distrust that recalls Spenser's handling of the
Bower of Blisse in *The Faerie Queene.* In pictorial terms, the grove is
a Claudian mythological landscape, peopled with figures from
Ovid. This ideal landscape is the symptomatic product of a mind
that avoids reality to indulge in fantasies of self-gratification.

She thought nothing of the evening light that lay gently in the
grassy alleys between the fern, and made the beauty of their
living green more visible than it had been in the overpowering
flood of noon: she thought of nothing that was present. She
only saw something that was possible: Mr Arthur Donnithorne
coming to meet her again along the Fir-tree Grove. That was
the foreground of Hetty's picture; behind it lay a bright hazy
something—days that were not to be as the other days of her life
had been. It was as if she had been wooed by a river-god, who
might any time take her to his wondrous halls below a watery
heaven. [13:201–02]

In other words, Hetty prefers a *Heroic Landscape with Poseidon and Tyro* to a more realistic picture along the lines of, say, Millais's *Waiting* (1854).[56] Claude's presumed avoidance of the nature immediately surrounding him makes him the chief villain in the historical drama of landscape painting presented by Ruskin in *Modern Painters.* By the same token, Claudian landscape is something of a villain in *Adam Bede.*

The aesthetic and the moral remain compatible in *Adam Bede.* Ruskin's critique of the surface-picturesque opens the way to a true landscape which intimates the possibility of salvation through moral struggle. The same is true in *Middlemarch,* but in the later novel the vision of true landscape is much more problematic. George Eliot explores more deeply than ever before the disturbing possibility that the aesthetic and the moral are incompatible, that art itself has no worthy human use. As Barbara Hardy has said: "The art/life antithesis is a very important subject in *Middlemarch.* . . . Many characters are defined and even tested by their response to art, and art itself is defined and even tested by its relevance and meaning for human beings of different kinds."[57]

These issues are crystallized in chapter 39, which narrates Mr. Brooke's visit to the farm of his tenant, Dagley. Here the lower picturesque is precisely what Ruskin called it: an eminently heartless ideal.

> It is true that an observer, under that softening influence of the fine arts which makes other people's hardships picturesque, might have been delighted with this homestead called Freeman's End: the old house had dormer-windows in the dark-red roof, two of the chimneys were choked with ivy, the large porch was blocked up with bundles of sticks, and half the windows were closed with grey worm-eaten shutters about which the jasmine-boughs grew in wild luxuriance; the mouldering garden wall with hollyhocks peeping over it was a perfect study of highly-mingled subdued colour, and there was an aged goat (kept doubtless on interesting superstitious grounds) lying against the open back-kitchen door. The mossy thatch of the cow-shed, the broken grey barn-doors, the pauper labourers in ragged

breeches who had nearly finished unloading a waggon of corn
into the barn ready for early thrashing [*sic*] ; the scanty dairy of
cows being tethered for milking and leaving one half of the shed
in brown emptiness; the very pigs and white ducks seemed to
wander about the uneven neglected yard as if in low spirits from
feeding on a too meagre quality of rinsings,—all these objects
under the quiet light of a sky marbled with high clouds would
have made a sort of picture which we have all paused over as a
"charming bit," touching other sensibilities than those which
are stirred by the depression of the agricultural interest, with the
sad lack of farming capital, as seen constantly in the newspapers
of that time. But these troublesome associations were just now
strongly present to Mr Brooke, and spoiled the scene for him.
[39:182–83]

At Freeman's End, picturesque unevenness betokens neglect and
brown emptiness signifies want. As Eliot says in *Daniel Deronda,*
again echoing Ruskin: "What horrors of damp huts, where human
beings languish, may not become picturesque through aerial distance!" (14:230).[58] The narrator of *Middlemarch* will not indulge
the nostalgia for "dear, old, brown, crumbling, picturesque inefficiency" which gives pleasure to the narrator of "Amos Barton"
(1:4). Even Mr. Brooke's connoisseurship gives way to a true perception of his tenant's misery.

The aestheticist view of life is questioned throughout *Middlemarch.* We have seen that Will Ladislaw accuses Naumann of looking
at the world "entirely from the studio point of view" (21:317).
By the same token Dorothea's conscience is troubled by aesthetic
apprehension as such. She is unable to bring the "severe classical
nudities and smirking Renaissance-Correggiosities" in her uncle's
art collection at Tipton Grange into "any sort of relevance with her
life" (9:109).[59] Her trip to Rome helps her better to understand
what Will calls the "old language" of classical and Renaissance art,
but it does not bridge the gap between that art and her own sense of
purpose. As Richard S. Lyons has pointed out, Dorothea renews her
attack upon Mr. Brooke's collection after her return from Rome:
"I used to come from the village with that dirt and coarse ugliness

like a pain within me, and the simpering pictures in the drawing-room seemed to me like a wicked attempt to find delight in what is false, while we don't mind how hard the truth is for the neighbours outside our walls" (39:175-76).[60] As the novel progresses, Ladislaw becomes less the aesthete, but Dorothea does not become more the connoiseuse.

Dorothea can find relevance in simple portraiture, which she values more for iconic than for aesthetic reasons. The miniature of Ladis-law's grandmother sustains her through some bad times because it reminds her of Will himself and of his great regard for her. Dorothea is also sustained by a hard-won vision of the English landscape, a vision that is partly pictorial but not sentimentally picturesque. She tends from the first to envision her own destiny as somehow involved with the midlands countryside. Even in the sculpture-gallery of the Vatican Museum her first thoughts are of the English landscape: "She did not really see the streak of sunlight on the floor more than she saw the statues: she was inwardly seeing the light of years to come in her own home and over the English fields and elms and hedge-bordered highroads; and feeling that the way in which they might be filled with joyful devotedness was not so clear to her as it had been" (20:311). Dorothea values nature and duty more highly than art, and her priorities reflect certain moments in George Eliot's own museum-going (Cross, II, 22, 88).

The landscape that matters most to Dorothea upon her return from Rome lies immediately outside the west window of her boudoir at Lowick. The window gives onto an avenue of lime-trees leading to an entrance-gate, beyond which may be seen a bit of road and a large expanse of open, flat field. Dorothea views this prospect under several different diurnal, seasonal, and emotional aspects, so that it affords a series of landscape images in which objective and subjec-tive elements strive to achieve a stable balance. E. D. H. Johnson has pointed out that the sequence of views from Dorothea's boudoir window provides an index to her growth toward self-knowledge.[61]

The most important views occur in chapters 28, 54, and 80; and they form a progression from despair through indifference to affir-mation which corresponds roughly with the progression outlined by Carlyle in *Sartor Resartus* from the Everlasting Nay through the

Centre of Indifference to the Everlasting Yea. In chapter 28 Dorothea is at an ebb, having suffered the disappointment of virtually all her marital hopes. The landscape outside her boudoir reflects her mood of cold constriction and drab imprisonment:

> she saw the long avenue of limes lifting their trunks from a white earth, and spreading white branches against the dun and motionless sky. The distant flat shrank in uniform whiteness and low-hanging uniformity of cloud. . . . Her blooming full-pulsed youth stood there in a moral imprisonment which made itself one with the chill, colourless, narrowed landscape. . . . [28:1-4]

Dorothea's subjectivity dominates this landscape of despair. The description borders on the pathetic fallacy, a concept which George Eliot noted with interest in her review of the third volume of *Modern Painters.*[62] The novelist here displays what John Stuart Mill called "the power of *creating* scenery, in keeping with some state of human feeling; so fitted to it as to be the embodied symbol of it, and to summon up the state of feeling itself, with a force not to be surpassed by anything but reality."[63] Mill was speaking of Tennyson's earliest poems, especially of "Mariana"; and indeed it is of "Mariana" and Millais's splendid painting of Tennyson's heroine (1851) that one is reminded most strongly by chapter 28 of *Middlemarch.*

Dorothea's duty is no clearer to her in chapter 54, but as a widow she suffers less acutely than she did as a wife. She has recuperated from the worst of her bereavement, and her condition is now comfortable but neutral and aimless. Again the landscape reflects her spiritual state:

> She had not yet applied herself to her work, but was seated with her hands folded on her lap, looking out along the avenue of limes to the distant fields. Every leaf was at rest in the sunshine, the familiar scene was changeless, and seemed to represent the prospect of her life, full of motiveless ease—motiveless, if her own energy could not seek out reasons for ardent action. [54: 11-12]

The prospect is no longer jaundiced by Dorothea's despair, but it is still dominated by her subjectivity. There is no fruitful interchange between objective and subjective, between nature and the perceiving mind.

The possibility of a more balanced relationship with the landscape is adumbrated in chapter 37 and realized in chapter 80. "She had been so used to struggle for and to find resolve in looking along the avenue towards the arch of western light," we are told in the earlier instance, "that the vision itself had gained a communicating power" (37:149). Once the vision itself communicates, it can offer the joy and moral strength that work through time and memory to make up Wordsworthian maturity. Dorothea attains such maturity in chapter 80, after suffering through a night of dark despair brought on by Will Ladislaw's apparent rejection of her love. Her psychic resurrection is assisted by her recognition of an independent life in the landscape outside her boudoir window.

> She opened her curtains, and looked out towards the bit of road that lay in view, with fields beyond outside the entrance-gates. On the road there was a man with a bundle on his back and a woman carrying her baby; in the field she could see figures moving—perhaps the shepherd with his dog. Far off in the bending sky was the pearly light; and she felt the largeness of the world and the manifold wakings of men to labour and endurance. She was a part of that involuntary, palpitating life, and could neither look out on it from her luxurious shelter as a mere spectator, nor hide her eyes in selfish complaining. [80:392]

The landscape is no longer problematic; its objective reality affords Dorothea an alternative to self-pity, and makes possible a creative interaction between her mind and the world outside it. Though faith is gone, the world remains; and work still has meaning, as it does for Carlyle's Teufelsdröckh in the phase of the Everlasting Yea. The perception of otherness is not sickening, as in Sartre's *La Nausée,* but healing. The recuperation of Rex Gascoigne in *Daniel Deronda* begins with a similar act of attention to a landscape peopled by working figures immediately outside his own window (8:122–23).

The vista in chapter 80 of *Middlemarch* holds its Wordsworthian and Carlylean elements within a highly pictorialized structure. The window provides a frame, and the prospect is divided into foreground, middle distance, and background. The lighting is specified and the figures in the scene are precisely located. Critics have sought analogues for the description in the paintings of Rubens and Millet, but the details given by Eliot are so minimal and generic as to defy identification with the work of any particular artist.[64] They are at any rate not conventionally picturesque; they manifest no roughness, irregularity, vivid chiaroscuro, or ruin. Eliot is evoking not the surface-picturesque but the noble picturesque, which consists, according to Ruskin, in the unconscious expression of human suffering "nobly endured by unpretending strength of heart . . . the world's hard work being gone through all the while, and no pity asked for, nor contempt feared."[65]

The best pictorial analogue for the window-scenes in *Middlemarch* is not to be found in landscape painting at all but in a popular motif of nineteenth-century Romantic genre painting: the figure looking out a window who presents his or her back to a viewer located inside the room. The motif is operative in European painting from the seventeenth century well into the twentieth; its classic nineteenth-century embodiment is in the work of Caspar David Friedrich, especially the *Frau am Fenster* of about 1822.[66] Millais's *Mariana* belongs to this tradition, as does Moritz von Schwind's *Morgenstunde*, a picture George Eliot might have seen at Munich in 1858. The real subject of such paintings, at least in the nineteenth century, is usually the spiritual interaction between the spectator and the prospect. Romantic *Fensterbilder* are an appropriate analogue to the window-scenes in *Middlemarch* because Dorothea's presence in those scenes is always visualized as carefully as the landscape itself, and because the quality of her apprehension is the true center of the audience's interest.

In natural description, then, no less than in characterization and domestic scenes, George Eliot was deeply influenced by pictorial conventions. Her vision of nature was shaped by eighteenth-century traditions of the picturesque and topographical, and by nineteenth-century modes of landscape sensibility which came to her through Wordsworth, Ruskin, and the Pre-Raphaelites. She was well aware that the beholder's share of perception may be conditioned by the experience of art. She lends this awareness to Daniel Deronda as he contemplates a Gothic capital at the Abbey:

> 'I wonder whether one oftener learns to love real objects through their representations, or the representations through the real objects,' he said, after pointing out a lovely capital made by the curled leaves of greens, showing their reticulated underside with the firm gradual swell of its central rib. 'When I was a little fellow these capitals taught me to observe, and delight in, the structure of leaves.' [35:220]

These remarks are in the spirit of Ruskin, as Henry Auster has pointed out, but they must also reflect many of George Eliot's own encounters with the natural world.[67] She knew that art can help one see and feel, and indeed she valued art chiefly because it can.

But what happened to Eliot's descriptive art when it became, in turn, subject to someone else's imagination—when, in short, an illustrator set about to render it into visual forms? Inevitably the pictures were modified from what the author had conceived. The next chapter will examine Frederic Leighton's illustrations of *Romola,* both for the light they throw upon the text and for the questions they raise concerning literary illustration in general.

9 Frederic Leighton's Illustrations of *Romola*

Romola was the only one of George Eliot's novels to be illustrated in its first edition. It acquired this distinction when the novelist decided to place the manuscript with George Smith instead of with her usual publisher, Blackwoods of Edinburgh. Smith was proprietor of *The Cornhill* magazine, one of the leading Victorian outlets for serialized, illustrated fiction. In *The Cornhill* Thackeray illustrated his late novels, *Lovel the Widower* and *The Adventures of Philip,* and Millais illustrated Trollope's *Framley Parsonage* and *The Small House at Allington.*[1] It was only natural that Smith should want a novel by the author of *Adam Bede* to receive similar honors. After all, literary illustration was to the Victorian publisher what literary pictorialism was to the Victorian novelist: an attempt to satisfy the boundless public appetite for visualized narrative.

In May of 1862, Smith gave the *Romola* commission to a rising young painter named Frederic Leighton. "It is to be illustrated by Leighton who is by far the *best* man to be had in England," Lewes wrote enthusiastically to his son (*Letters,* IV, 37). Leighton seemed clearly the best man because he had lived in Florence and studied in its academy in 1845–46, and because he had made rather a specialty of Florentine Renaissance subjects in his early work.[2] In pictures such as *Cimabue Finding Giotto in the Fields of Florence* (1850), *The Plague in Florence* (1851), *Signorelli Painting His Dead Son* (1851), *The Death of Brunelleschi* (1852), and *Cimabue's Celebrated Madonna Is Carried in Procession through the Streets of Florence*

157

(1855) Leighton met the demand for what he called "correctly drawn historical genre."[3] Ruskin praised *Cimabue's Madonna* for the realism of its costumes, setting, and vegetation; and Queen Victoria purchased the painting for 600 guineas.[4]

Leighton rode the fashion for subjects from Vasari well into the 1860s.[5] Of the six paintings he displayed at the Royal Academy in the year of the *Romola* commission, *Michael Angelo Nursing His Dying Servant* impressed the Leweses most powerfully (*Letters,* IV, 37n.).[6] The artist had already demonstrated his abilities in black and white by successfully illustrating two of Elizabeth Barrett Browning's poems for *The Cornhill* in 1860.[7] And he was later to contribute nine highly distinguished illustrations to the *Dalziel's Bible Gallery.*[8] All told, it would be difficult to imagine a better-qualified illustrator for George Eliot's historical novel of Florence in the 1490s.

Romola appeared in twelve installments between July of 1862 and August of 1863. Leighton contributed twenty-four illustrations (two for each number) together with fourteen initial letters and a tail-piece to the Proem. His commission brought him £40 per number or £480 in all.[9] He worked from the page proofs of each installment, without an overview of the finished story. He first sketched his designs in black and white chalk on gray paper; then he recast them in pen-and-ink on woodblocks.[10] Photographs of the drawings were made by Smith before the blocks were turned over to the engravers, Joseph Swain and W. J. Linton, who cut away those portions of the blocks that were to appear as white in the finished illustrations, leaving in relief the portions that were to print black. The blocks were then locked directly into the printer's form, and inked on their raised surfaces at the same time as the type. This was the technique of wood-engraving that Thomas Bewick had revived late in the eighteenth century.[11] The original chalk drawings by Leighton are now in the hands of Mr. Philip Hofer and Professor Gordon S. Haight (*Letters,* IV, 39). Either the drawings or the photographs (probably the latter) hung for a time in George Eliot's drawing room at the Priory (*Letters,* V, 8). The photographs are now owned by Leighton House.

In style Leighton's black-and-white work belongs to the "Sixties" school of English illustration, so named by Gleeson White even though it arose in the mid-1850s and continued well into the 1870s.[12] The Sixties school represented a departure from the tradition of comical-satirical caricature in English illustration, the tradition of Hogarth, Rowlandson, Gillray, Cruikshank, Leech, Seymour, Browne, Doyle, May, Meadows, and Thackeray. Many of the Sixties illustrators were academically trained and therefore brought to their work a classical sense of the human form and a mimetic mode of representation derived from the life-classes of the academy.[13] Pre-Raphaelite ideals of naturalism and precise symbolic detail also influenced the movement through the black-and-white work of Rossetti, Millais, and Holman Hunt—especially their contributions to the Moxon edition of Tennyson's *Poems* (1857). The tone of Sixties illustration was predominantly serious and sentimental. The artists aimed to bestow some of the dignity of painting upon their medium, and to that end invested great care in the conception and execution of their designs. Millais remained the dominant figure of the new school, which also included Charles Keene, Ford Madox Brown, Fred Walker, Frederick Sandys, Arthur Boyd Houghton, Arthur Hughes, George du Maurier, Frederick Shields, George J. Pinwell, William Small, Thomas and Edward Dalziel, Luke Fildes, Edward J. Poynter, Whistler, the early Burne-Jones, and Leighton.

Partaking in the style of Sixties illustration did not, of course, guarantee a picture's success. Leighton's illustrations of *Romola* are in fact highly uneven, and much less consistently effective than his designs for *Dalziel's Bible Gallery*.[14] Although some of the *Romola* designs are strikingly good both as pictures and as interpretations of the novel, others are stiff, inanimate, and heedless of the text. For several important characters in the story—Savonarola, Baldassarre, and Piero di Cosimo—Leighton never found adequate pictorial forms; indeed, he positively avoided the well-known features of Savonarola.[15] Leonée and Richard Ormond rightly observe that the best illustrations in the series tend to be "those with one or two figures, placed in a landscape setting or a domestic interior"; whereas the more crowded scenes of Florentine street life are rarely effective.[16]

Perceiving this unevenness, George Eliot herself had mixed feelings about her collaborator's work. Her side of an extensive and detailed correspondence with Leighton survives.[17] In it can be glimpsed her deep disappointment with some of his pictures, her genuine delight in others, and finally her resignation to the inevitable discrepancy between the artist's conception of the scenes and her own. Her mature position is well represented by the following passage:

> But I am quite convinced that illustrations can only form a sort of overture to the text. The artist who uses the pencil must otherwise be tormented to misery by the deficiencies or requirements of the one who uses the pen, and the writer, on the other hand, must die of impossible expectations.[18] [*Letters,* IV, 55–56]

Only "a mind well accustomed to resignation," George Eliot told John Blackwood in 1877, can bear to see its vivid conceptions altered by the mind and hand of another person (*Letters,* VI, 335).[19]

The experience of being illustrated brought home to Eliot the truth which Lewes articulated in his 1867 introduction to Wilhelm von Kaulbach's illustrations of Goethe: "no two minds form precisely similar conceptions of the same poetic presentation; each mind forms its own Gretchen and Lotte, its own Frederike and Leonore, its own Dorotea and Ottilie; none of these having more than a general resemblance to the images in the poet's mind."[20] Illustration, in other words, always involves an interpretive restatement of its subject.[21] It is never a simple transcription. At the beginning of her collaboration with Leighton, George Eliot harbored the naïve ideal of a "perfect correspondence between the text and the illustration" (*Letters,* IV, 41). But she had to abandon the dream of complete mimesis as soon as she realized that the literary text is seldom the sole determinant of the illustrator's rendition. The text is only one of several important factors that enter into the creation and interpretation of literary illustration, as J. Hillis Miller and Ronald Paulson have recently emphasized.[22]

Like paintings, illustrations also acquire meaning from their relation to other pictures. As the identification of a biblical or literary source is only one step in the analysis of a Renaissance painting, so comparison with the text is only one step in the analysis of a Victorian illustration. In either case the artist's choice and handling of his subject may be determined more by established stylistic and iconographic traditions in the visual arts than by an author's words. Catherine Gordon has shown, for example, that early illustrations of Scott are decisively shaped by late eighteenth-century historical literary painting such as the Boydell Shakespeare Gallery.[23] Likewise, Hillis Miller has argued that "Cruikshank's pictures draw their meaning from their relation to other works of art [in the tradition of English caricature] to which they implicitly refer and on which they depend for the creation of their own significance."[24]

Furthermore, any illustration has a place in the illustrator's personal oeuvre, and may gain significance from its developmental relationship to other pictures within that oeuvre.[25] Finally, an illustration may, if it belongs to a set, generate meanings by repeating and varying visual forms that appear in other pictures within the set. To elucidate such meanings, Miller notes, "the investigation moves back and forth from one plate to another in an attempt to identify the motifs and structuring forms which recur from one picture to another."[26] In short, the pictorial contexts of an illustration are at least as important to its interpretation as the literary context. Unfortunately, those best qualified to provide and evaluate the relevant pictorial contexts—namely, the art historians—have with a few notable exceptions treated illustration as infra dig and have ignored it completely.

The rest of this chapter will consider the pictorial contexts of several of Leighton's *Romola* illustrations. The first example will involve a design whose main formal source is an identifiable picture that has no connection with George Eliot's text. Then I shall place several of the *Romola* illustrations in the context of Leighton's oeuvre, noting their developmental affinities with earlier and later pictures. The final group of illustrations to be considered will include several examples of the repetition and variation of pictorial structures within the *Romola* series, a technique by which the artist can imitate temporal narrative sequence. In this interpretation of

Leighton's images, the criterion of fidelity to the text will not be abandoned; but it will be applied flexibly enough to accommodate the meanings revealed by a pictorial approach.

The tenth picture in the *Romola* series is entitled "Niccolò at Work," and shows Tito Melema entering the workshop of the blacksmith, Niccolò Cappara, to buy a shirt of chain mail (fig. 27). The composition of the illustration derives directly from Joseph Wright's *An Iron Forge* (1772), which was displayed at the South Kensington Museum in the International Exhibition of 1862 (fig. 28).[27] The exhibition opened in May, several months before Leighton set to work on the illustrations for part 5 of *Romola*.[28] When he encountered George Eliot's description of a smith's shop, Leighton conceived the scene in terms of Wright's striking picture.

Following his eighteenth-century model, Leighton centers his composition upon a powerful workman frontally placed who turns his head to the viewer's right. The artificial sources of light in both pictures are to the left of the principal figures and are related to the business in hand: a white-hot piece of iron in Wright's painting, and the forge in Leighton's drawing. The strong diagonal line provided by the pole which runs from lower right to upper left in *An Iron Forge* is echoed by the handles of the hammer and spear which Niccolò and his apprentice hold, while the group of rods on the right side of *An Iron Forge* are replaced by the rods emerging from Niccolò's Gothic lantern.[29] Both pictures are framed on the left by a jutting wall and a figure whose back is to the viewer. There are, of course, some compositional differences between the two pictures, as well as "period" differences of costume and technology. But these modifications do not obscure Leighton's indebtedness to Wright for the basic form of his design. "Niccolò at Work," then, belongs to a tradition of forge-painting that extends from Wright of Derby back through the Dutch Caravaggists to Renaissance depictions of Vulcan's smithy.[30]

A pictorial source in this case determined the illustration far more decisively than did the literary text. In fact, Leighton's picture does not follow George Eliot's text very closely. Here is the passage which "Niccolò at Work" purports to illustrate:

Preoccupied as [Tito] was, he could not help pausing a moment in admiration as he came in front of the workshop. The wide doorway, standing at the truncated angle of a great block or "isle" of houses, was surmounted by a loggia roofed with fluted tiles, and supported by stone columns with roughly carved capitals. Against the red light framed in by the outline of the fluted tiles and columns stood in black relief the grand figure of Niccolò, with his huge arms in rhythmic rise and fall, first hiding and then disclosing the profile of his firm mouth and powerful brow. Two slighter ebony figures, one at the anvil, the other at the bellows, served to set off his superior massiveness.

Tito darkened the doorway with a very different outline, standing in silence, since it was useless to speak until Niccolò should deign to pause and notice him. That was not until the smith had beaten the head of an axe to the due sharpness of edge and dismissed it from his anvil. But in the meantime Tito had satisfied himself by a glance around the shop that the object of which he was in search had not disappeared.

Niccolò gave an unceremonious but good-humoured nod as he turned from the anvil and rested his hammer on his hip.

"What is it, Messer Tito? Business?" [26:336]

The description is highly pictorialized, perhaps even preconcerted expressly for the illustrator. The workshop is viewed from the street through a frame-within-a-frame, and the figures are silhouetted by a red light which bestows infernal connotations upon the business about to be transacted.

The organization and implications of the scene are quite different from those of Leighton's illustration. Leighton has ignored both the viewpoint and the lighting suggested by his author. By moving his light-source from the anvil to the furnace he has actually diminished the effect of silhouette and chiaroscuro, which are stronger in Wright's *Iron Forge.* And Leighton's Niccolò is not particularly dark or vulcanic; indeed, he is altogether cleaner and more statuesque than the unwashed, barrel-chested figure described in chapter 1 of *Romola.* Leighton's departures from the text were prompted by his

admiration for Wright's *Iron Forge,* but they were not equally inspired by a coherent interpretive vision of his literary source. The
illustration loses in force what it gains in prettiness.

As his experimentation with Wright of Derby suggests, Leighton's
art was in a transitional phase during the early 1860s. He was
moving, as he himself later put it, from the Gothicism of his early
work to the classicism of his maturity.[31] As a result, his *Romola*
illustrations have interesting developmental affinities with both
earlier and later pictures in the artist's oeuvre. A case in point is
"Tessa at Home," the twenty-first of the *Romola* series. This design
represents an important stage in Leighton's handling of the motif of
the seated, sleeping female figure. This motif, which may derive
from the Demeter-and-Persephone group of the Elgin Marbles,[32]
arises in one of the artist's early neomedieval pictures, *Lieder ohne
Worte* (1860–61), and comes to fruition in several of his later neoclassical paintings: *Summer Moon* (c. 1872), *The Garden of the
Hesperides* (1891), and *Flaming June* (c. 1895). The affinities between *Lieder ohne Worte,* "Tessa at Home" and *Summer Moon* are
especially strong (figs. 29–31). The illustration, then, shows Leighton on his way to becoming the great Victorian painter of lassitude,
the artist for whom, as Disraeli observed, beauty is inseparable from
"the sentiment of repose."[33]

"Tessa at Home" is not only profoundly characteristic of its
creator but also entirely faithful to the details of George Eliot's
text. The scene in question shows Tessa as Romola sees her through
an open door at the beginning of the providential visit which reveals
to the heroine the existence of her husband's "other wife":

> On a low chair at the farther end of the room, opposite the light,
> sat Tessa, with one hand on the edge of the cradle, and her head
> hanging a little on one side, fast asleep. Near one of the win-
> dows, with her back turned towards the door, sat Monna Lisa at
> her work of preparing salad, in deaf unconsciousness. [56:261]

The point of view, the attitudes and relationships of the figures, and
the function of the window in George Eliot's description are all
carefully rendered in Leighton's version of the scene. Both pictorially and interpretively, the illustration is an admirable success.

The *Romola* illustrations repeat or anticipate many other details of costume, attitude, expression, and landscape composition that appear elsewhere in Leighton's work. The Ormonds have noted the similarity between the slightly sinister hooded cloaks worn in many of the illustrations and those worn in Leighton's frescoes of *The Wise and Foolish Virgins* at Lyndhurst (1862–64) and his *Dante at Verona* (1864).[34] The eloquent attitude of Romola in "Coming Home" is repeated in *Salomé Dancing* (1863?) and much later in *The Last Watch of Hero* (ca. 1887).[35] The heroine's figure and facial expression in "At the Well" look forward to one of Leighton's worst paintings, *Clytemnestra from the battlements of Argos watches for the beacon fires which are to announce the return of Agamemnon* (ca. 1874). This Clytemnestra, as the Ormonds have observed, "is based on a caryatid"; she is "stilted and operatic," achieving "monumentality, but no more."[36] The same strictures apply to the Romola of "At the Well." But the landscape background in the same illustration is far more imaginative than the figures, dropping suddenly away to a panoramic, bird's-eye view of the bay which Romola's boat has just crossed. The same abrupt landscape vista occurs in "Escaped" and "'You Didn't Think It Was So Pretty, Did You?'" The technique anticipates what the Ormonds have called the "vertiginous composition" of the landscape backgrounds in *Daedalus and Icarus* and a number of Leighton's other late pictures.[37] In the *Romola* illustrations, then, Leighton first tested many of the pictorial formulae that were to reappear in his best-known paintings.

Leighton also repeated and varied motifs within the series to generate pictorial meanings. A set of novel illustrations, as Anthony Burton has pointed out, can "take on a sequential or narrative force" because the artist has twenty or more opportunities to represent the beginning, middle, and end of a story.[38] He can render narrative contrasts and developments by repeating the patterns of earlier pictures in the set while varying them dramatically. A group of illustrations, in other words, can generate an internal iconography.[39]

Leighton created a deliberate pictorial contrast in the two illustrations which he designed for the opening number of *Romola* (figs. 32–33). The pictures introduce the heroine and the hero-villain,

Tito Melema, in complementary scenes which form a sort of diptych. The characters are related by the repetition of pictorial motifs but distinguished by significant variations in treatment. In "The Blind Scholar and His Daughter" Romola stands erect and central, one hand resting on her father's chair, the other out-stretched towards the lamp and the book she is reading aloud. In "Suppose You Let Me Look at Myself" Nello usurps, nearly par-odies, Romola's attitude, as he rests one arm on the barber's chair and flamboyantly stretches the other toward the mirror imaging Tito's enigmatic face. Whereas Romola contemplates light and knowledge, Tito reenacts the traditional emblem of vanity ("it is a Venetian mirror from Murano, the true *nosce teipsum,*" says Nello). The question raised in the novel about the moral reality behind Tito's physical appearance is also raised in the illustration, where the newly shaven face seems not quite unmasked and rather perplexed by its own reflection. George Eliot accurately praised the picture of the barbershop because "it makes so good a variety with Bardo and Romola" (*Letters,* IV, 41).

Having established these motifs, Leighton repeated them in a later picture where Tito's image is also at issue. In "The Painted Record" Romola contemplates Piero di Cosimo's portrait of Tito as a fearful reveller (fig. 34). Her attitude, one hand on the back of a chair and the other outstretched toward what she sees, is a third variation of the central attitude used in "The Blind Scholar and His Daughter" and "Suppose You Let Me Look at Myself." The props and the lighting deliberately echo those of the earlier pictures, while Piero replaces Nello on the right side of the picture as the maker of the framed image on the left. Romola has undergone a pictorial transi-tion from the independent maiden in the library to the implicated wife burdened by the question of her husband's identity that was first raised in the barbershop. The transition is manifested by the repetition and variation of motifs within the structurally coherent group of three illustrations.

Considered individually, however, these pictures are not equally successful. "Suppose You Let Me Look at Myself" is a magnificent triumph of expressive and energetic design. Leighton's barber is more imposing than George Eliot's, even a little frightening as he ushers Tito into the story ("better than my Nello," said the author, impressed). The unpleasantness of the smile on Nello's harlequin-like mask of a face is emphasized by its visual association with the grimace of the satyr's bust in the garden.

The satyr-face reappears in "The Painted Record," but generates no energy in that relatively lifeless design. Romola and Piero are too inert for the occasion: she is serene and static, slightly worried rather than deeply anxious; and he is a wooden Don Quixote with a tall, inordinately skinny body, gigantic artist's hands, and amusingly baggy hose. Here and throughout the series Leighton's Piero is a comical figure, entirely lacking the visionary power of his namesake in the novel.[40]

The figures are also unsatisfactory in "The Blind Scholar and His Daughter," though the setting is skillfully composed in the mode of conversation pieces which portray a gentlemanly collector amidst his collection.[41] Leighton's Romola is indecisively drawn and, as George Eliot herself pointed out, very different from the Romola of the text.[42] The illustrator has reversed nearly every important visual association connected with the heroine in the author's introductory word-portrait. Eliot's "square-cut gown of black *rascia,*" which reflects the ascetic side of Romola's character, gives way to Leighton's light and ornamented gown (5:72). In the novel Romola's "reddish gold" hair is the principal source of light in Bardo's library, a naturalistic nimbus which hallows the reader's first impression of a secular Madonna. But in Leighton's illustration Romola is not blonde and the principal source of light is the sun, which the novel explicitly describes as "not yet high enough to send gleams of brightness through the narrow windows" (5:72). Tonally, the illustration is to the text very nearly what a negative is to a photograph.

As for Bardo, George Eliot specifies that he "sat with head uplifted and turned a little aside towards his daughter, as if he were looking at her" (5:72-73). Leighton has ignored these details and drawn instead a head very like the one he gave to *Signorelli Painting His Dead Son* in the chalk drawing of 1851.[43] That is why, when Romola views Piero di Cosimo's portrait of Bardo later in the novel, she says to the artist: "Ah . . . you have done what I wanted. You have given it more of the listening look" (28:392). Leighton's liberties with the text in "The Blind Scholar and His Daughter" are not dictated by the logic of its pictorial grouping with the two other illustrations we have just examined. That logic does not prescribe the gratuitous changes of tone and attitude which the illustrator chose to make.

But Leighton is at his very best in another pair of designs which employ the technique of repetition and variation. The artist depicted Romola and Tito alone together only twice in the set of twenty-four illustrations. The pictures in question represent the dramatically different stages of courtship and marriage (figs. 35, 36). Presenting images of "before and after," the illustrations give an illusion of narrative growth and development, rather like two photographs of the same person in the same setting at different times in his or her life.

In "The First Kiss" Tito has just followed Romola into a small book-lined cabinet adjoining her father's library. Here they first declare their mutual love: "The faces just met, and the dark curls mingled for an instant with the rippling gold" (12:184). In Leighton's illustration the cabinet becomes a stage. There is just the faintest hint of books in the upper left corner. The more prominent overhead beam and curtain constitute a distinct proscenium, and one has the sensation of witnessing an intimate scene from which the curtain has only moments ago been drawn back.

"Coming Home" reflects the changes that have taken place in the eighteen months since the lovers were married. The narrative has just entered Romola's mind for a lengthy analysis of her marital disillusionment. The objective correlative of the change that has come over her is seen at the end of her meditation, when Tito comes home wearing the chain-mail shirt we have seen him purchase from Niccolò Cappara as protection against Baldassarre's dagger.

She waited and listened long, for Tito had not come straight home after leaving Niccolò Cappara, and it was more than two hours after the time when he was crossing the Ponte Rubaconte that Romola heard the great door of the court turning on its hinges, and hastened to the head of the stone steps. There was a lamp hanging over the stairs, and they could see each other distinctly as he ascended. The eighteen months had produced a more definable change in Romola's face than in Tito's; the expression was more subdued, less cold, and more beseeching, and, as the pink flush overspread her face now, in her joy that the long waiting was at an end, she was much lovelier than on the day when Tito had first seen her. [27:379]

Leighton's illustration, perhaps the finest of the entire series, emphasizes not so much the change in Romola as the change in the relationship between the two characters. It shows Romola holding open the curtain on a landing of the stairs, her arms, her dress, and the curtains themselves forming a graceful harmony of S-shaped curves picked up below in the contours of Tito's cloak. The artist has been astonishingly successful in suggesting the effort with which Tito toils up the steps under the unfamiliar weight of his new coat of mail. The drawn curtain recalls the proscenium effect of "The First Kiss," but the moral change in the relationship between the two characters is visually underlined by the change in their physical positions. The figures stood on an equal plane in the earlier illustration, but now Tito is below Romola's level and seems to conceal his face as well as his chain mail and his treachery. The lighting and the handling of draperies give the two pictures a stylistic kinship which complements their structural similarities.

A pictorial approach to literary illustration can discover visual meanings that a narrowly literary approach might overlook. The illustrator, after all, is primarily a picture-maker; and pictures, as Gombrich and other art historians have demonstrated, are largely born of other pictures which establish the conventions that our minds use to order their perceptual experiences.[44] It is natural for the illustrator to ask, as Leighton did when confronted by George Eliot's description of the blacksmith's shop, what kind of painting the literary scene calls to mind. It is equally natural for the scene to mold itself around a visual motif which the illustrator has used before. To ignore this pictorial modeling may be to overlook the most decisive influence upon a given illustration. The text, to be sure, establishes certain limits of permissible meaning, and the illustration ought not to violate those limits without good reason.

But departures from the letter of the text may serve the spirit if they are governed by a coherent interpretive vision expressed in distinctively pictorial terms. As George Eliot learned, the illustrator's barber may well be better than the author's.

10   Conclusion

The first important biography of Leighton carries a quotation from *Romola* on its second page.[1] "*Va!* your human talk and doings are a tame jest; the only passionate life is in form and colour" (8:134). Walter Pater liked to quote this aphorism, too, enchanted no doubt by its formalist implications.[2] But George Eliot was not a forerunner of Roger Fry or Clive Bell in her approach to visual art. As Gillian Beer has noted, "pure pattern has no appeal for her . . . [her] emphasis is on art straining to become life . . . the human model is always more vital than the picture."[3] Art serves life in George Eliot's scheme of values; pictures are but an imperfect means to a higher end—the truthful representation of life in its dynamic complexity. That is why Daniel Deronda's mother has "an expression of living force beyond anything that the pencil could show" (53:138).

Ruskin, more than anyone else, taught George Eliot to value art as the servant of a greater reality. "The truth of infinite value that he teaches is *realism,*" she declared, "the doctrine that all truth and beauty are to be attained by a humble and faithful study of nature and not by substituting vague forms, bred by imagination on the mists of feeling, in place of definite, substantial reality."[4] For Ruskin and Eliot, the faithful study of nature is not an end in itself but a means of attaining a selfless perception of truth and beauty. Ruskin's belief in the spiritual significance of nature was no less important to Eliot than his empiricism. She learned from him to seek what Richard L. Stein has called "an intense spiritual appre-

hension of nature from a detailed examination of its physical characteristics."[5] She learned or relearned, in other words, the great lesson
of Romantic aesthetics: to be attentive to the veil of appearances in
the hope of seeing through it to a profounder truth. A Ruskinian
conviction that visual and literary art deals with two planes of
reality—one visible, the other invisible—pervades her theory and
practice of literary pictorialism.

In portraiture, the two planes are the physical appearance and the
inner nature of the sitter. All of Eliot's speculations about physiognomical expression presuppose a correlation between the two. But
the correlation becomes complex and problematic once naïve systems of interpretation such as phrenology are abandoned. Then the
portraitist must, like Piero di Cosimo in *Romola,* ponder the surfaces
until his penetrative imagination intuits the truth behind them. And
he must remain alert to the possibility that good looks mask selfish
or evil inclinations.

Idealizing portraiture depends upon the double reality of type and
antitype in figural symbolism. The type has a concrete existence in
history or literature yet prefigures or postfigures an absent antitype
which fulfills its meaning. Thus Daniel Deronda achieves his full
meaning only in his figural relation to Titian's exemplary image of
Christ giving the world its due. In secular or humanistic typology,
the figure may be valued more highly than the paradigm of which it
is the shadow. Thus Eliot criticizes Naumann's symbolism because it
is inattentive to the empirical reality of its vehicles. Both the flesh
and the spirit must be honored in the incarnations of art.

In narrative and problem pictures, the spectator infers a state of
affairs from the visual clues given him, comprehending the unseen
through a careful scrutiny of the seen. By the same token, the reader
must scan George Eliot's literary problem pictures carefully if he is
to perceive how the absence of an unlawful member of the family
group subverts the benign conventions of the conversation piece.
Eliot invites us to consult appearances but teaches us to look well
beyond them.

She values accurate empirical detail in representations of landscape because the attention paid to such detail ultimately yields a
spiritual insight into the larger reality of the human condition. For

both Eliot and Ruskin, a true vision of landscape is at once faithful to material surfaces yet aware that suffering and evil may be present in the most idyllic scenes, that mountain gloom is no less real than mountain glory, that the picturesque may have a dark underside of squalor and decay. It was chiefly Ruskin who taught Eliot to see the art of landscape as a marriage of naturalistic and emblematic techniques.

Although she had ceased to share the Evangelical faith that informs *Modern Painters* and *The Stones of Venice,* George Eliot was nonetheless profoundly influenced by Ruskin's conceptions of nature, imagination, and art. She incorporates his vivid sense of a world that is intensely present in its own right, yet intensely meaningful to humankind. She believes with him that imagination is the agency by which this physical/spiritual world is apprehended, and that art is the means by which the truthful apprehensions of the imagination are conveyed. Her realism, like Ruskin's, is essentially a subspecies of Romanticism.

Illustrations

Figure 1. Raphael, *The Sistine Madonna.* Dresden, Gemäldegalerie Alte Meister.

Figure 2. Titian, *The Assumption of the Virgin.* Venice, Chiesa di Santa Maria Gloriosa dei Frari.

Figure 3. Peter Paul Rubens, *The Crucifixion*. Munich, Alte Pinakothek.

Figure 4. Sir Peter Lely, *Sir John Skeffington, Viscount Massareene.*
Arbury Hall, Nuneaton, Warwickshire.

Figure 5. Sir Peter Lely, *Mary Bagot, Wife of Sir Richard Newdigate, 2d Bart.* Arbury Hall, Nuneaton, Warwickshire.

Figure 6. Robert Smirk, *The Marys at the Sepulchre* (detail). Engraved by William Sharp.

Figure 7. Johann Friedrich Overbeck, *The Triumph of Christianity in the Arts*. Frankfurt, Städelsches Kunstinstitut.

Figure 8. Josef von Führich, *The Triumph of Christ*. Poznań, Museum Narodowe.

Figure 9. Raphael, *The Coronation of the Virgin*. Rome, Vatican Museum.

Figure 10. *Ariadne.* Rome, Vatican Museum.

Figure 11. Palma Vecchio, *Santa Barbara*. Venice, Chiesa di
Santa Maria Formosa.

Figure 12. Sir Godfrey Kneller, *John Locke.* Engraved by Robert Graves.

Figure 13. Raphael, *Saint Catherine of Alexandria.* London, National Gallery.

Figure 14. Wilhelm von Schadow, *Pietas und Vanitas.* Bonn, Rheinisches Landes-museum.

Figure 15. Adam Buck, *Mrs. Siddons as Hermione*. Engraved by J. Alais.

Figure 16. Johann Zoffany, *Miss Farren in 'The Winter's Tale.'* Engraved by Edward Fisher.

Figure 17. Sir Godfrey Kneller, *Lady Elizabeth Cromwell as Saint Cecilia.* From a private collection.

Figure 18. Sir Joshua Reynolds, *Mrs. Sheridan as Saint Cecilia.* Waddesdon Manor, Aylesbury, Buckinghamshire.

Figure 19. Rembrandt, *Bust of a Bearded Man in a Cap.* London, National Gallery.

Figure 20. Titian, *The Annunciation*. Venice, Scuola di San Rocco.

Figure 21. Titian, *The Young Man with a Glove.* Paris, Musée du Louvre.

Figure 22. Titian, *The Tribute Money*. Dresden, Gemäldegalerie Alte Meister.

Figure 23. Gerard Dou, *The Spinner's Grace.* Munich, Alte Pinakothek.

Figure 24. Edward H. Corbould, *Hetty and Captain Donnithorne in Mrs. Poyser's Dairy*. Collection of Her Majesty the Queen. Copyright reserved.

Figure 25. Edward H. Corbould, *Dinah Morris Preaching on Hayslope Green.*
Collection of Her Majesty the Queen. Copyright reserved.

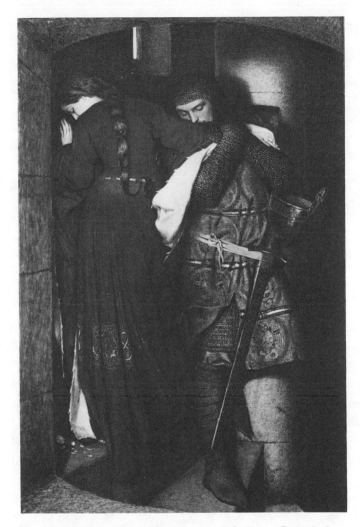

Figure 26. Frederic Burton, *The Meeting on the Turret Stairs*. Dublin, National Gallery of Ireland.

Figure 27. Frederic Leighton, *Niccolò at Work*. Engraved by Joseph Swain and William James Linton.

Figure 28. Joseph Wright, *An Iron Forge*. From a private collection in England.

Figure 29. Frederic Leighton, *Lieder ohne Worte* (study). London, Leighton House.

Figure 30. Frederic Leighton, *Tessa at Home*. Engraved by Joseph Swain and William James Linton.

Figure 31. Frederic Leighton, *Summer Moon*. From a private collection in India.

Figure 32. Frederic Leighton, *The Blind Scholar and His Daughter.* Engraved by Joseph Swain and William James Linton.

Figure 33. Frederic Leighton, *Suppose You Let Me Look at Myself.* Engraved by Joseph Swain and William James Linton.

Figure 34. Frederic Leighton, *The Painted Record*. Engraved by Joseph Swain and William James Linton.

Figure 35. Frederic Leighton, *The First Kiss*. Engraved by Joseph Swain and
William James Linton.

Figure 36. Frederic Leighton, *Coming Home*. Engraved by Joseph Swain and William James Linton.

Notes

Chapter 1

1 *The Correspondence of Gerard Manley Hopkins and Richard Watson Dixon,* ed. Claude Colleer Abbott (London: Oxford University Press, 1935), p. 61.

2 *The Letters of Gerard Manley Hopkins to Robert Bridges,* ed. Claude Colleer Abbott (London: Oxford University Press, 1935), p. 267. Both this and the previous quotation from Hopkins appear in Josephine Miles, *Eras and Modes in English Poetry,* 2d ed. (Berkeley: University of California Press, 1964), p. 168. On Hopkins's theory and practice of *ut pictura poesis,* see Jerome Bump, "Hopkins and Keats," *Victorian Poetry,* 12 (1974), 36–38, and "Hopkins' Drawings," in *All My Eyes Can See: The Visual World of Gerard Manley Hopkins,* ed. R. K. R. Thornton (Sunderland: Ceolfrith Press, 1975), p. 80. See also Robert C. Wilson, "Hopkins and the Art of Painting," *Thought,* 51 (1976), 147–60.

3 Henry James, *The Painter's Eye,* ed. John L. Sweeney (London: Rupert Hart-Davis, 1956), p. 90, and *The Letters of Aubrey Beardsley,* ed. Henry Maas, J. L. Duncan, and W. G. Good (London: Cassell, 1970), p. 61, quoted by John Dixon Hunt, "'Story Painters and Picture Writers': Tennyson's Idylls and Victorian Painting," in *Tennyson,* ed. D. J. Palmer (Athens: Ohio University Press, 1973), p. 180.

4 For recent descriptions of this interchange, see Hunt, p. 180; Peter Conrad, *The Victorian Treasure-House* (London: Collins, 1973), p. 134; Ian Fletcher, "Some Types and Emblems in

Victorian Poetry," *The Listener,* 77 (25 May 1967), 679; and Norman Page, "Visual Techniques in Hardy's 'Desperate Remedies,'" *Ariel,* 4 (1973), 70–71.

5 See "L'Oeuvre et la vie d'Eugene Delacroix" (1863), in *Oeuvres Complètes de Charles Baudelaire,* ed. Jacques Crépet (Paris: Louis Conard, 1925), II, 5: "C'est, du reste, un des diagnostics de l'etat spirituel de notre siècle que les arts aspirent, sinon à se suppléer l'un l'autre, du moins à se preter réciproquement." This passage is quoted in a slightly different translation by Jeffrey Meyers, *Painting and the Novel* (New York: Barnes and Noble, 1975), p. 1.

6 Joseph Conrad, "Preface" (1897) to *The Nigger of the 'Narcissus'* (New York: Doubleday and Page, 1918), p. x.

7 John Morley, [unsigned review of *Felix Holt*], *Saturday Review,* 21 (16 June 1866); rpt. *George Eliot: The Critical Heritage,* ed. David Carroll (London: Routledge and Kegan Paul, 1971), p. 252. George Saintsbury [review of *Daniel Deronda*], *Academy,* 10 (9 September 1876); rpt. *George Eliot: The Critical Heritage,* p. 373.

8 Morley, p. 252.

9 See *Letters,* II, 274, 406–07, and G. H. Lewes, "The Novels of Jane Austen," *Blackwood's Edinburgh Magazine,* 86 (1859), 105.

10 G. H. Lewes, "A Word about Tom Jones," *Blackwood's Edinburgh Magazine,* 87 (1860), 335.

11 "The Novels of Jane Austen," pp. 105–06. Lewes's ideas about description and drama may owe something to those of Bulwer-Lytton; see Harold H. Watts, "Lytton's Theories of Prose Fiction," *Publications of the Modern Language Association,* 50 (1935), 214.

12 Throughout this study I assume that Eliot and Lewes thought alike on important questions of aesthetic theory. Gordon S. Haight has challenged Alice R. Kaminsky for making the same assumption, but Bernard J. Paris seems to accept it; see Haight, "George Eliot's Theory of Fiction," *The Victorian Newsletter,* 10 (1956), 1–3, and Paris, *Experiments in Life: George Eliot's Quest for Values* (Detroit: Wayne State University Press, 1965), pp. 37–38. I have never seen it clearly demonstrated that Eliot and Lewes *disagreed* on any major issue, and anyone who reads the essays of both cannot help being struck by the many parallels of thought and phrasing.

13   See Donald A. Ringe, *The Pictorial Mode: Space and Time in the Art of Bryant, Irving and Cooper* (Lexington: University of Kentucky Press, 1971), pp. 2, 10, 15.

14   Barbara Smalley, *George Eliot and Flaubert: Pioneers of the Modern Novel* (Athens: Ohio University Press, 1974), p. 9.

15   See Reva Stump, *Movement and Vision in George Eliot's Novels* (Seattle: University of Washington Press, 1959), and Paris, pp. 34-39.

16   See Mario Praz, *The Hero in Eclipse in Victorian Fiction,* trans. Angus Davidson (London: Oxford University Press, 1956), pp. 319-83; Peter Conrad, *The Victorian Treasure-House,* pp. 39-40, 80-82, 105, 119; John Bayley, "The Pastoral of Intellect," in *Critical Essays on George Eliot,* ed. Barbara Hardy (London: Routledge and Kegan Paul, 1970), pp. 200-04; Michael Squires, *The Pastoral Novel: Studies in George Eliot, Thomas Hardy, and D. H. Lawrence* (Charlottesville: The University Press of Virginia, 1974), pp. 68, 75-77; and Ann Ronald, "George Eliot's Florentine Museum," *Papers on Language and Literature,* 13 (1977), 260-69. For more sympathetic treatments, see John Goode, "Adam Bede," in Hardy, ed., *Critical Essays on George Eliot,* p. 22; William J. Sullivan, "George Eliot and the Fine Arts," Diss. Wisconsin 1970; Norma Jean Davis, "Pictorialism in George Eliot's Art," Diss. Northwestern 1972; and Bernard A. Richards, "The Use of the Visual Arts in the Nineteenth-Century Novel," Diss. Oxford 1972. For excellent illustrations of Eliot's life and works, see Marghanita Laski, *George Eliot and Her World* (London: Thames and Hudson, 1973).

17   The dependence of Victorian novel-reviewers in general upon the vocabulary of painting is amply illustrated in Richard Stang, *The Theory of the Novel in England, 1850-1870* (London: Routledge and Kegan Paul, 1959). For an impressive list of the terms which William Hazlitt adapted to literary criticism from art criticism, see Roy Park, *Hazlitt and the Spirit of the Age: Abstraction and Critical Theory* (Oxford: Clarendon Press, 1971), pp. 108-09.

18   Edward Dowden [essay on George Eliot], *Contemporary Review,* 20 (1872); rpt. Carroll, ed., *George Eliot: The Critical Heritage,* pp. 320-21. For an interesting comment on "the metaphor of the portrait gallery . . . in Victorian reviewing," see James D. Benson, "'Sympathetic Criticism': George Eliot's

Response to Contemporary Reviewing," *Nineteenth-Century Fiction,* 29 (1975), 434.

19 See, for example, Derek Oldfield, "The Language of the Novel: The Character of Dorothea," in *Middlemarch: Critical Approaches to the Novel,* ed. Barbara Hardy (London: The Athlone Press, 1967), p. 85.

20 See Mario Praz, *The Hero in Eclipse* and *Mnemosyne: The Parallel between Literature and the Visual Arts* (Princeton: Princeton University Press, 1974); Wylie Sypher, *Four Stages of Renaissance Style: Transformations in Art and Literature 1400–1700* (New York: Doubleday, 1955) and *Rococo to Cubism in Art and Literature* (New York: Vintage Books, 1960); and Jean Hagstrum, *The Sister Arts: The Tradition of Literary Pictorialism and English Poetry from Dryden to Gray* (Chicago: University of Chicago Press, 1958). For a method that is similar to Praz's and Sypher's, though more telegraphic in its exposition, see Marshall McLuhan and Harley Parker, *Through the Vanishing Point: Space in Poetry and Painting* (New York: Harper & Row, 1968). See also Helmut A. Hatzfield, *Literature through Art: A New Approach to French Literature* (New York: Oxford University Press, 1952).

21 Praz, *Mnemosyne,* p. 29. For other expressions of distrust, see John Dixon Hunt, "Preface" to *Encounters: Essays on Literature and the Visual Arts* (London: Studio Vista, 1971), pp. 8–9; Jean Seznec, *Literature and the Visual Arts in Nineteenth-Century France* (Hull, Eng.: University of Hull Publications, 1963), pp. 4–5; and James D. Merriman, "The Parallel of the Arts: Some Misgivings and a Faint Affirmation," *Journal of Aesthetics and Art Criticism,* 31 (1972), 153–64, 309–21.

22 Bernard Richards, "Ut Pictura Poesis," *Essays in Criticism,* 21 (1971), 321–23.

23 See Giovanni Giovannini, "Method in the Study of Literature in Its Relation to the Other Fine Arts," *Journal of Aesthetics and Art Criticism,* 8 (1950), 185–95; John B. Bender, *Spenser and Literary Pictorialism* (Princeton: Princeton University Press, 1972), pp. 18–20; H. James Jensen, *The Muses' Concord: Literature, Music, and the Visual Arts in the Baroque Age* (Bloomington: Indiana University Press, 1976), pp. xiv–xv; and Merriman, "Parallel of the Arts," pp. 154, 160. Thus I cannot follow Viola Hopkins Winner when she argues that

Henry James's style is Mannerist in the same sense as Tintoretto's, and compares "James's often tortuous, involuted late style" to "Tintoretto's twisted lines and tormented restless forms"; see *Henry James and the Visual Arts* (Charlottesville; The University Press of Virginia, 1970), pp. 89–93. Surely the similarity here is more in the critic's adjectives than in the things compared.

24 See G. H. Ford, [review of *The Hero in Eclipse in Victorian Fiction*], *Modern Philology*, 54 (1957), 215–16. Praz defines Biedermeier as "both a style and a conception of the world," but he nearly always uses the term in the latter sense, to refer to "the whole bourgeois *Weltanschauung*" (*The Hero in Eclipse*, p. 118).

25 Hagstrum, *The Sister Arts*, pp. xxi–xxii.

26 In *Spenser and Literary Pictorialism*, John B. Bender has made an interesting attempt to update the theory of literary pictorialism by combining it with E. H. Gombrich's conception of the beholder's share in the perception of art and with Paul J. Alpers's affective approach to *The Faerie Queene*. Bender argues that a passage is pictorial not when its language reminds us of the visual arts, but only when its language imitates the psychological process of visual perception. He distinguishes three kinds of perception re-created in the poetry of Spenser: focusing, framing, and scanning. The main weakness of Bender's theory is that it does not discriminate sufficiently between the visual and the pictorial. Many of the examples he cites, especially under the headings of "focusing" and "scanning," are visual but not in any strict sense pictorial; and conversely, many traditionally structured descriptive word-portraits he refuses to call pictorial because they do not mime perceptual processes. Nevertheless, Bender has provided useful definitions of three effects which literary pictorialism *can* create, and his terms will no doubt help students of the sister arts to speak with greater precision in the future. On framing, see also Winner, *Henry James and the Visual Arts*, pp. 72–77.

27 Hagstrum, *The Sister Arts*, pp. 17–36.

28 On Fielding's pictorialism, see Sean Shesgreen, *Literary Portraits in the Novels of Henry Fielding* (De Kalb: Northern Illinois University Press, 1972) and Martin C. Battestin, *The Providence of Wit: Aspects of Form in Augustan Literature and*

the Arts (Oxford: Clarendon Press, 1974), pp. 179–92. On Scott's pictorialism, see J. D. W. Murdoch, "Scott, Pictures, and Painters," *Modern Language Review*, 67 (1972), 31–43, and Marcia Allentuck, "Scott and the Picturesque: Afforestation and History," in *Scott Bicentenary Essays*, ed. Alan Bell (Edinburgh: Scottish Academic Press, 1973), pp. 188–98.

29 Alastair Smart, "Pictorial Imagery in the Novels of Thomas Hardy," *Review of English Studies*, 12 (1961), 263. On Hardy's pictorialism, see also Gunther Wilmsen, *Thomas Hardy als impressionistischer Landschaftsmaler* (Marburg: G. H. Nolte, 1934); Carl J. Weber, *Hardy of Wessex* (New York: Columbia University Press, 1940), pp. 26–27; Richard C. Carpenter, "Hardy and the Old Masters," *Boston University Studies in English*, 5 (1961), 18–28; James F. Scott, "Thomas Hardy's Use of the Gothic," *Nineteenth-Century Fiction*, 17 (1963), 363–80; Lloyd Fernando, "Thomas Hardy's Rhetoric of Painting," *Review of English Literature*, 6 (1965), 62–73; F. B. Pinion, *A Hardy Companion* (New York: St. Martin's Press, 1968), pp. 193–200; John Peck, "Hardy and the Figure in the Scene," *Agenda*, 10 (1972), 117–25; Bernard Richards, "The Use of the Visual Arts in the Nineteenth-Century Novel," pp. 171–209; Norman Page, "Visual Techniques in Hardy's 'Desperate Remedies'"; and Penelope Vigar, *The Novels of Thomas Hardy: Illusion and Reality* (London: The Athlone Press, 1974).

Chapter 2

1 W. J. Harvey, "The Intellectual Background of the Novel: Casaubon and Lydgate," in Hardy, ed., *Middlemarch: Critical Approaches to the Novel*, p. 37.

2 Her first book was *The Linnet's Life: Twelve Poems, with a copper plate engraving to each* (London: G. & W. B. Whittaker, B. J. Holdsworth, 1822). She kept this book until the end of her life, and said that she had "thought the pictures beautiful, especially the one where the linnet is feeding her young" (Cross, I, 15). Her watercolors included two pictures of "floral arrangements—honeysuckle, moss rose, auricula, and so on, the stems lightly caught in a bow of blue ribbon" (Haight, p. 11).

3 On Eliot and Thackeray, see Richards, "The Use of the Visual Arts in the Nineteenth-Century Novel," pp. 22–90, 137–70,

563-67, 575. On James, see F. O. Matthiessen, "James and the Plastic Arts," *Kenyon Review,* 5 (1943), 535-50; Henry James, *The Painter's Eye;* Edwin T. Bowden, *The Themes of Henry James: A System of Observation through the Visual Arts* (New Haven: Yale University Press, 1956); Robert L. Gale, "Art Imagery in Henry James's Fiction," *American Literature,* 29 (1957), 47-63; Bernard Richards, "Henry James's Use of the Visual Arts," Diss. Oxford 1965; Winner, *Henry James and the Visual Arts*; and Susan P. Ward, "Painting and Europe in *The American,*" *American Literature,* 46 (1975), 566-74.

4   The importance to George Eliot's childhood of such illustrated books as the Bible, *Pilgrim's Progress,* Defoe's *Satan's Devices, Pug's Tour through Europe,* the *Keepsake,* and *The Vicar of Wakefield* is suggested by passages in *Adam Bede* (14:211, 51:317-19), *The Mill on the Floss* (I, 3:21-23; I, 4:37, 40; IV, 3:22), and *Letters* (IV, 354). Reproductions of works by Overbeck, Canaletto, Gavarni, Retzsch, Delaroche, Kaulbach, and Titian are mentioned in, respectively, "Janet's Repentance" (11:170), "The Lifted Veil" (1:289), *Daniel Deronda* (18: 295, 37:271), and *Letters* (I, 206; II, 454-55; V, 8). In *Daniel Deronda* Mrs. Meyrick's front parlour contains engravings from Titian, Dürer, Michelangelo, Raphael, Leonardo da Vinci, Holbein, Rembrandt, and Reynolds (20:312-13).

5   Her *Letters* contain clear evidence that George Eliot visited the Royal Academy Exhibition in 1852 (II, 29-30), 1854 (II, 154-55), 1859 (III, 388), 1862 (IV, 37), 1872 (V, 277), and 1877 (VI, 365); and the Old Water-Colour Society Exhibition in 1862 (IV, 30) and 1864 (IV, 147). Moreover, her journals mention visits to the Royal Academy in 1867 (Cross, III, 14) and to the Old Water-Colour in 1869 (Cross, III, 82).

6   She attended the French Exhibition in 1854 (*Letters,* II, 154-55), 1857 (*Letters,* II, 377), and 1867 (Cross, III, 14). For details of these exhibitions and the amazing career of Gambart, see Jeremy Maas, *Gambart: Prince of the Victorian Art World* (London: Barrie and Jenkins, 1975).

7   *Letters,* IV, 144 and VI, 228-29. George Eliot first expressed her admiration for Walker in a letter to Barbara Bodichon of 4 June 1872 (V, 277). The Leweses especially admired Walker's *Harbour of Refuge* in the Royal Academy Exhibition of that year.

8 Cross, II, 87–88, and *Letters,* V, 329. At Bethnal Green the Leweses saw the Hertford Gallery of Pictures, the core of what is now the Wallace Collection. The *Illustrated London News* (29 June 1872, p. 631) called it "unquestionably the most important private collection in the world," and spoke of "more than 600 oil paintings, about 200 water colour drawings and miniatures, and over 1000 objects of art in Sèvres and other porcelain, bronzes, decorative furniture, &c." The Leweses were particularly struck by Constant Troyon's *Landscape with Cattle* (1857?), and they also mentioned works by Hobbema, Gainsborough, Reynolds, and Decamps.

9 *Letters,* IV, 476. The National Art-Exhibition (19 May to 26 October 1868) was the most important provincial show since the Manchester Art-Treasures Exhibition of 1857. Many of the pictures came from distinguished private collections. Mounted in the wards of the new Infirmary building, the displays included "three galleries of oil paintings by the old masters, and a collection of their drawings and sketches; two galleries of oil paintings of the English school by deceased and living artists; a gallery of oil paintings by modern foreign artists; a gallery of English water-colour drawings"; and several other sections. See *The Illustrated London News,* 23 May 1868, pp. 512–13.

10 The visit to Leighton's studio took place in 1864 (*Letters,* IV, 143); to Hunt's, in 1868 (Cross, III, 32); to Watts's, in 1870 (Haight, p. 422); to Rossetti's, in 1870 (*Letters,* V, 78–79; to Burne-Jones's, in 1873 (*Letters,* V, 391); and to Mrs. Allingham's, in 1877 (*Letters,* VI, 424).

11 *Letters,* I, 347 and VI, 162. According to the *Dictionary of National Biography,* Morrison specialized in autographs, Persian carpets, Chinese porcelain, Greek gems and gold work, miniatures, cameos, inlaid metals, and enameled glass. He also had an extensive collection of engravings, and a "small but choice" collection of paintings. On their second visit, the Leweses noted a watercolor of a bird's wing by Albrecht Dürer.

12 "Recollections of Berlin," Beinecke Rare Book and Manuscript Library, Yale University. Excerpts from this journal appear in Cross, I, 269–306. On *Middlemarch,* see Chapter 6 below.

13 See Volker Plagemann, *Das deutsche Kunstmuseum 1790–1870* (Munich: Prestel Verlag, 1967), p. 135. The Neue Pinakothek in Munich had opened in 1854; the Neues Museum in Berlin, in 1855.

14 Cross, II, 47–49; *Letters*, II, 471–74; Haight, p. 264. The Leweses returned to Dresden and Berlin in 1867, but the pictorial record of the trip is sparse (Haight, p. 403). So are the records of their second visits to Antwerp in 1866 (*Letters*, IV, 270) and Vienna in 1870 (*Letters*, V, 88–89).

15 *Letters*, III, 294. Among the "centres" mentioned in her journal are the Brera and the Ambrosian Library in Milan; the Vatican, Lateran, and Capitoline museums in Rome; the Museo Borbonico in Naples; the Uffizi, the Pitti, the Academy, the Bargello, and the monastery of San Marco in Florence; the Academy in Bologna; the Arena Chapel in Padua; the Scuola di San Rocco, the Academy, and the Church of the Frari in Venice. George Eliot studied painting and sculpture not only in the famous museums but also in a great many churches, palaces, villas, and ateliers. In Rome, for example, she visited the Borghese Palace, the Villa Farnesina, and the studio of Johann Friedrich Overbeck, the great Nazarene painter. All of these details come from "Recollections of Italy 1860" (Cross, II, 140–211).

16 *Letters*, IV, 43, 55–56. G. H. Lewes's journal for 17 May 1862 reports: "On Wednesday we hired a Brougham for the day; went to the Printroom of the British Museum to Italian portraits of 15th cent." (*Letters*, IV, 34).

17 "Italy 1864," Beinecke Rare Book and Manuscript Library, Yale University. This journal mentions visits to the Louvre, the Gallery in Turin, the Brera in Milan, the Arena Chapel in Padua, and the Galleries in Verona and Brescia.

18 Haight, p. 376, and Laski, *George Eliot and Her World*, p. 85.

19 "Normandy and Brittany 1865," Beinecke Rare Book and Manuscript Library, Yale University.

20 Haight, p. 402. Lewes's journal mentions the following paintings at the Prado: Titian's *The Emperor Charles V on Horseback* and *The Bacchanal*, Murillo's *The Appearance of the Virgin to Saint Bernard*, and Velasquez's *The Drunkards, Aesop*, and *Menippus*. I am indebted to Professor Haight for this information.

21 On Cara Bray, see Haight, p. 45 and Plate IV. On Sara Hennell, see Haight, Plate II, and *Letters*, I, 148, 275–76, 332; II, 27.

22 The information in this paragraph comes from Haight, pp. 105, 204–05, 334; from the *Dictionary of National Biography*, vol. 22; and from Hester Burton, *Barbara Bodichon 1827–1891* (London: John Murray, 1949).

23 *Letters,* III, 124. The "illustrious predecessor" was David Cox,
    whose watercolors were shown at the French Gallery in May,
    June, and July of 1859. Most of Mme. Bodichon's pictures were
    drawings of Algerian landscapes and vegetation; she spent part
    of each year in Algiers after marrying Dr. Eugène Bodichon,
    French physician and radical, in 1857. For a review of the exhi-
    bition, see *The Illustrated London News,* 30 July 1859, p. 105.
    Another Bodichon show, featuring forty-three of her drawings,
    was held at the French Gallery in April of 1861; see Maas, *Gam-
    bart,* pp. 113, 137.

24 *Letters,* III, 134. Roberts's statement seemed borne out by the
    success of Rosa Bonheur, the French landscape, history, and
    animal painter whose work Gambart vigorously promoted in
    Britain after 1854. After seeing *Bourcairos Crossing the Pyr-
    enees,* one of three Bonheur paintings exhibited at the French
    Gallery in 1857, George Eliot wrote to Sara Hennell: "We went
    to see Rosa Bonheur's picture the other day. What power! That
    is the way women should assert their rights" (*Letters,* II, 377).
        Although George Eliot preferred to assert her rights through
    her work, Barbara Bodichon engaged in more direct forms of
    action as well. In 1856 she persuaded George Eliot to sign a
    petition urging Parliament to enact a law that would permit
    married women to own property. And the energetic artist later
    helped to enlist George Eliot as a founder of Girton College
    (Haight, pp. 204, 396–97). Another French woman painter
    promoted by Gambart and admired by George Eliot was
    Henriette Browne, whose *Sisters of Mercy* created a minor
    sensation when shown in London in August of 1859; see Maas,
    Gambart, p. 113, and *Letters,* III, 134.

25 Haight, pp. 371, 376–78, Plate IX. The finished version, in
    chalks, now hangs in the National Portrait Gallery.

26 On Leslie, see Haight, p. 83; on Cruikshank, Haight, pp. 110–11;
    on Hay, Haight, p. 345, and *Letters,* III, 388; on Laurence,
    Haight, p. 338; on Leighton, *Letters,* IV, 39; on Lehmann,
    Haight, p. 389; on Scott, Haight, p. 406, and Hock Guan Tjoa,
    George Henry Lewes: A Victorian Mind (Cambridge, Mass.:
    Harvard University Press, 1977), p. 17; on Howard, Haight, p.
    392; on Smith, Haight, pp. 432–33; on d'Aubigny, *Letters,* V,
    134–35; and on du Maurier, Haight, p. 422. George Eliot's
    library contained a copy of Scott's *Mural Paintings* (1868);

see William Baker, *The George Eliot-George Henry Lewes Library: An Annotated Catalogue of Their Books at Dr. Williams's Library, London* (New York and London: Garland, 1977), #1982.

27 *Letters,* II, 228; "Art and Belles Lettres," *The Westminster Review,* 65 (April 1856), 625-50; and Haight, p. 183.

28 Passages from volumes I and III of *The Stones of Venice* are copied into an undated commonplace book of George Eliot's now at the Beinecke Library. On Ruskin's letter to *The Times,* see *Letters,* II, 156. On the Edinburgh lectures, see Haight, p. 144, and *The Leader,* 10 June 1854, pp. 545-46. On *The Political Economy of Art,* see *Letters,* II, 422. George Eliot's library contained a copy of Joseph Milsand's *L'Esthétique anglaise, étude sur John Ruskin* (Paris, 1864); see Baker, *The George Eliot-George Henry Lewes Library,* #1479.

29 See "Belles Lettres," *The Westminster Review,* 66 (October 1856), 566; G. H. Lewes, "Lessing," *The Edinburgh Review,* 82 (October 1845), 451-70; and Joseph Wiesenfarth, *George Eliot's Mythmaking* (Heidelberg: Carl Winter Universitätsverlag, 1977), p. 46.

30 "Recollections of Berlin" and *Essays,* pp. 86-89.

31 Cross, I, 290-91, 304-05. Part I of *Torso* is noticed in *The Leader,* 6 (17 March 1855), 257-58, and Part II, in *The Westminster Review,* 65 (1856), 633-37. On the importance of *Torso* to George Eliot, see Joseph Wiesenfarth, "George Eliot's Notes for *Adam Bede,*" *Nineteenth-Century Fiction,* 32 (1977), 148-49.

32 See Baker, *The George Eliot-George Henry Lewes Library,* #1590, where the author is incorrectly identified.

33 Cross, II, 267, 275. In a diary at the Beinecke Library, Eliot notes that she has "copied out the lives of some saints from Mrs. Jamieson [*sic*]" on 31 August 1861. She had met Mrs. Jameson at the home of Barbara Leigh Smith in 1852 (Haight, p. 106).

34 Haight, pp. 324-25. The books in question are John Coindet, *Histoire de la peinture en Italie: guide de l'amateur des beaux-arts* (1849; new edition, Paris: J. Renouard, 1856), and Franz Theodor Kugler, *A Handbook of the History of Painting, from the Age of Constantin the Great to the Present Time,* trans. Mrs. M. Hutton and ed. C. L. Eastlake (London: John Murray, 1842; 3d ed. 1855). Coindet's book is still in George Eliot's library;

see Baker, *The George Eliot-George Henry Lewes Library*, #457.

35 On Rio, see "Belles Lettres," *The Westminster Review*, 65 (January 1856), 290–312. George Eliot's library contained an Italian translation of Rio's *Leonardo da Vinci e la sua Scuola* by V. G. de Castro (Milan, 1856) and a copy of Rio's seminal *De la poésie chrétienne* (Paris, 1836); see Baker, *The George Eliot-George Henry Lewes Library*, #1831, 1832. On Pater, see Haight, p. 461. In 1870 George Eliot dined with Pater at Oxford (*Letters*, V, 100).

36 Baker, *The George Eliot-George Henry Lewes Library*, #1322, 1758, 1818, 1938, 2044, 637, 1994, 2312, 2311, 1387, 1851, 2118.

37 She did, however, read the pioneering account of Pre-Columbian art in J. L. Stephens, *Incidents of Travel in Central America, Chiapas, and Yucatan*, 2 vols. (London: John Murray, 1841); see Haight, p. 302.

Chapter 3

1 Henry James, [review of *George Eliot's Life*], *Atlantic Monthly*, 55 (May 1885); rpt. *George Eliot: The Critical Heritage*, p. 499.

2 On George Eliot and music, see Sullivan, "George Eliot and the Fine Arts," pp. 6–20, 38–68 and "Music and Musical Allusion in *The Mill on the Floss*," *Criticism*, 16 (1974), 232–46; Shirley F. Levenson, "The Use of Music in *Daniel Deronda*," *Nineteenth-Century Fiction*, 24 (1969), 317–34; Ruby V. Redinger, *George Eliot: The Emergent Self* (New York: Alfred A. Knopf, 1975), pp. 87–90; and Marghanita Laski, "The Music of *Daniel Deronda*," *The Listener*, 96 (23 September 1976), 373–74.

3 G. H. Lewes's journal for 20 July 1858 (*Letters*, II, 472). A more articulate discussion of the painting occurs in Lewes's essay on "Realism in Art: Recent German Fiction," *Westminster Review*, 70 (1858), 493–94; rpt. *Literary Criticism of George Henry Lewes*, ed. Alice R. Kaminsky (Lincoln: University of Nebraska Press, 1964), p. 88. Furthermore, the *Sistine Madonna* is mentioned twice in Lewes's early novel, *Ranthorpe* (London: Chapman and Hall, 1847), pp. 12, 284. The half-Italian heroine, Isola Churchill, has "a pale, olive

complexion, large lustrous eyes, black hair, and a certain look of Raffaelle's Sistine Madonna." Later, the hero, Percy Ranthorpe, spends "some months" in Dresden, returning to London only "when he knew by heart every tint of the Sistine Madonna."

4 Cross, II, 47; *Letters,* II, 472; and "Life of Goethe," *The Leader,* 6 (1855), 1060. James himself acknowledged the importance of the *Sistine Madonna* to George Eliot when he placed two photographs of it, together with all of her writings, in the Cape Cod cottage of his feminists in *The Bostonians* (chap. 36). Philip Wakem refers to the *Sistine Madonna* in *The Mill on the Floss* when he tells Maggie: "The greatest of painters only once painted a mysteriously divine child" (V, 1:58). Mrs. Jameson called *The Sistine Madonna* "probably the most perfect picture in the world" in *Memoirs of the Early Italian Painters* (London: Charles Knight & Co., 1845), II, 147. Ruskin ranked the painting among the "few works of man so perfect as to admit of no conception of their being excelled"; see "Preface to the Second Edition" of *Modern Painters I,* in *Works,* III, 13.

5 I use the terms "High Renaissance" and "baroque" in the sense given them by Heinrich Wölfflin in *Principles of Art History,* trans. M. D. Hottinger (New York: Henry Holt & Co., 1932).

6 *Letters,* II, 450–51. For other references to Rubens, see *Letters,* IV, 270 and Cross, I, 269–70; II, 20–21, 43, 49, 189.

7 See Cross, II, 33, 187–90, 206–07; *Letters,* VII, 288; "Italy 1864," entries for May 9–11 and June 5–10.

8 On Michelangelo, see Cross, II, 155, 157, 162, 182–85, 188, 197. On Tintoretto, see Cross, II, 201–04, and "Italy 1864," entry for May 16. Here is an important difference between George Eliot's taste and that of Henry James. As Viola Hopkins Winner has shown (*Henry James and the Visual Arts,* pp. 83–93), James preferred the mannerist style above all others. He was therefore not disposed to think well of George Eliot's taste when he learned that she had described Michelangelo's manneristic statues of Night, Day, and Dawn in the Medici Chapel at Florence as "affected and exaggerated" (Cross, II, 184, and Carroll, ed., *George Eliot: The Critical Heritage,* p. 499).

9 On Rembrandt, see Cross, II, 49, 190; *Letters,* V, 89; "Art and Belles Lettres," *Westminster Review,* 65 (1856), 628–29,

and "Impressions of Theophrastus Such" (13:197). Rembrandt's squalling, pissing *Ganymede* at Dresden offended George Eliot (Cross, II, 49) and inspired the following passage in *Adam Bede*: "What little child ever refused to be comforted by that glorious sense of being seized strongly and swung upward? I don't believe Ganymede cried when the eagle carried him away, and perhaps deposited him on Jove's shoulder at the end" (30:52).

10   Ruskin, *Modern Painters*, vol. III, pt. IV, chap. iii, para. 5, in *Works*, V, 49. Eliot emphasized "the choice of noble subjects" in her review of Ruskin's third volume; see "Art and Belles Lettres," *Westminster Review*, 65 (1856), 627.

11   "Realism in Art," p. 499. Cf. Lewes's essay on "The Novels of Jane Austen," p. 102: "It is obvious that the thing represented will determine degrees in art. Raphael will always rank higher than Teniers; Sophocles and Shakespeare will never be lowered to the rank of Lope de Vega and Scribe." On Lewes's objections to "ugliness" and "horrible realities" in fiction, see Alice R. Kaminsky, *George Henry Lewes as Literary Critic* (Syracuse, N.Y.: Syracuse University Press, 1968), pp. 80, 90, and Walter M. Kendrick, "Balzac and British Realism: Mid-Victorian Theories of the Novel," *Victorian Studies*, 20 (1976), 13–14.

12   The Madonna described in this passage is Titian's *The Assumption of the Virgin* (fig. 2). The angel is probably one of Fra Angelico's.

13   Martin Price, "The Picturesque Moment," in *From Sensibility to Romanticism: Essays Presented to Frederick A. Pottle*, ed. Frederick W. Hilles and Harold Bloom (New York: Oxford University Press, 1965), p. 283.

14   In the opening chapters of the third volume of *Modern Painters*, Ruskin attacks Sir Joshua Reynolds's notion of the grand style in painting and refutes Reynolds's criticism of the Dutch school. These chapters, which George Eliot reviewed in 1856, are the most important source of the ideas propounded in chapter 17 of *Adam Bede;* see Darrell Mansell, Jr., "Ruskin and George Eliot's 'Realism,'" *Criticism*, 7 (1965), 203–16. Mansell points out that Eliot even borrows Ruskin's famous example of the real griffin from chapter 8 of *Modern Painters III*. Clearly Eliot had Ruskin's rebuttal of Reynolds in mind when she wrote to William Blackwood on 4 February 1857, defending *Scenes of Clerical*

Life against some reported objections: "much adverse opinion will of course arise from a dislike to the *order* of art rather than from a critical estimate of the execution. Any one who detests the Dutch school in general will hardly appreciate fairly the merits of a particular Dutch painting" (*Letters*, II, 292).

15 "Ruskin and George Eliot's 'Realism,'" p. 206. See also *Adam Bede* (17:265); *Essays*, p. 89; and Richard Stang, "The Literary Criticism of George Eliot," *Publications of the Modern Language Association*, 72 (1957), 956. Other critics who recognize the active role of the artist's imaginative mind in George Eliot's theory of realism are Ian Gregor and Brian Nichols, *The Moral and the Story* (London: Faber and Faber, 1962), p. 31; Dorothy Van Ghent, *The English Novel: Form and Function* (New York: Harper & Row, 1967), p. 210; U. C. Knoepfl-macher, *George Eliot's Early Novels: The Limits of Realism* (Berkeley: University of California Press, 1968), pp. 24–37; Bernard Richards, "The Use of the Visual Arts in the Nineteenth-Century Novel," pp. 222–28; Elizabeth Ermarth, "Method and Moral in George Eliot's Narrative," *Victorian Newsletter*, 47 (Spring 1975), 4; J. Hillis Miller, "Optic and Semiotic in *Middlemarch*," in *The Worlds of Victorian Fiction*, ed. Jerome H. Buckley (Cambridge, Mass.: Harvard University Press, 1975), pp. 138, 143; E. S. Shaffer, *"Kubla Khan" and the Fall of Jerusalem: The Mythological School in Biblical Criticism and Secular Literature 1770–1880* (Cambridge: Cambridge University Press, 1975), pp. 248–49; and Robert Langbaum, "The Art of Victorian Literature," in *The Mind and Art of Victorian England*, ed. Josef L. Altholz (Minneapolis: University of Minnesota Press, 1976), pp. 27–28. For the contrary view that the mind is essentially a passive recorder of externals in George Eliot's theory of realism, see Kenneth Graham, *English Criticism of the Novel, 1865–1900* (Oxford: Clarendon Press, 1965), p. 21, and Peter Jones, *Philosophy and the Novel* (Oxford: Clarendon Press, 1975), p. 67. On the expressive elements in Ruskin's aesthetic theory, see George P. Landow, *The Aesthetic and Critical Theories of John Ruskin* (Princeton: Princeton University Press, 1971), pp. 69–74, and Robert Hewison, *John Ruskin: The Argument of the Eye* (London: Thames and Hudson, 1976), pp. 65–71.

16 "Realism in Art," p. 499.

17 *Modern Painters,* vol. III, pt. IV, chap. iii, para. 9 in *Works,* V, 51.

18 Titian's *Assumption* is alluded to by the narrator of *Adam Bede* (17:270), and an engraving of it hangs in the Meyricks' parlour in *Daniel Deronda*: "the Virgin soaring amid her cherubic escort" (20:312).

19 Of *St. Peter Martyr,* she wrote: "In this picture, as in that of the Tribute-money at Dresden, Titian seems to have surpassed himself, and to have reached as high a point in expression as in colour" (Cross, II, 203). On the high regard in which *St. Peter Martyr* was held in nineteenth-century England generally, see Leslie Parris, *Landscape in Britain c. 1750–1850* (London: Tate Gallery, 1973), p. 22. The painting was destroyed by fire in 1867.

20 See Jean Hagstrum's account of "sacramental pictorialism" in *The Sister Arts,* pp. 128–29.

21 Louis L. Martz, *The Poetry of Meditation* (New Haven: Yale University Press, 1954). See especially chapter 4, "Problems in Puritan Meditation," pp. 153–75.

22 Haight, p. 58. Pictures of both the cast and the engraving are reproduced in Laski, *George Eliot and Her World,* p. 30. The print was made by Blanchard in 1844 for the Paris firm of Goupil and Vibert; it was published and marketed in London by their agents, Gambart and Junin (Maas, *Gambart,* p. 35).

23 See Wiesenfarth, *George Eliot's Mythmaking,* p. 30.

24 "Recollections of Italy 1860," Beinecke Library. Wordsworth expressed a similar anxiety during his tour of the Alps: "Ten thousand times in the course of this tour have I regretted the inability of my memory to retain a more strong impression of the beautiful forms before me, and again and again in quitting a fortunate station have I returned to it with the most eager avidity, with the hope of bearing away a more lively picture. At this moment, when many of these landscapes are floating before my mind, I feel a high [enjoyment] in reflecting that perhaps scarce a day in my life will pass [in which] I shall not derive some happiness from these images." See *The Letters of William and Dorothy Wordsworth,* ed. Ernest de Selincourt, 2d ed. rev. by Chester L. Shaver (Oxford: Clarendon Press, 1967), I, 35–36.

25 "Recollections of Berlin," Beinecke Library.

Chapter 4

1   On the theory of *ut pictura poesis* before the nineteenth cen-
    tury, see William Guild Howard, "Ut Pictura Poesis," *Publica-
    tions of the Modern Language Association,* 17 (1909), 40–123;
    Cicely Davies, "Ut Pictura Poesis," *Modern Language Review,*
    30 (1935), 159–69; Rensselaer W. Lee, "Ut Pictura Poesis:
    The Humanistic Theory of Painting," *Art Bulletin,* 22 (1940),
    197–269 (rpt. New York: W. W. Norton & Co., 1967); Jean
    Hagstrum, *The Sister Arts;* Ralph Cohen, *The Art of Discrimi-
    nation: Thomson's* The Seasons *and the Language of Criticism*
    (Berkeley: University of California Press, 1964), pp. 188–247;
    Dean Tolle Mace, *"Ut pictura poesis*: Dryden, Poussin and the
    Parallel of Poetry and Painting in the Seventeenth Century,"
    in Hunt, ed., *Encounters,* pp. 58–81; and James S. Malek, *The
    Arts Compared: An Aspect of Eighteenth-Century British
    Aesthetics* (Detroit: Wayne State University Press, 1974).
2   Ian Jack, *Keats and the Mirror of Art* (Oxford: Clarendon Press,
    1967); Roy Park, "'Ut Pictura Poesis': The Nineteenth-Century
    Aftermath," *Journal of Aesthetics and Art Criticism,* 28 (1969),
    155–64, and *Hazlitt and the Spirit of the Age;* George P.
    Landow, "Ruskin's Versions of 'Ut Pictura Poesis,'" *Journal of
    Aesthetics and Art Criticism,* 26 (1967), 521–28, and *The
    Aesthetic and Critical Theories of John Ruskin*; Viola Hopkins
    Winner, "Pictorialism in Henry James's Theory of the Novel,"
    Criticism, 9 (1967), 1–21, and *Henry James and the Visual
    Arts.*
3   Henry James, "The Art of Fiction," in *Partial Portraits* (1888;
    rpt. New York: Haskell House, 1968), p. 378. Cf. Bulwer-
    Lytton in his 1843 preface to *The Last of the Barons*: "To my
    mind, a writer should sit down to compose a fiction as a painter
    prepares to compose a picture"; quoted by Richard Stang, *The
    Theory of the Novel in England, 1850–1870,* p. 12.
4   Praz, *The Hero in Eclipse,* p. 29.
5   Richards, "Henry James's Use of the Visual Arts," pp. 46–51,
    and "The Use of the Visual Arts in the Nineteenth-Century
    Novel," pp. 215–17.
6   Landow, *The Aesthetic and Critical Theories of John Ruskin,*
    p. 49.

7   William Hazlitt, *Complete Works*, ed. P. P. Howe (London: J. M. Dent & Sons, 1930–34), XI, 166; quoted by Park, *Hazlitt and the Spirit of the Age*, p. 104.

8   On the eighteenth-century backgrounds of this distrust, see Cohen, *The Art of Discrimination*, pp. 135–42; and Ronald Paulson, *Emblem and Expression: Meaning in English Art of the Eighteenth Century* (London: Thames and Hudson, 1975), pp. 48–49. On Mill and landscape painting, see Anna J. Mill, "John Stuart Mill and the Picturesque," *Victorian Studies*, 14 (1970), 151–63.

9   Lewes, "Hegel's Philosophy of Art," *British and Foreign Review*, vol. 13 (1842); quoted from Kaminsky, ed., *Literary Criticism of George Henry Lewes*, p. 49. Coleridge, *Shakespearian Criticism*, ed. T. M. Raysor (Cambridge, Mass.: Harvard University Press, 1930), II, 134; I am indebted to Roy Park's work for the quotation from Coleridge.

10 Philip Gilbert Hamerton, "Word Painting and Colour Painting," in *A Painter's Camp in the Highlands and Thoughts about Art* (Cambridge: Macmillan, 1862), II, 251.

11 Hagstrum, *The Sister Arts*, p. 11.

12 See Alice R. Kaminsky, *George Henry Lewes as Literary Critic*, pp. 22, 38.

13 Lewes, "The Principles of Success in Literature," *Fortnightly Review*, I (1865), 190–91. The role of images in the epistemology and aesthetics of the Scottish "Common Sense" school of British empiricism is well summarized by Ringe, *The Pictorial Mode*, pp. 3–8.

14 Lewes, "Principles of Success," p. 190.

15 Ibid., p. 574.

16 Ibid., p. 583. On the tradition of the primacy of the sense of sight, see Paulson, *Emblem and Expression*, p. 235n.

17 Lewes, "Principles of Success," 190. See, too, the excellent discussion of "vision" in Paris, *Experiments in Life*, pp. 34–39.

18 Lewes, "Imaginative Artists," *The Leader*, 7 (1856), 545. Michael York Mason has noted Ruskin's profound influence upon Lewes's "Principles of Success"; see "*Middlemarch* and Science: Problems of Life and Mind," *Review of English Studies*, 22 (1971), 152. See also Tjoa, *George Henry Lewes*, pp. 63, 71–72.

19 Lewes, "Principles of Success," pp. 586–87. Likewise George

Eliot, in a letter praising Ruskin, spoke of "the falsity that paints what the painter does not see" (*Letters,* II, 422).

20 Lewes, "Principles of Success," p. 188. On Ruskin's aim "to vivify our sight," see George P. Landow, "There Began To Be a Great Talking about the Fine Arts," in Altholz, ed., *The Mind and Art of Victorian England,* p. 137.

21 Eliot, "Belles Lettres," *Westminster Review,* 65 (1856), 294. The italics are George Eliot's.

22 Joseph Hornung (1792–1870) was a Swiss painter and the mentor of George Eliot's friend d'Albert-Durade. Thomas Pinney (*Essays,* p. 270) associates Eliot's "group of chimney-sweepers" with Hornung's *The Little Chimney-sweep.* The scene in Luckie Mucklebackit's cottage occurs in chapter 31 of Scott's *The Antiquary,* and contains a famous allusion to the Scottish genre painter, David Wilkie: "In the inside of the cottage was a scene which our Wilkie alone could have painted, with the exquisite feeling of nature that characterises his enchanting productions." The scene in Kingsley's *Alton Locke* (chap. 11) contains a good deal of picturesque description.

23 William J. Hyde, "George Eliot and the Climate of Realism," *Publications of the Modern Language Association,* 72 (1957), 151.

24 Eliot, "Belles Lettres," *Westminster Review,* 67 (1857), 321.

25 For the word *art* in this passage, should we read *out* "to make *out* a sufficiently real background"?

26 Eliot uses the same picture-diagram metaphor in "The Sad Fortunes of the Reverend Amos Barton," where she contrasts picturesque architecture with the modern architecture that is displacing it: "dear, old, brown, crumbling, picturesque inefficiency is everywhere giving place to spick-and-span new-painted, new-varnished efficiency, which will yield endless diagrams, plans, elevations, and sections, but alas! no picture" (1:4).

27 Hagstrum, *The Sister Arts,* p. 153.

28 Edmund Burke, *A Philosophical Enquiry into the Origin of Our Ideas of the Sublime and Beautiful,* 2d ed. (London: R. & J. Dodsley, 1759), pt. II, sec. iv, p. 108 (rpt. New York: Garland Publishing Co., 1971). A neatly bound copy of Burke's essay ornaments the bookcase of Miss Linnet in "Janet's Repentance" (3:71). For the influence of Burke's *Enquiry* upon Hardy, see S. F. Johnson, "Hardy and Burke's 'Sublime,'"

in *Style in Prose Fiction,* ed. Harold C. Martin (New York: Columbia University Press, 1959), pp. 55–86.

29   Lewes, "Principles of Success," p. 583. See also Lewes's introduction to *Female Characters of Goethe, from the Original Drawings of William Kaulbach,* 2d ed. (London: Frederick Bruckmann, 1874).

30   "Principles of Success," p. 585. This was not always Lewes's position. Earlier in his career he had agreed with Burke's view of poetic language; see "Hegel's Aesthetics: Philosophy of Art," *British and Foreign Review,* vol. 13 (1842); rpt. Kaminsky, ed., *Literary Criticism of George Henry Lewes,* pp. 47–49.

31   See Hagstrum, *The Sister Arts,* pp. 155–56.

32   See *Laokoön,* sec. xvii. We do not know which German edition the Leweses used; the earliest complete English translation was by William Ross (London: J. Ridgway & Sons, 1836).

33   Eliot, "Belles Lettres," *Westminster Review,* 66 (1856), 566.

34   E. H. Gombrich has argued, contra Lessing, that the visual arts can, within limits, represent movement and temporal sequences of events, and that our perception of painting is a more time-consuming process than Lessing allowed. Gombrich contends that Lessing's denial of time to painting is based upon the false premise of a *punctum temporis,* a static point in time. See "Moment and Movement in Art," *Journal of the Warburg and Courtauld Institutes,* 27 (1964), 293–306. See also Etienne Souriau, "Time in the Plastic Arts," *Journal of Aesthetics and Art Criticism,* 7 (1949), 294–307, and Bender, *Spenser and Literary Pictorialism,* pp. 25–27.

35   *Daniel Deronda,* 11:170. See also Sullivan, "George Eliot and the Fine Arts," pp. 70–71, and Gillian Beer, "Music and the Visual Arts in the Novels of George Eliot," *The George Eliot Fellowship Review,* 5 (1974), 17–20.

36   Eliot calls attention to Laokoön's voice in her remarks on Lessing in "Belles Lettres," *Westminster Review,* 66 (1856), 566.

37   By "picture" James did not mean passages rich in descriptive visual detail; rather, he meant nondramatic narrative passages centered in the consciousness of a single character. See Winner, "Pictorialism in Henry James's Theory of the Novel," pp. 14–15, and Peter K. Garrett, *Scene and Symbol from George Eliot to James Joyce: Studies in Changing Fictional Modes* (New Haven: Yale University Press, 1969), p. 11.

38 Fletcher, "Some Types and Emblems in Victorian Poetry," p. 679.
39 See Joseph Frank, "Spatial Form in Modern Literature," in *Criticism: The Foundations of Modern Literary Judgment,* ed. Mark Schorer, Josephine Miles, Gordon McKenzie (New York: Harcourt, Brace, & Co., 1958), pp. 379–92. An interesting modification of Frank's theory is proposed by Ellen Stewart Spangler in "The Book As Image: Medieval Form in the Modern Spatialized Novel of Marcel Proust and His Contemporaries," Diss. New Mexico 1975.
40 Meyers, *Painting and the Novel,* p. 1.
41 Ibid., pp. 19–82, 96–123; Maurice Chernowitz, *Proust and Painting* (New York: International University Press, 1945); and Keith Alldritt, *The Visual Imagination of D. H. Lawrence* (Evanston, Ill.: Northwestern University Press, 1971).
42 On James's use of Bronzino, see Miriam Allott, "The Bronzino Portrait in *The Wings of the Dove," Modern Language Notes,* 68 (1953), 23–25; Winner, *Henry James and the Visual Arts,* pp. 81–85; and Meyers, *Painting and the Novel,* pp. 19–25. Allott's identification of Lord Mark's Bronzino with the Uffizi portrait of Lucrezia Panciatichi is not universally accepted; for another suggestion, see Richards, "Henry James's Use of the Visual Arts," pp. 131–34.

Chapter 5

1 G. H. Lewes, "The Novels of Jane Austen," p. 106.
2 On the tradition of the literary portrait, see Blanchard W. Bates, *Literary Portraiture in the Historical Narrative of the French Renaissance* (New York: G. T. Stechert, 1945); Alice M. Colby, *The Portrait in Twelfth Century French Literature* (Geneva: Droz, 1965); and Shesgreen, *Literary Portraits in the Novels of Henry Fielding.*
3 George Eliot's description of Amos Barton may have influenced Thomas Hardy's description of Dick Dewy in the first chapter of *Under the Greenwood Tree* (1872): "Having come more into the open he could now be seen rising against the sky, his profile appearing on the light background like the portrait of a gentleman in black cardboard. It assumed the form of a low-crowned hat, an ordinary-shaped nose, an ordinary chin, an ordinary neck, and ordinary shoulders."

4   For a different view, see Knoepflmacher, *George Eliot's Early Novels*, p. 49: "Barton is grossly caricatured."

5   See E. H. Gombrich, "On Physiognomic Perception," in *Meditations on a Hobby Horse and Other Essays on the Theory of Art* (London: Phaidon, 1963), pp. 45–55; and David Piper, *The English Face* (Aylesbury, Eng.: Thames and Hudson, 1957), p. 216.

6   See Brewster Rogerson, "The Art of Painting the Passions," *Journal of the History of Ideas*, 14 (1953), 68–94; George Levitine, "The Influence of Lavater and Girodet's *Expression des sentiments de l'ame*," *Art Bulletin*, 36 (1954), 33–45; Wylie Sypher, "The Mechanics of Expression," in *Four Stages of Renaissance Style*, pp. 274–81; Alastair Smart, "Dramatic Gesture and Expression in the Age of Hogarth and Reynolds," *Apollo*, 82 (1965), 90–97; and Jensen, *The Muses' Concord*, pp. 102–08.

7   Sir Charles Bell, *Essays on the Anatomy of Expression in Painting* (London: Longmans & Co., 1806), pp. vi–vii.

8   George Combe, *Phrenology Applied to Painting and Sculpture* (London: Simpkin, Marshall, & Co., 1855), p. 78. The Leweses owned a copy of this book; see Baker, *The George Eliot-George Henry Lewes Library*, #464. Combe was converted to phrenology by Spurzheim around 1817 and became the leading spokesman and popularizer of the movement in Britain.

9   For general accounts of the phrenological system, see John D. Davies, *Phrenology: Fad and Science* (New Haven: Yale University Press, 1955), and David de Giustino, *Conquest of Mind: Phrenology and Victorian Social Thought* (London: Croom Helm, 1975).

10 See Davies, *Phrenology*, pp. 118–25; Edward Hungerford, "Poe and Phrenology" and "Whitman and His Chart of Bumps," *American Literature*, 2 (1930–31), 209–31, 350–84; Arthur Wrobel, "Whitman and the Phrenologists: The Divine Body and the Sensuous Soul," *Publications of the Modern Language Association*, 89 (1974), 17–23; Wilfred M. Senseman, "Charlotte Brontë's Use of Physiognomy and Phrenology," *Papers of the Michigan Academy of Science, Arts, and Letters*, 38 (1953), 475–86; Herbert R. Brown, *The Sentimental Novel in America, 1789–1860* (Durham, N.C.: Duke University Press, 1940), pp. 189–96; and Conrad, *The Victorian Treasure-House*, pp. 59–60.

11 Maurice L. Johnson, "George Eliot and George Combe," *Westminster Review,* 166 (1906), 561.

12 Ibid. For other phrenological portraits in *Scenes of Clerical Life,* see "Amos Barton" (3:48, 3:56) and "Mr Gilfil's Love-Story" (2:153, 5:209).

13 Combe, *Phrenology Applied to Painting and Sculpture,* p. 40.

14 Orson S. Fowler, *Phrenological Chart* (Baltimore, 1836), quoted by Davies, *Phrenology,* p. 181.

15 This loss of faith was probably due to the influence of Lewes, who accepted Gall's principle of the physical basis of mind but rejected the cranioscopy of Spurzheim, Combe, and their followers. See Haight, p. 188; N. N. Feltes, "Phrenology: From Lewes to George Eliot," *Studies in the Literary Imagination,* 1 (1968), 13–22; Anna Theresa Kitchel, *George Lewes and George Eliot* (New York: John Day Co., 1933), pp. 92–93; T. L., "Applications of Phrenological Doctrines," *Encylopedia Britannica,* 8th ed. (Edinburgh: A. and C. Black, 1853–60), XVII, 565–67; and John R. Reed, *Victorian Conventions* (Athens: Ohio University Press, 1975), pp. 336–37. For an example of physiognomical portraiture by Lewes himself, see *Ranthorpe,* p. 4.

16 The drawing in question is probably the *Hamlet and Ophelia* of 1866 rather than the earlier version of 1858; see John Nicoll, *Dante Gabriel Rossetti* (London: Studio Vista, 1975), p. 133. A square anterior lobe would imply that Hamlet's organs of ideality and wonder are highly developed; see Johnson, "George Eliot and George Combe," p. 558.

17 *Adam Bede* (12:192–94, 13:204, 15:228) and Squires, *The Pastoral Novel,* pp. 60–67.

18 *Adam Bede* (37:145) and Wiesenfarth, *George Eliot's Mythmaking,* pp. 43–44.

19 Davies, *Phrenology,* p. 8.

20 *Modern Painters,* vol. II, pt. III, sec. I, chap. xiv, paras. 9, 14, in *Works,* IV, 184, 187.

21 *Letters,* III, 300. Hawthorne's influence upon *Romola* was first pointed out by Curtis Dahl, "When the Deity Returns: *The Marble Faun* and *Romola,*" *Papers on Language and Literature,* 5 (Summer Supplement, 1969), 82–99.

22 See Paul Brodtkorb, "Art Allegory in *The Marble Faun,*" *Publications of the Modern Language Association,* 77 (1962),

254-67; Gary Scrimgeour, "*The Marble Faun:* Hawthorne's Faery Land," *American Literature,* 36 (1964), 271-87; Spencer Hall, "Beatrice Cenci: Symbol and Vision in *The Marble Faun,*" *Nineteenth-Century Fiction,* 25 (1970), 85-95; Judith Kaufman Budz, "Cherubs and Humblebees: Nathaniel Hawthorne and the Visual Arts," *Criticism,* 17 (1975), 168-81; Rita K. Gollin, "Painting and Character in *The Marble Faun,*" *Emerson Society Quarterly,* 21 (1975), 1-10; and Meyers, *Painting and the Novel,* pp. 6-18.

23   When Nello says that Tito would "make a Saint Sebastian . . . that will draw troops of devout women" (4:63), George Eliot is probably thinking of the copy of Guido Reni's *Saint Sebastian* in the Dulwich College Gallery. She saw it on 9 May 1859 and judged it "no exception to the usual 'petty prettiness' of Guido's conceptions" (Cross, II, 88).

24   See Dahl, "When the Deity Returns," pp. 83-86, 92-93; and Wiesenfarth, *George Eliot's Mythmaking,* pp. 152-55. On "the conception of Bacchus as the Care-Dispeller," see also George Eliot, "Art and Belles Lettres," *Westminster Review,* 65 (1856), 637. There may be a reminiscence of Hawthorne's Faun of Praxiteles in Tito's totemic statue of "a young faun playing the flute, modelled by a promising youth named Michelangelo Buonarotti" (20:303).

25   The allegory presents "three masks—one a drunken laughing Satyr, another a sorrowing Magdalen, and the third, which lay between them, the rigid, cold face of a Stoic: the masks rested obliquely on the lap of a little child, whose cherub features rose above them with something of the supernal promise in the gaze which painters had by that time learned to give to the Divine Infant" (3:51-52). This design resembles no known work by the original Piero di Cosimo. It is a nineteenth-century historical allegory devised by George Eliot herself to represent the three phases of western religious sensibility that preceded Christianity. Reading the masks from left to right, we encounter a progression from an animalistic paganism that takes pleasure in this world, to a philosophical stoicism that endures this world, to a metaphysical sorrow that yearns to transcend this world. The cherubic, Christ-like child is the new dispensation of Christianity, which promises transcendence and thereby absorbs its predecessors. But Tito interprets the child as "the Golden

Age . . . [or] the wise philosophy of Epicurus" (3:52), failing to see that those stages of mind are represented by the masks of the satyr and the Stoic. For differing interpretations of this "symbolical picture," as Tito calls it, see Barbara Hardy, *The Novels of George Eliot* (New York: Oxford University Press, 1967), p. 176; William J. Sullivan, "The Sketch of the Three Masks in *Romola*," *Victorian Newsletter*, 41 (1972), 9–13; and Richards, "The Use of the Visual Arts in the Nineteenth-Century Novel," pp. 302–03.

26 See *Modern Painters*, vol. II, pt. III, sec. I, chap. ii, in *Works* IV, 42–50. *Aesthesis* is the "mere sensual perception of the outward qualities and necessary effects of bodies," whereas *theoria* is "the exulting, reverent, and grateful perception" of beauty as a creation and gift of God.

27 Romola is first attracted to Savonarola by the physiognomy of his hands and face (15:240). Eliot's description of Savonarola's face is modeled upon Fra Bartolommeo's famous portrait in the Accademia at Florence (*Letters*, III, 295).

28 The most famous version is Titian's *Bacchus and Ariadne* (1523), which the National Gallery of London purchased in 1826. George Eliot may also have known Garofalo's *Triumph of Bacchus* at Dresden. Bacchus and Ariadne do appear in one of the original Piero di Cosimo's Bacchanals, *The Discovery of Honey*, now in the Worcester Art Museum (Worcester, Mass.). But this painting bears no resemblance to the picture commissioned by Tito.

29 This conflation was first noted by Edward T. Hurley, "Piero di Cosimo: An Alternate Analogy for George Eliot's Realism," *Victorian Newsletter*, 31 (1967), 54–56. George Eliot had seen a cartoon for Buonaventura Genelli's unfinished *Bacchus verwandelt die Seeräuber in Delphine* when she visited the artist's studio in Munich in 1858; see "Germany," Beinecke Library, entry for 10 May 1858. The cartoon has since been destroyed; see Hans Ebert, *Buonaventura Genelli: Leben und Werk* (Weimar: Hermann Böhlaus, 1971), pp. 48, 218.

30 *Modern Painters*, vol. II, pt. III, sec. II, chap. iii, paras. 3, 29, in *Works*, IV, 251, 285.

31 See Lawrence Poston III, "Setting and Theme in *Romola*," *Nineteenth-Century Fiction*, 20 (1965), 358–59. As a choral observer rather than a participant, Piero fulfills a dictum of

Ruskin's that George Eliot copied into her commonplace book around the time she was creating *Romola:* "Of course, a painter of men must be *among* men; but it ought to be as a watcher, not as a companion." See George Eliot's commonplace book, Beinecke Library, p. 99, and Ruskin, *The Stones of Venice,* vol. III, chap. ii, para. 13n, in *Works,* XI, 53.

32 Most commentators on Piero have connected his aesthetic with George Eliot's, though none has noted that the most important similarities derive from Ruskin. See Hurley, "Piero di Cosimo," pp. 54–56; Davis, "Pictorialism in George Eliot's Art," p. 48; and William J. Sullivan, "Piero di Cosimo and the Higher Primitivism in *Romola,*" *Nineteenth-Century Fiction,* 26 (1972), 390–405. Sullivan, I think, underestimates the extent to which Piero is a seer and a Christian artist.

33 On the special vividness of Vasari's life of Piero, see Erwin Panofsky, *Studies in Iconology* (New York: Harper & Row, 1962), pp. 65–67; and R. Langton Douglas, *Piero di Cosimo* (Chicago: University of Chicago Press, 1946), p. 7. The vita was immensely popular among the German Romantics, thanks to W. H. Wackenroder's *Herzensergiessungen eines kunstliebendes Klosterbruders* (1797). Many of the eccentricities attributed to Piero in *Romola* come straight from Vasari, as do the descriptions of the studio in chapter 18 and the allegorical procession in chapter 20. Except for the picture of *Venus, Cupid, and Mars* placed on the easel in the studio scene, however, not one of the paintings given to the artist in the novel recreates an actual work by the historical Piero di Cosimo. There is no evidence that George Eliot knew any of his work at first hand, beyond what she learned from the *ecphrases* of Vasari. Barbara Hardy (*The Novels of George Eliot,* p. 173) argues that some of the details in Tito's wedding-portrait derive from Vasari.

34 *Modern Painters,* vol. V, pt. IX, chap. iii, para. 7, in *Works,* VII, 283. Wiesenfarth (*George Eliot's Mythmaking,* p. 155) argues persuasively that the corporal attitude of Piero's reveller is modeled upon Michelangelo's *Bacchus,* which was on display at Florence in George Eliot's time.

35 Hardy, *The Novels of George Eliot,* pp. 176–77.

36 *Modern Painters,* vol. V, pt. IX, chap. iii, para. 1, in *Works,* VII, 279.

37 Barbara Hardy (*The Novels of George Eliot,* p. 174) refers to

the portrait of Tito as a "prophetic picture," but claims that it anticipates Baldassarre's interruption of the supper in the Rucellai Gardens (chap. 39) rather than the scene on the Duomo steps (chap. 22). The most important prophetic images in *The Marble Faun* are the so-called *Portrait of Beatrice Cenci*, whose ambiguous expression of guilty innocence is shared by both Miriam and Hilda as they come into contact with evil, and the clay model for a bust of Donatello, in which the sculptor Kenyon inadvertently creates an expression of pure ferocity that is true to character even though the artist has never actually seen it on the model's face (chap. 30).

38 See Richards, "Henry James's Use of the Visual Arts," pp. 104–20, and "The Use of the Visual Arts in the Nineteenth-Century Novel," pp. 416–51, and Theodore Ziolkowski, *Disenchanted Images: A Literary Iconology* (Princeton: Princeton University Press, 1977), pp. 78–148.

39 Dahl, "When the Deity Returns," p. 92. See also Richards, "The Use of the Visual Arts," p. 303.

40 On *Romola* and Paterian aestheticism, see David J. DeLaura, "*Romola* and the Origin of the Paterian View of Life," *Nineteenth-Century Fiction*, 21 (1966), 225–33; Donald L. Hill, "Pater's Debt to *Romola*," *Nineteenth-Century Fiction*, 22 (1968), 361–77; Redinger, *George Eliot*, p. 452; and Jerome Bump, "Hopkins, Pater, and Medievalism," *Victorian Newsletter*, 50 (Fall 1976), 10–15.

41 See Robert Preyer, "Beyond the Liberal Imagination: Vision and Unreality in *Daniel Deronda*," *Victorian Studies*, 4 (1960), 33–54.

42 On the portraiture in *Felix Holt*, see Richards, "The Use of the Visual Arts in the Nineteenth-Century Novel," pp. 391–93; Peter Coveney, "Introduction" to *Felix Holt, the Radical* (Harmondsworth: Penguin Books, 1972), pp. 47–48; and Nicholas Rance, *The Historical Novel and Popular Politics in Nineteenth-Century England* (London: Vision Press, 1975), p. 122.

43 Laski, *George Eliot and Her World*, p. 75.

44 *Letters*, III, 307–08. For Eliot's view of photography, see also *Letters*, III, 449; VI, 385; VII, 213, 233.

45 Gwendolen's similar habit of imagining herself the heroine of a play is discussed by Brian Swann in "George Eliot and the Play:

Symbol and Metaphor of the Drama in *Daniel Deronda,*" *Dalhousie Review,* 52 (1972), 191–202.

46 George Eliot could have seen a number of Moroni's works in London in the 1860s and 1870s. The National Gallery purchased the famous *Portrait of a Tailor* in 1862, another portrait in 1865, and three more in 1876. Sir A. H. Layard loaned three Moronis to the South Kensington Museum in 1869, two of which had been displayed at the great Leeds Exhibition of 1868, which George Eliot attended (*Letters,* IV, 476). Eliot also knew the two portraits by Moroni in the Museo Civico at Brescia (see "Italy 1864," Beinecke Library, entry for 4 June). If she had a specific portrait in mind when describing Grandcourt, I suspect that it was one of Layard's, the *Portrait Said to Represent Count Lupi,* which was shown at Leeds and now hangs in the National Gallery (no. 3129); see Cecil Gould, *The Sixteenth-Century Italian Schools* (*excluding the Venetian*) (London: Publications Department of the National Gallery, 1962), p. 118.

47 The National Portrait Gallery opened in 1857. The secretary of the Gallery, George Scharf, was a friend of the Lewes family. George Eliot met him early in 1862 and visited the gallery on her spring tour of the exhibitions in that year (*Letters,* IV, 13, 37).

48 *Letters,* IV, 363–64. The National Portrait Exhibition took place at the South Kensington Museum in 1866–67. The first section of the exhibition opened in 1866 and included portraits from the reign of the Plantagenets through that of the Stuarts. The second section, which George Eliot attended, opened on 3 May 1867 and contained 866 pictures from the period 1688–1800, including more than 150 by Hogarth, Reynolds, and Gainsborough. See *The Illustrated London News,* 11 May 1867, p. 462.

49 See Haight, p. 221, and Laski, *George Eliot and Her World,* plate 56.

50 George Eliot apparently confused these portraits with those of Sir Richard Newdegate, 1st Bart., and his wife, Juliana Leigh, which hang in the same room. Sir Richard, not his nephew, was in fact "the renovator of the family splendour."

51 Anthony is described as an "Antinous in a pigtail" (2:155), and his verbal portrait is modeled upon classical sculpture in

marble: "Nothing could be more delicate than the blond complexion—its bloom set off by the powdered hair—than the veined overhanging eyelids, which gave an indolent expression to the hazel eyes; nothing more finely cut than the transparent nostril and the short upper lip. Perhaps the chin and lower jaw were too small for an irreproachable profile, but the defect was on the side of that delicacy and *finesse* which was the distinctive characteristic of the whole person, and which was carried out in the clear brown arch of the eyebrows, and the marble smoothness of the sloping forehead" (2:154). Later Anthony is compared to "an Olympian god" with an "exquisite outline and rounded fairness" (2:171), and to "a fine cameo in high relief" (2:172).

52 A gallery located over cloisters is a recurrent setting in George Eliot's country houses. It appears in "Mr Gilfil's Love-Story" (chap. 2), *Adam Bede* (chap. 22), and *Daniel Deronda* (chap. 16).

53 The self-possession of Lady Cheverel's portrait is shared by the portrait of her husband, Sir Anthony: "A very imposing personage was this Sir Anthony, standing with one arm akimbo, and one fine leg and foot advanced, evidently with a view to the gratification of his contemporaries and posterity" (2:165; see fig. 4).

54 Cf. William E. Buckler, "Memory, Morality, and the Tragic Vision in the Early Novels of George Eliot," in *The English Novel in the Nineteenth Century: Essays on the Literary Mediation of Human Values,* ed. George Goodin (Urbana: University of Illinois Press, 1972), p. 147: "In imagining herself a 'great lady,' she creates in the mirror an ironic image of a courtesan."

55 See Coveney, "Introduction," pp. 48–50.

56 On the change in English portraiture after 1830, see Piper, *The English Face,* p. 255.

Chapter 6

1 *Adam Bede* (10:162, 14:208, 51:319). R. Smirk's illustration of "The Marys at the Sepulchre" was engraved by W. Sharp and published on 16 July 1791 by Thomas Macklin of Fleet Street.

2 The cherub in question is probably "the little cherub riding astride a cloud" whom George Eliot noted in Correggio's

Madonna with Saint Sebastian at Dresden in 1858 (Cross, II, 48). Lucy's cherub-face returns to haunt Maggie later in the novel: "the picture grew and grew into more speaking definiteness under the avenging hand of remorse" (VII, 4:380).

3 Hagstrum, *The Sister Arts,* p. 8.

4 Trollope, *The Last Chronicle of Barset* (London: Smith, Elder, & Co. [1867]), II, 84:383.

5 Lewes, "Realism in Art," pp. 493–94.

6 See Alice R. Kaminsky, "George Eliot, George Henry Lewes, and the Novel," *Publications of the Modern Language Association,* 70 (1955), 1009–10, and Eliot, "Impressions of Theophrastus Such" (13:196–97).

7 See Bernard J. Paris, "George Eliot's Religion of Humanity," *Journal of English Literary History,* 29 (1962), 418–43; rpt. *George Eliot: A Collection of Critical Essays,* ed. George R. Creeger (Englewood Cliffs: Prentice-Hall, 1970), pp. 11–36.

8 On typological characterization in *Romola,* see Wiesenfarth, *George Eliot's Mythmaking,* p. 149. See also Howard Rodee's discussion of the angel motif in Victorian paintings of charity scenes, "Scenes of Rural and Urban Poverty in Victorian Painting and Their Development, 1850–1900," Diss. Columbia 1975, p. 53.

9 Ludwig Feuerbach, *The Essence of Christianity,* trans. Marian Evans (London: John Chapman, 1854), p. 74. Feuerbach wrote: "Den sinnlichen und gemüthlichen Menschen beherrscht und beseligt nur das Bild. Die bildliche, die gemüthliche, die sinnliche Vernunft ist die Phantasie"; see *Das Wesen Christentums* (Leipzig: Otto Wigand, 1841), p. 89.

10 See Erich Auerbach, *Mimesis: The Representation of Reality in Western Literature,* trans. Willard R. Trask (New York: Doubleday & Co., 1975), pp. 42–43, 64–66, 136–41, 170–76. On the gradual liberation of typological signification from its original biblical applications, see Paul J. Korshin, "The Development of Abstracted Typology in England, 1650–1820," in *Literary Uses of Typology from the Middle Ages to the Present,* ed. Earl Miner (Princeton: Princeton University Press, 1977), pp. 147–203. On the "tradition of secularized and immediate typology" in nineteenth-century English literature in general and George Eliot in particular, see John R. Reed, *Victorian Conventions,* pp. 5, 20–24, 38–39.

11 See Paulson, *Emblem and Expression,* pp. 35–47.
12 See ibid., pp. 202–03; Edgar Wind, "The Revolution of History Painting," *Journal of the Warburg and Courtauld Institutes,* 2 (1938), 116–27; Charles Mitchell, "Benjamin West's 'Death of General Wolfe' and the Popular History Piece," *Journal of the Warburg and Courtauld Institutes,* 7 (1944), 20–33; Robert Rosenblum, *Transformations in Late Eighteenth Century Art* (Princeton: Princeton University Press, 1967); and Theodore Ziolkowski, *Fictional Transfigurations of Jesus* (Princeton: Princeton University Press, 1972), p. 11.
13 See Fletcher, "Some Types and Emblems in Victorian Poetry," pp. 679–81, and Ziolkowski, *Fictional Transfigurations,* pp. 7, 49–54.
14 See George P. Landow, "William Holman Hunt's 'The Shadow of Death,'" *Bulletin of the John Rylands University Library of Manchester,* 55 (1972), 197–239; Herbert Sussman, "Hunt, Ruskin, and 'The Scapegoat,'" *Victorian Studies,* 12 (1969), 83–90; and John Dixon Hunt, "The Poetry of Distance: Tennyson's *Idylls of the King,"* in *Victorian Poetry,* ed. M. Bradbury and D. J. Palmer (London: Edward Arnold, 1972), p. 108. For uses of typology in Victorian poetry, see Landow, "Moses Striking the Rock: Typological Symbolism in Victorian Poetry," in Miner, ed., *Literary Uses of Typology,* pp. 315–44; and Jerome Bump, "Hopkins' Imagery and Medievalist Poetics," *Victorian Poetry,* 15 (1977), 99–119.
15 On *Take Your Son, Sir!,* see Helene E. Roberts, "Marriage, Redundancy, or Sin: The Painter's View of Women in the First Twenty-five Years of Victoria's Reign," in *Suffer and Be Still: Women in the Victorian Age,* ed. Martha Vicinus (Bloomington: Indiana University Press, 1972), p. 75.
16 The resemblance between *The Blind Girl* and the emblem "Superna Respicit" in Otto van Veen's *Amoris Divini Emblemata* (Antwerp: Martin Nut and Johannis Meurs, 1615), pp. 38–39, is so strong as to suggest a possible source for the painting. The emblem was available to Millais in the Royal Academy library, and is reproduced in Mario Praz, *Studies in Seventeenth Century Imagery,* 2d ed. (Rome: Edizioni di Storia e Letteratura, 1964), fig. 53.
17 Fletcher, "Some Types and Emblems in Victorian Poetry," p. 680.

18 See Landow, *The Aesthetic and Critical Theories of John Ruskin,* pp. 333–70; Hewison, *John Ruskin,* pp. 26–28; and Thomas M. Davis, "The Traditions of Puritan Typology," in *Typology and Early American Literature,* ed. Sacvan Bercovitch (Amherst: University of Massachusetts Press, 1972), pp. 11–45.

19 For a nonpictorial example of George Eliot's transformation of Christian motifs, see U. C. Knoepflmacher's analysis of the secularized communion scenes in *Adam Bede:* "George Eliot, Feuerbach, and the Question of Criticism," *Victorian Studies,* 7 (1964), 306–09; rpt. Creeger, ed., *George Eliot: A Collection of Critical Essays,* pp. 79–85.

20 For a succinct account of the most important similarities and differences between the two brotherhoods, see L. D. Ettlinger, "Nazarener und Praeraffaeliten," in *Festschrift für Gert von der Osten* (Cologne: Verlag M. du Mont Schauberg, 1970), pp. 205–20.

21 Theological distaste was a common feature of the mid-Victorian reaction to both the Nazarenes and the Pre-Raphaelites; see Francis Haskell, *Rediscoveries in Art: Some Aspects of Taste, Fashion, and Collecting in England and France* (Ithaca, N.Y.: Cornell University Press, 1976), pp. 49–57, and the review by E. H. Gombrich, *The Times Literary Supplement,* 27 February 1976, pp. 210–11.

22 See John Duncan Macmillan, "Holman Hunt's *Hireling Shepherd:* Some Reflections on a Victorian Pastoral," *The Art Bulletin,* 54 (1972), 187–97, and chapter 8, n. 46, below.

23 On the similarities between George Eliot's naturalism and that of the Pre-Raphaelites, see John Murdoch, "English Realism: George Eliot and the Pre-Raphaelites," *Journal of the Warburg and Courtauld Institutes,* 37 (1974), 313–29.

24 See Keith Andrews, *The Nazarenes: A Brotherhood of German Painters in Rome* (Oxford: Clarendon Press, 1964), pp. 29, 67.

25 Lewes, "Realism in Art," p. 497.

26 See William Vaughan, "The German Manner in English Art, 1815–1861," Diss. Courtauld Institute 1977, pp. 18, 25, 35.

27 See Andrews, *The Nazarenes,* p. 69.

28 This connection was first noticed in a review of Cross's *Life* by Joseph Jacobs, *George Eliot, Matthew Arnold, Browning, Newman: Essays and Reviews from the 'Athenaeum'* (London: D. Nutt, 1891), p. 72.

29 On display in Overbeck's studio, the Leweses saw cartoons of *The Savior Withdraws from His Followers on the Hill at Nazareth* (1857) and *Allegory of the Arts* (1860).

30 For 1829 as the year of Dorothea's honeymoon, see Jerome Beaty, "History by Indirection: The Era of Reform in *Middlemarch*," *Victorian Studies*, 1 (1957), 173–79.

31 See Andrews, *The Nazarenes*, p. 51.

32 See Heinrich von Wörndle, *Josef Führichs Werke* (Vienna: Verlag von Artaria, 1914), pp. 58, 83.

33 See Erwin Panofsky, *Problems in Titian, Mostly Iconographic* (New York: New York University Press, 1969), pp. 58–63.

34 "Recollections of Berlin," Beinecke Library.

35 She may also have remembered Otto van Veen's *Der Triumph der katholischen Kirche in sechs Bildern allegorisch dargestellt*, which she might have seen at Munich in 1858; see *Verzeichnis der Gemälde in der königlichen Pinakothek zu München* (Munich, 1858), pp. 197–200.

36 Vaughan, "The German Manner in English Art," p. 46.

37 In "Recollections of Berlin," Eliot mentions Kaulbach's frescoes in the Neues Museum of the *Deutsche Sage, The Destruction of the Tower of Babel, Homer and the Greeks*, and *The Destruction of Jerusalem;* his cartoons for the Neues Museum frescoes of the *Deutsche Sage*, the figures of *Architecture, Sculpture, History*, and *The Battle of the Huns;* and his illustrations of Shakespeare. She also saw Cornelius's *Christ in Limbo* (1843) and cartoons for the Royal Mausoleum. At Munich in 1858 she saw Kaulbach's frescoes in the Neue Pinakothek, his easel-painting of *The Destruction of Jerusalem*, his illustrations of *Reineke Fuchs*, and Cornelius's frescoes in the Glyptothek and Ludwigskirche. She disliked Cornelius's work, and once quoted a parody of it by the French critic, Edmond About; see "Belles Lettres," *Westminster Review*, 65 (1856), 308–09.

38 See Vaughan, "The German Manner in English Art," pp. 18, 70, 115.

39 G. H. Lewes, *The Life and Works of Goethe* (London: D. Nutt, 1855), II, 216–20.

40 For a different view of Naumann's achievement, see Barbara Hardy, *"Middlemarch:* Public and Private Worlds," *English*, 25 (1976), 22.

41 "Recollections of Berlin." George Eliot read (Cross, II, 21)

a warmer appreciation of Kaulbach's symbolism by Anna Mary Howitt, *An Art-Student in Munich* (London: Longman, Brown, Green, and Longmans, 1853), I, 20–35. In 1867, G. H. Lewes contributed an introduction to an English edition of *Female Characters of Goethe, from the Original Drawings of William Kaulbach,* first published in Germany in 1859.

42 See *Laokoön,* sec. xviii. The engravings of "mystic groups where far-off ages made one moment" in Mrs. Meyrick's front parlor in *Daniel Deronda* (20:313) are probably reproductions of modern German history paintings such as Kaulbach's.

43 Richard Ellmann, *Golden Codgers: Biographical Speculations* (New York: Oxford University Press, 1973), p. 33, and A. E. S. Viner, *George Eliot* (Edinburgh: Oliver and Boyd, 1971), p. 86.

44 See Eliot's review of R. W. Mackay's *The Progress of the Intellect* (*Essays,* p. 36), and W. J. Harvey, "The Intellectual Background of the Novel: Casaubon and Lydgate," in Hardy, ed., *Middlemarch: Critical Approaches to the Novel,* pp. 33–34. Harvey notes that although Casaubon's mythography is not strictly speaking an allegorical method, its basic affinities are nevertheless with "the Renaissance approach . . . [which] reconciles pagan fable to Christianity by allegory." See also Wiesenfarth, *George Eliot's Mythmaking,* pp. 205–06.

45 Vaughan, "The German Manner in English Art," p. 48.

46 "Recollections of Berlin." The painting in question is *The Marriage of the Virgin,* then in Graf Raczinsky's collection and now in the Museum Narodowe, Poznań, Poland. For a reproduction, see my "George Eliot, Naumann, and the Nazarenes," *Victorian Studies,* 18 (1974), 154.

47 Lewes, *Life and Works of Goethe,* II, 216.

48 Ibid., p. 219.

49 See Andrews, *The Nazarenes,* pp. 75–76. Overbeck and Cornelius were personally acquainted with Alexis-Francois Rio, whose *De la poésie chrétienne* (1836) inspired pioneering British studies in iconography such as Lord Lindsay's *Sketches in the History of Christian Art* (1847) and Mrs. Anna Jameson's *The Poetry of Sacred and Legendary Art* (1848), *Legends of the Monastic Orders* (1850), and *Legends of the Madonna* (1852). Didron's *Iconographie chrétienne* (1843) was translated into English in 1851, and Louisa Twining published *Symbols and Emblems of Early and Medieval Christian Art* in 1852. A good

summary of the literature available to English readers by 1848 may be found in Charles Lock Eastlake, *Contributions to the Literature of the Fine Arts,* 1st ser. (London: John Murray, 1848), pp. 18–19. George Eliot owned a copy of Rio's *De la poésie chrétienne;* see Baker, *The George Eliot-George Henry Lewes Library,* #1831.

50 Lewes, *Life and Works of Goethe,* II, 220.

51 Eliot, "Church History of the Nineteenth Century," *The Leader,* 7 (1856), 331. On Gerard Manley Hopkins's interest in Nazarene medievalism, see Bump, "Hopkins, Pater, and Medievalism," p. 12.

52 Hazlitt was first identified as George Eliot's source by Mrs. E. E. Duncan-Jones, "Hazlitt's Mistake," *The Times Literary Supplement,* 27 January 1966, p. 68.

53 Hazlitt, *Notes of a Journey through France and Italy* (London: Hunt and Clarke, 1826), p. 294.

54 Anna B. Jameson, *Legends of the Madonna as Represented in the Fine Arts,* 2d ed. (London: Longmans, Green, & Co., 1857), pp. 326, 329. On the possible influence of Mrs. Jameson's *Sacred and Legendary Art* upon *Middlemarch,* see Gillian Beer, "Myth and the Single Consciousness: *Middlemarch* and *The Lifted Veil,*" in *This Particular Web,* ed. Ian Adam (Toronto: University of Toronto Press, 1975), pp. 107–09.

55 Naumann's long hair marks him a Nazarene. The Brothers of St. Luke came to be called "Nazarenes" by witty detractors alluding to the Old Testament priests (Nazarites) who refrained from cutting their hair as a sign of their dedication to God; see Andrews, *The Nazarenes,* p. 29. George Eliot noted Overbeck's "long grey hair" at their meeting in 1860 (Cross, II, 158).

56 See *Modern Painters,* vol. III, pt. IV, chap. iii, paras. 7, 11, 14; III, IV, iv, 24; III, IV, vi, 9; III, IV, xvi, 10, in *Works,* V, 50, 54, 57, 89–90, 109, 323. George Eliot quoted the third of these passages in her review of Ruskin, "Art and Belles Lettres," *Westminster Review,* 65 (1856), 628. See also *The Stones of Venice,* vol. III, chap. iii, para. 60n., in *Works,* XI, 179, where Ruskin connects "the huge German cartoon" with human vanity.

57 Compare Naumann's description of Dorothea with Walter Pater's description of Leonardo's *Mona Lisa;* in both, the lady's beauty is a synthesis of the major phases of western civilization,

an incarnation of the collective wisdom and experience of her kind. Pater's essay on Leonardo was first published in 1869; in 1870 George Eliot dined at Oxford with "Mr. Pater, writer of articles on Leonardo da Vinci, Morris, etc." (*Letters*, V, 100).

58   As Mario Praz points out (*The Hero in Eclipse*, p. 358), the comparison of Dorothea with "a picture of Santa Barbara looking out from her tower into the clear air" (10:131) probably refers to Palma Vecchio's Santa Barbara altarpiece in the Church of Santa Maria Formosa at Venice, which George Eliot noticed in 1860 (Cross, II, 205).

59   The "portrait of Locke" is most likely to be Kneller's of 1698, of which at least fourteen different engravings exist; see Freeman O'Donoghue, *Catalogue of Engraved British Portraits Preserved in the Department of Prints and Drawings in the British Museum* (London: Trustees of the British Museum, 1912), III, 79–81. Dorothea might have seen the version by R. Graves (no. 13 in O'Donoghue) which appeared as the frontispiece to Locke's *An Essay Concerning Human Understanding* (London: J. F. Dove, 1828). The Leweses owned a copy of this edition; see Baker, *The George Eliot-George Henry Lewes Library*, #1311.

60   W. J. Harvey, *The Art of George Eliot* (London: Chatto and Windus, 1969), pp. 193–95. For a different interpretation of the mythological allusions in chapter 19 of *Middlemarch*, see Wiesenfarth, *George Eliot's Mythmaking*, pp. 194–97.

61   In *Yeast: A Problem* (London: John W. Parker, 1851), p. 17, Charles Kingsley describes Argemone Lavington in terms of the same picture: "With her perfect masque, and queenly figure, and earnest upward gaze, she might have been the very model from which Raphael conceived his glorious St. Catherine—the ideal of the highest womanly genius, softened into self-forgetfulness by girlish devotion." This characterization is discussed by John R. Reed, *Victorian Conventions*, p. 38.

62   It is not altogether clear which statue Eliot had in mind when she wrote: "A woman's arm touched the soul of a great sculptor two thousand years ago, so that he wrought an image of it for the Parthenon which moves us still as it clasps lovingly the time-worn marble of a headless trunk. Maggie's was such an arm as that. . ." (VI, 10:274–75). The likeliest candidate among the Elgin Marbles is the left arm of the leftmost figure in the

Demeter-and-Persephone group; see *The Mill on the Floss,* ed. Gordon S. Haight (Boston: Houghton Mifflin, 1961), p. 387n. But Eliot may have been thinking instead of another arm which she had seen in the Griechischer Saal of the Neues Museum at Berlin in 1854–55 and described in "Recollections of Berlin" as follows: "The backs of a male and female figure, the latter with her lovely arm round the neck of her companion—these were our favourites, and made everything else seem mean or lifeless in comparison." Eliot seems wrongly to have thought that this "male and female figure" was one of the Parthenon sculptures, copies of which stood in the same room. I have not been able to identify the statue she was recalling.

63 *Ranthorpe,* p. 12.

64 On a smaller scale, Mirah is visualized as "an onyx cameo" (17:281), "a perfect cameo" (32:144). As in the case of Mirah's suicidal despair, George Eliot often represents states of extreme emotional stress through an imagery of sculpture. See, for example, *Adam Bede,* (27:10, 27:19, 43:223).

65 See Constance Marie Fulmer, "Contrasting Pairs of Heroines in George Eliot's Fiction," *Studies in the Novel,* 6 (1974), 288–94.

66 See Herbert Rudolph, "'Vanitas': Die Bedeutung mittelalter-licher und humanistischer Bildinhalt in der niederlandischer Malerei des 17. Jahrhunderts," in *Festschrift Wilhelm Pinder* (Leipzig: E. U. Seemann, 1938), pp. 405–33; Ingvar Bergstrom, *Dutch Still-Life Painting in the Seventeenth Century,* trans. Christina Hedström and Gerald Taylor (London: Faber and Faber, 1950), pp. 154–90; F.-C. Legrand, *Les peintres fla-mandes de genre au XVIIe siècle* (Brussels: Editions Meddens, 1963), pp. 6, 10, 241–42; Jakob Rosenberg, Seymour Slive, and E. H. Ter Kuile, *Dutch Art and Architecture: 1600–1800* (Harmondsworth: Penguin Books, 1966), pp. 101–02, 146, 194–95; Seymour Slive, "Realism and Symbolism in Seventeenth-Century Painting," *Daedalus,* 91 (1962), 469–500; and Paulson, *Emblem and Expression,* p. 95.

67 David Leon Higdon, "The Iconographic Backgrounds of *Adam Bede,* Chapter 15," *Nineteenth-Century Fiction,* 27 (1972), 155–70. Only one clear connection between a specific emblem and a specific passage in George Eliot has been demonstrated to date. Gordon S. Haight has linked Quarles's emblem I, 12 with the image of "the world as an udder" in *Middlemarch* (21:323);

see *Middlemarch,* ed. Gordon S. Haight (Boston: Houghton Mifflin, 1956), p. 156n. Professor Haight has also pointed out in correspondence that the same emblem informs Book 1, lines 104–05 of *The Spanish Gypsy.*

68 R. T. Jones, *George Eliot* (Cambridge: Cambridge University Press, 1970), p. 17.

69 See *Wilhelm von Schadow 1788–1862: Gedächtnis-Ausstellung aus Anlass seines 100. Todesjahres* (Düsseldorf: Kunstmuseum der Stadt Düsseldorf, 1962), pp. 29, 36. Die deutsche allgemeine und historische Kunst-Ausstellung opened in July (see *Morgenblatt für gebildete Leser,* 8 August 1858, p. 760). George Eliot had left Munich in May. She knew Schadow from her visit to Berlin in 1854 (Cross, I, 285).

70 A comparable Victorian painting, though done too late to have influenced *Adam Bede,* is Arthur D. Lemon's *Pure Innocence and Pure in No Sense* (ca. 1880); see Rodee, "Scenes of Rural and Urban Poverty," p. 141 and illus. 52.

71 See Hagstrum, *The Sister Arts,* p. 144; Edgar Wind, "Studies in Allegorical Portraiture," *Journal of the Warburg and Courtauld Institutes,* 1 (1937–38), 138–62; and Praz, *Mnemosyne,* p. 7. Praz writes: "the custom dated from the times of Alexandria and Imperial Rome, when sovereigns were represented with attributes of divinity, and lasted until the time of Canova, who represented Ferdinand IV of Naples . . . in the garb of Minerva, the goddess of wisdom and culture."

72 See Gustav Glück, ed., *Van Dyck: Des Meisters Gemälde in 571 Abbildungen,* 2d ed. (Stuttgart and Berlin: Klassiker der Kunst, 1931), pp. 399, 455, 489; and David Piper, *The English Face,* p. 97.

73 Hagstrum, *The Sister Arts,* p. 146.

74 See Ellis K. Waterhouse, *Reynolds* (London: Kegan Paul, Trench, Trübner, 1941), and Edgar Wind, "Borrowed Attitudes in Reynolds and Hogarth," *Journal of the Warburg and Courtauld Institutes,* 2 (1938–39), 182–85. A late version of the Diana motif is Raimundo de Madrazo's *The Marquise d'Hervey as Diana* (1888); see Aleksa Celebonović, *The Heyday of Salon Painting: Masterpieces of Bourgeois Realism* (London: Thames and Hudson, 1974), p. 29.

75 Chauncey Brewster Tinker, *Painter and Poet: Studies in the Literary Relations of English Painting* (Cambridge, Mass.:

Harvard University Press, 1939), p. 14. That George Eliot was familiar with the term is shown by the fact that Latimer, the narrator of "The Lifted Veil," has been "the model of a dying minstrel in a fancy-picture" (1:295).

76 See A. Dwight Culler, "Monodrama and the Dramatic Monologue," *Publications of the Modern Language Association,* 90 (1975), 373–75; Kirsten Gram Holmström, *Monodrama, Attitudes, Tableaux Vivants: Studies on Some Trends of Theatrical Fashion, 1770–1815* (Stockholm: Almquist and Wiksell, 1967), pp. 110–40; and Ziolkowski, *Disenchanted Images,* pp. 34–35. That George Eliot knew the scene in *Die Wahlverwandtschaften* is clear from an entry in her Berlin journal of 1854–55: "I was pleased also to recognize among the pictures the one by Jan Steen, which Goethe describes in the 'Wahlverwandtschaften' as the model of a *tableau vivant,* presented by Luciane and her friends. It is the daughter being reproved by her father, while the mother is emptying the wineglass" (Cross, I, 299). The picture is actually by Terborch, not Steen, and Goethe refers specifically to "Wille's admirable engraving" (pt. 2, chap. 5).

77 Edgar Wind, "Humanitätsidee und heroisiertes Porträt in der englischen Kultur des 18. Jahrhunderts," in *England und die Antike: Vorträge der Bibliothek Warburg 1930–31,* ed. Fritz Saxl (Leipzig and Berlin: B. G. Teubner, 1932), pp. 222–24 and Tafel XXIX. Another excellent example of the motif, not cited by Wind, is Reynold's *Mrs. Abington as the Comic Muse* (1764–69), now at Waddesdon Manor, Buckinghamshire. This was shown at the National Portrait Exhibition of 1867, which George Eliot attended (*Letters,* IV, 363–64). See Ellis K. Waterhouse, *The James A. DeRothschild Collection at Waddesdon Manor: Paintings* (London: The National Trust for Places of Historic Interest or Natural Beauty, 1967), pp. 67–69.

78 Wind, "Humanitätsidee," pp. 222, 224. Wind reproduces a drawing of Mrs. Siddons as Hermione from the sketchbook of a young lady, Mary Hamilton, who depicted the attitudes and costumes of Mrs. Siddons in a variety of roles, with a view to recreating them in private entertainments.

79 *Modern Painters,* vol. III, pt. IV, chap. v, para. 7, in *Works,* V, 96.

80 *Mrs. Sheridan as Saint Cecilia* was shown at the National Portrait

Exhibition of 1867; see Waterhouse, *The James A. DeRothschild Collection,* pp. 86–89.

81 Hagstrum, *The Sister Arts,* pp. 204–06, cites this passage after listing the representations of Saint Cecilia best known in the seventeenth century. Fancy portraits were also satirized by Oliver Goldsmith in chapter 16 of *The Vicar of Wakefield.*

82 *Modern Painters,* vol. III, pt. IV, chap. v, para. 5 in *Works,* V, 93–94. For a spirited defense of Reynolds's fancy portraits, see Robert E. Moore, "Reynolds and the Art of Characterization," in *Studies in Criticism and Aesthetics, 1660–1800,* ed. Howard Anderson and John S. Shea (Minneapolis: University of Minnesota Press, 1967), pp. 336–37.

83 See Davis, "Pictorialism in George Eliot's Art," pp. 210–37.

84 See Neil MacLaren, *The Dutch School* (London: Publications Department of the National Gallery, 1960), pp. 316–17. The painting is now called *Bust of a Bearded Man in a Cap.* As MacLaren notes, "the man here may possibly be Jewish and is bearded; there is no other reason for supposing him a rabbi." Like many of Rembrandt's so-called "Jewish" subjects, this painting first received the appellation in the nineteenth century. George Eliot may also have known the Rembrandt "Rabbi" in the Queen's collection at Hampton Court.

85 Harold Fisch, *"Daniel Deronda,* or *Gwendolen Harleth?" Nineteenth-Century Fiction,* 19 (1965), 354–55.

86 Cf. Ruskin, *The Seven Lamps of Architecture,* VI, 13, in *Works,* VIII, 237–38: "In the case of Rembrandt there is often an essential sublimity in invention and expression besides, and always a high degree of it in the light and shade itself; but it is, for the most part, parasitical or engrafted sublimity as regards the subject of the painting, and, just so far, picturesque."

87 Disraeli's hero in *Lothair* (1870) makes a similar point when discussing the influence of "Semitism" upon "Aryan art" (chap. 29).

88 For evidence that Klesmer is Jewish, see Gordon S. Haight, "George Eliot's Klesmer," in *Imagined Worlds: Essays on Some English Novels and Novelists in Honour of John Butt,* ed. Maynard Mack and Ian Gregor (London: Methuen, 1968), pp. 205–14; and Levenson, "The Use of Music in *Daniel Deronda."*

89 Hans's projected series belongs to a Haydonesque tradition of neoclassical history-painting for which George Eliot had little

sympathy. Fortunately, Hans himself does not take it seriously. What is valid about the series is the idealizing portraiture of Mirah as Berenice. George Eliot wholly approves Hans's remark that "every painter worth remembering has painted the face he admired most, as often as he could. . . . He puts what he adores into some sacred, heroic form. If a man could paint the woman he loves a thousand times as the *Stella Maris* to put courage into the sailors on board a thousand ships, so much the more honour to her" (37:280).

90 *Modern Painters,* vol. V, pt. IX, chap. iii, paras. 30–31, in *Works,* VII, 296–98.

91 Ibid., vol. II, pt. III, sec. I, chap. xiv, para. 19, in *Works,* IV, 193. See also "Sir Joshua and Holbein," *Works,* XIX, 5–12.

92 *Modern Painters,* vol. V, pt. IX, chap. iii, para. 12, in *Works,* VII, 286.

93 *The Stones of Venice,* vol. II, chap. iii, para. 37, and vol. II, chap. v, para. 32, in *Works,* X, 64, 174. See also John Gage *Colour in Turner: Poetry and Truth* (London: Studio Vista, 1969), p. 91.

94 Structurally, the scene is a conversation piece (see chap. 7, below). It may recall Simeon Solomon's "Illustrations of Jewish Customs," *The Leisure Hour,* vol. 15 (1866).

95 Hagstrum, *The Sister Arts,* p. 164.

96 Lewes, "Realism in Art," p. 499. Earlier in the novel the Meyrick girls create their own portrait of "Deronda as an ideal" when they set about "to paint him as Prince Camaralzaman," hero of one of the *Arabian Nights* (16:275).

97 Cross, II, 96 and "Italy 1864," Beinecke Library, entry for 6 May.

98 See Laski, *George Eliot and Her World,* p. 84.

99 Albert Cirillo, "Salvation in *Daniel Deronda:* The Fortunate Overthrow of Gwendolen Harleth," in *Literary Monographs,* ed. Eric Rothstein and Thomas K. Dunseath, vol. 1 (Madison: University of Wisconsin Press, 1970), p. 204.

100 Cf. Shaffer, *'Kubla Khan' and the Fall of Jerusalem,* p. 250: "the main characters [in *Daniel Deronda*] are . . . consciously modelled on the historical and legendary figures of their religious literature, the Old Testament prophets, the Christian saints and martyrs, and not least Jesus himself."

101 Lewes, "Realism in Art," p. 494.

102 Lewes, "The Principles of Success in Literature," p. 187.

103   Henry James, [review of Cross's *Life*], *Atlantic Monthly,* 55
       (May 1885); rpt. Carroll, ed., *George Eliot: The Critical Her-
       itage,* p. 498.
104   See Ian Milner, *The Structure of Values in George Eliot* (Prague:
       Universita Karlova, 1968), p. 121.

Chapter 7

1   George Scharf, *A Handbook to the Gallery of British Paintings
     in the Art Treasures Exhibition* (London: Bradbury and Evans,
     1857), p. 95.
2   Oliver Millar, *Dutch Pictures from the Royal Collection* (Lon-
     don: Lund Humphries, 1971), pp. 6–36.
3   Stang, *The Theory of the Novel in England,* p. 149, refers to
     Arsène Houssaye, *Histoire de la peinture flamande et hol-
     landaise* (1846; 2d ed., Paris: Jules Hetzel, 1866). Houssaye
     speaks (p. 179) of Terborch's "gout tout hollandais, empreint
     de poésie réaliste," and argues that "l'oeuvre de Gérard de Ter-
     burg est le roman intime de la Hollande, comme l'oeuvre de
     Gérard Dow en est le roman familière." See also Peter Demetz,
     "Defences of Dutch Painting and the Theory of Realism,"
     Comparative Literature, 15 (1963), 97–115.
4   Charles Sumner Olcott, *George Eliot: Scenes and People in Her
     Novels, Illustrated from Photographs* (New York: Thomas Y.
     Crowell, 1910) and Laski, *George Eliot and Her World.*
5   Walter Pater, "Sebastian van Storck," *Imaginary Portraits,* in
     The Works of Walter Pater, Library ed., 10 vols. (London:
     Macmillan, 1910), p. 88.
6   See above, pp. 10–11. On the inadequacies of "Biedermeier" as
     a critical term, see Alex Preminger, ed., *The Princeton Encyclo-
     pedia of Poetry and Poetics* (Princeton: Princeton University
     Press, 1965), p. 77; and Ulrich Finke, *German Painting from
     Romanticism to Expressionism* (London: Thames and Hudson,
     1974), p. 68.
7   Mansell, "Ruskin and George Eliot's 'Realism.'"
8   William Bell Scott, *Gems of Modern German Art* (London:
     George Routledge, 1873), p. 81. On the varieties of painting to
     which the term *genre* could refer in the eighteenth century, see
     Wolfgang Stechow and Christopher Comer, "The History of the

Term Genre," *Bulletin of the Allen Memorial Art Museum, Oberlin College,* 33 (1975–76), 89–94

9 See Legrand, *Les peintres flamandes de genre;* H. Gerson and E. H. Ter Kuile, *Art and Architecture in Belgium 1600 to 1800* (Harmondsworth: Penguin Books, 1960); and Rosenberg, et al., *Dutch Art and Architecture.*

10 James, *The Painter's Eye,* p. 77.

11 See A. Staring, *De Hollanders Thuis: Gezelschapstukken uit drie eeuwen* (The Hague: Martinus Nijhoff, 1956).

12 See Gerson and Ter Kuile, *Art and Architecture in Belgium,* pp. 172–73, and Paulson, *Emblem and Expression,* pp. 123–25.

13 Davis, "Pictorialism in George Eliot's Art," p. 71; and Richards, "The Use of the Visual Arts in the Nineteenth-Century Novel," p. 152. On Dou's picture, see W. Martin, *Gerard Dou: Des Meisters Gemälde in 247 Abbildungen* (Stuttgart: Deutsche Verlags-Anstalt, 1913), p. 100.

14 The correspondence is far less exact in the case of Nicolaes Maes's *Grace before Meat* in the Louvre, the painting which Mario Praz has nominated as the source of Eliot's description (*The Hero in Eclipse,* p. 385 and pl. 37). Dou's *Alte Frau am Fenster, Blumen begiessend* in the Kunsthistorisches Museum at Vienna (Martin, *Gerard Dou,* p. 106) is probably the original of George Eliot's "old woman bending over her flower-pot" in chapter 17 of *Adam Bede.* The painting was acquired in 1811, and Eliot might have seen it in 1858; see *Katalog der Gemäldegalerie: Holländische Meister des 15., 16., und 17. Jahrhunderts* (Vienna: Kunsthistorisches Museum, 1972), p. 26. The other Dutch pictures evoked in chapter 17 are described too generically to be identifiable, but some of them have strong affinities with Adriaen van Ostade's work at Munich.

15 See Davis, "Pictorialism in George Eliot's Art," pp. 28–43, and John Goode, "Adam Bede," p. 22. For an excellent analysis of the prose style of the pictorialized passages in *Adam Bede,* see Ian Adam, "The Structure of Realisms in *Adam Bede,*" *Nineteenth-Century Fiction,* 30 (1975), 127–49.

16 *Middlemarch,* ed. Gordon S. Haight (Boston: Houghton Mifflin, 1956), p. 178.

17 Paulson, *Emblem and Expression,* p. 121.

18 See Mario Praz, *Conversation Pieces: A Survey of the Informal Group Portrait in Europe and America* (London: Methuen,

1971). See also G. C. Williamson, *English Conversation Pieces of the Eighteenth and Early Nineteenth Centuries* (London: B. T. Batsford, 1931); Sacheverell Sitwell, *Conversation Pieces: A Survey of English Domestic Portraits and Their Painters* (London: B. T. Batsford, 1936); Ralph Edwards, *Early Conversation Pictures from the Middle Ages to about 1730: A Study in Origins* (London: Country Life, 1954); and Edwards, "Georgian Conversation Pictures," *Apollo,* 105 (1977), 252–61.

19 Paulson, *Emblem and Expression,* pp. 154–55.

20 Some of the same connotations are present in a series of three portraits of Mary Garth in orchard or garden settings (40:203, 52:367, 86:448–49). These portraits punctuate her relations with Mr. Farebrother and Fred Vincy.

21 Paulson, *Emblem and Expression,* pp. 121–22.

22 On the importance of Wilkie to the genre tradition, see Odette Aubrat, *La peinture de genre en Angleterre de la mort de Hogarth (1764) au Préraphaélisme (1850)* (Paris: Maison du livre francais, 1935), and Lord Ronald Charles Sutherland Gower, *Sir David Wilkie* (London: George Bell, 1902).

23 "Recollections of Berlin," Beinecke Library. On Hasenclever, see Wolfgang Hütt, *Die Düsseldorfer Malerschule 1819–1869* (Leipzig: E. A. Seemann, 1964), pp. 59–65.

24 Jones, *George Eliot,* p. 6.

25 On *Work,* see Ford Madox Hueffer, *Ford Madox Brown: A Record of His Life and Work* (London: Longmans and Co., 1896), pp. 189–95, and Mary Bennett, *Ford Madox Brown 1821–1893* (Liverpool: Walker Art Gallery, 1964), pp. 18–20. On *Newcastle Quay in 1861,* see Quentin Bell, *Victorian Artists* (London: Routledge and Kegan Paul, 1967), p. 38. On *From under the Sea,* see Rodee, "Scenes of Rural and Urban Poverty," 22–24.

26 Scharf, *A Handbook to the Gallery of British Paintings,* p. 58. See also Edgar Wind, "The Revolution of History Painting," *Journal of the Warburg and Courtauld Institutes,* 2 (1938), 116–27.

27 Scharf, *A Handbook to the Gallery of British Paintings,* p. 58.

28 On the Düsseldorf school, see Finke, *German Painting,* pp. 100–01, and Hütt, *Die Düsseldorfer Malerschule.* On George Eliot's interest in the school, see Haight, p. 151, and "Recollections of Berlin."

29 Robert Rosenblum, *Modern Painting and the Northern Romantic Tradition: Friedrich to Rothko* (New York: Harper & Row, 1975), pp. 26–27, 57.

30 See Michael Fried, "Absorption: A Master Theme in Eighteenth-Century Painting and Criticism," *Eighteenth-Century Studies*, 9 (1975–76), 139–77.

31 See Ronald Paulson, *Hogarth: His Life, Art, and Times*, 2 vols. (New Haven: Yale University Press, 1971).

32 See Raymond Lister, *Victorian Narrative Paintings* (London: Museum Press, 1966), and anon., "Critic and Connoisseur," *The Times Literary Supplement*, 7 January 1972, p. 13.

33 Conrad, *The Victorian Treasure-House*, pp. 25, 46.

34 Sitwell, *Conversation Pieces*, p. 86.

35 Praz, *Conversation Pieces*, p. 172; Paulson, *Emblem and Expression*, p. 124.

36 Conrad, *The Victorian Treasure-House*, p. 105.

Chapter 8

1 On Scott, see Murdoch, "Scott, Pictures, and Painters," and Allentuck, "Scott and the Picturesque." On Cooper, see Ringe, *The Pictorial Mode*, and Blake Nevius, *Cooper's Landscapes: An Essay on the Picturesque Vision* (Berkeley: University of California Press, 1976).

2 Lewes, "The Novels of Jane Austen," p. 109.

3 See Christopher Hussey, *The Picturesque: Studies in a Point of View* (1927; rpt. London: Archon Books, 1967); Walter J. Hipple, Jr., *The Beautiful, the Sublime, and the Picturesque in Eighteenth-Century British Aesthetic Theory* (Carbondale: Southern Illinois University Press, 1957); and Luke Herrmann, *British Landscape Painting of the Eighteenth Century* (London: Faber and Faber, 1973), chapter 4.

4 William D. Tempelman, *The Life and Work of William Gilpin (1724–1804): Master of the Picturesque and Vicar of Boldre* (Urbana: University of Illinois Press, 1939), p. 82. See also C. P. Barbier, *William Gilpin: His Drawings, Teaching, and Theory of the Picturesque* (Oxford: Clarendon Press, 1963).

5 Hussey, *The Picturesque*, p. 2. Hussey is wrong, however, when he says that "it was only the second-rate novelists who visualized through a picture frame after Mrs. Radcliffe" (p. 237).

6 On Gilpin's drawings, see Barbier, *William Gilpin*, p. 107. George Eliot's distaste for Claudian techniques may account for her inability to admire Karl Rottmann's Greek landscapes, which she saw at Munich in 1858 (Cross, II, 33).

7 On the difference between the picturesque and the local, see John Barrell, *The Idea of Landscape and the Sense of Place 1730-1840: An Approach to the Poetry of John Clare* (Cambridge: Cambridge University Press, 1972).

8 John Steegman, *The Artist and the Country House* (London: Country Life, 1949).

9 Ibid., p. 15.

10 John Preston Neale, *Views of the Seats of Noblemen and Gentlemen in England, Wales, Scotland, and Ireland*, 6 vols. (London: 1818-23); and John Dixon Hunt and Peter Willis, *The Genius of the Place: The English Landscape Garden, 1620-1820* (London: Paul Elek, 1975), p. 1. See also F. O. Morris, *A Series of Picturesque Views of Seats of the Noblemen and Gentlemen of Great Britain and Ireland*, 6 vols. (London: William MacKenzie, 1864?-80).

11 Herrmann, *British Landscape Painting*, p. 105. See also Ellis Waterhouse, *Painting in Britain: 1530-1790* (London: Penguin, 1953), pp. 123, 125; *Philip Mercier 1689-1760: An Exhibition of Paintings and Drawings* (York: City Art Gallery, and London: Iveagh Bequest, Kenwood House, 1969), pp. 7, 15-16; Praz, *Conversation Pieces*, p. 125; and Paulson, *Emblem and Expression*, pp. 104, 123-25. Through Watteau's Flemish connections, this kind of group portrait can be traced back to seventeenth-century Flemish aristocratic conversation pieces by such painters as Gonzales Coques; see Staring, *De Hollanders Thuis*, p. 64.

12 See *Adam Bede* (6:102-03, 22:383), *Felix Holt* (1:15-16), and *Daniel Deronda* (3:27, 10:144-45, 30:92, 31:119-20, 35:215-17).

13 Laski, *George Eliot and Her World*, p. 57.

14 For another example of Watteau's influence upon the English conversation piece, see M. J. H. Livesridge, "An Elusive Minor Master: J. F. Nollekens and the Conversation Piece," *Apollo*, 15 (1972), 34-41. On Watteau's continued popularity in England throughout the nineteenth century, see Haskell, *Rediscoveries*, pp. 51, 57. For a suggestion that George Eliot's

description of Cheverel Manor influenced Henry James's description of Matcham in *The Wings of the Dove,* which also mentions Watteau, see Richard Gill, *Happy Rural Seat: The English Country House and the Literary Imagination* (New Haven: Yale University Press, 1972), p. 251.

15 *Philip Mercier 1689–1760,* pp. 15–16.

16 Joseph Nash, *The Mansions of England in the Olden Time,* 4 vols. (1839–49; rpt. London: Offices of 'The Studio,' 1906). On the importance of Nash's *Mansions* to Henry James, see Winner, *Henry James and the Visual Arts,* p. 1.

17 G. H. Lewes, *Sea-Side Studies at Ilfracombe, Tenby, the Scilly Isles, and Jersey* (Edinburgh: William Blackwood and Sons, 1858), pp. 30–31.

18 See also "Ferny Combes," *The Leader,* 7 (1856), 787. On Charles Kingsley and the cult of outdoor naturalism, see the novel *Two Years Ago* (1857) and W. H. Brock, "Glaucus: Kingsley and the Seaside Naturalists," *Cerve,* vol. 3 (1976).

19 *British Quarterly Review,* 16 (1852), 205.

20 G. H. Lewes, "Imaginative Artists," *The Leader,* 7 (1856), 545–46. This article is a review of volume IV of *Modern Painters.*

21 Praz, *Mnemosyne,* p. 172.

22 Most of the hedgerows in the midlands were planted between 1750 and 1780 as a result of the Parliamentary Enclosure Acts; see W. G. Hoskins, *The Making of the English Landscape* (1955; rpt. London: Hodder and Stoughton, 1977), pp. 195–200.

23 Hamerton, *Thoughts about Art,* II, 254.

24 On the Wordsworthian elements in *Modern Painters,* see John D. Rosenberg, *The Darkening Glass: A Portrait of Ruskin's Genius* (New York: Columbia University Press, 1961), pp. 5–7, 14–16, 22–24, 27, 33–34; and Hewison, *John Ruskin,* pp. 16–19, 28.

25 See Thomas Pinney, "George Eliot's Reading of Wordsworth: The Record," *Victorian Newsletter,* 24 (Fall 1963), 20–22.

26 "Impressions of Theophrastus Such" (2:36–37). On George Eliot's temperamental affinities with Wordsworth, see Christopher Salvesen, *The Landscape of Memory: A Study of Wordsworth's Poetry* (London: Edward Arnold, 1965), pp. 19–22.

27 J. R. Watson, *Picturesque Landscape and English Romantic Poetry* (London: Hutchinson, 1970), p. 22. On Wordsworth and the picturesque, see also Salvesen, *The Landscape of*

Memory; Patricia M. Ball, *The Science of Aspects* (London: The Athlone Press, 1971), pp. 5–47; Russell Noyes, *Wordsworth and the Art of Landscape* (Bloomington: Indiana University Press, 1968); John R. Nabholtz, "Wordsworth's *Guide to the Lakes* and the Picturesque Tradition," *Modern Philology,* 61 (1964), 288–97; and W. P. Ker, *On Modern Literature: Lectures and Addresses* (Oxford: Clarendon Press, 1955), pp. 102–03.

28 Wordsworth, *The Prelude,* ed. Ernest de Selincourt and Helen Darbishire, 2d ed. (Oxford: Clarendon Press, 1959), Bk. 2, ll. 336–37 (1805) or 317–18 (1850), pp. 60–61. Wordsworth's objections to the picturesque are expressed most explicitly in *The Prelude,* Bk. XI, ll. 152–64 (1805) or Bk. XII, ll. 111–21 (1850), pp. 438–39.

29 Salvesen, *The Landscape of Memory,* p. 69. The absence of pictorial qualities in Wordsworth's best poetry undermines most critical attempts to compare it with painting; see, for example, Karl Kroeber, *Romantic Landscape Vision: Constable and Wordsworth* (Madison: University of Wisconsin Press, 1975), and the critical review by E. D. H. Johnson in *Victorian Studies,* 19 (1976), 432–33.

30 On Dorothy Wordsworth's descriptive prose, see John R. Nabholtz, "Dorothy Wordsworth and the Picturesque," *Studies in Romanticism,* 3 (1964), 118–28.

31 Stump, *Movement and Vision,* pp. 70–71.

32 On Constable and Wordsworth, see Kroeber *Romantic Landscape Vision;* Kenneth Clark, *English Romantic Poets and Landscape Painting* (London, 1945); Martha Hale Shackford, *Wordsworth's Interest in Painters and Pictures* (Wellesley, Mass., 1945); R. T. Storch, "Wordsworth and Constable," *Studies in Romanticism,* 5 (1966), 121–38; and J. R. Watson, "Wordsworth and Constable," *Review of English Studies,* 13 (1962), 361–67.

33 Eliot did know Constable's biographer, C. R. Leslie (Haight, p. 83), and she could have seen the six important Constable pictures in the Sheepshanks bequest, which came to the South Kensington Museum in 1857. But Ruskin's low estimate of Constable's art would hardly have escaped her notice.

34 *The Mill on the Floss* (V, 1:49 and V, 3:92–93). This vision is affirmed both by Philip Wakem and by the narrator. It is the

sort of Ovidian fancy that George Eliot treats ironically in the cases of Hetty Sorrel and Gwendolen Harleth.

35   These monitory images include "a remarkable series of pictures representing the Prodigal Son in the costume of Sir Charles Grandison: (I, 4:43), and "a dreadful picture" of a witch's trial by water (I, 3:21). The former is an English version of one of the favorite moral themes of Dutch and Flemish genre painting, and the latter is "Ducking a Witch," drawn by G. M. Brighty and engraved by T. Wallis for a new edition of Daniel Defoe's *Satan's Devices: or the Political History of the Devil: Ancient and Modern* (London: T. Kelley, 1819), p. 229.

36   Davis, "Pictorialism in George Eliot's Art," p. 72.

37   See Jones, *George Eliot,* p. 97.

38   Edward Dowden, *Contemporary Review,* 29 (1877); rpt. Carroll, ed., *George Eliot: The Critical Heritage,* p. 440. See also John P. Kearny, "Time and Beauty in *Daniel Deronda,*" *Nineteenth-Century Fiction,* 26 (1971), 301.

39   See John Gage, "Turner and the Picturesque," *The Burlington Magazine,* 107 (1965), 16–25, 75–81.

40   *Modern Painters,* vol. IV, pt. V, chap. i, paras. 12–13, in *Works,* VI, 19. See also *The Stones of Venice,* vol. III, chap. iii, para. 35, in *Works,* XI, 159–60; and *The Seven Lamps of Architecture,* VI, 11–12, in *Works,* VIII, 234–36.

41   See the excellent discussions of Ruskin's conception of the picturesque in Landow, *The Aesthetic and Critical Theories of John Ruskin,* pp. 222–38, and Hewison, *John Ruskin,* pp. 32–53. See also John Alford, "Romanticism via Ruskin," *Art News,* 42 (December 1943), 11–13.

42   See Hussey, *The Picturesque,* p. 70, and Hipple, *The Beautiful, the Sublime, and the Picturesque,* p. 220.

43   See Thomas Love Peacock, *Works,* ed. Henry Cole (London, 1875), I, 213; Hunt and Willis, *The Genius of the Place,* pp. 376–79; Kingsley, *Yeast,* chapter 3; *Birket Foster's Pictures of English Landscape with Pictures in Words by Tom Taylor* (London: Routledge, Warne, and Routledge, 1863), no. 18; Conrad, *The Victorian Treasure-House,* pp. 78–79; William D. Tempelman, "Thoreau, Moralist of the Picturesque," *Publications of the Modern Language Association,* 47 (1932), 879, 884; and Leo Levy, "Picturesque Style in *The House of the Seven Gables,*" *New England Quarterly,* 39 (1966), 150.

44 See Price, "The Picturesque Moment," p. 283.

45 *Modern Painters*, vol. IV, pt. V, chap. xix, para. 6, in *Works*, VI, 390.

46 Eliot praises "the pictures of Teniers" and "the ragged boys of Murillo" for their "truthfulness." The latter are probably the two beggar-boys in the Dulwich College Gallery, whom she admired in 1859 and may have seen earlier (Cross, II, 88). Eliot criticizes the figures in Holman Hunt's *The Hireling Shepherd* as "not much more real than the idyllic swains and damsels of our chimney ornaments." She was thinking of the stylized rococo shepherds and shepherdesses to be found on many Dresden-china statuettes. Her instinct about Hunt's source was accurate enough, for the iconography of the central figures in *The Hireling Shepherd* comes from an erotic pastoral painting by Boucher entitled *Pensent-t-ils à ce mouton?*; see Macmillan, "Holman Hunt's *Hireling Shepherd*." But Eliot failed to see the moral criticism of the rococo pastoral tradition involved in Hunt's use of the figures and of monitory emblematic details such as the death's-head moth. *The Hireling Shepherd* is actually much closer than Eliot supposed to the Ruskinian version of pastoral advocated in her essay and exemplified in *Adam Bede*.

47 See Rodee, "Scenes of Rural and Urban Poverty," pp. 4, 37, 91. On English rural genre painting before 1855, see Roberts, "Marriage, Redundancy, or Sin," p. 55.

48 Arnold Kettle, "Felix Holt the Radical," in Hardy, ed., *Critical Essays on George Eliot*, p. 100. For an opposing view, see Conrad, *The Victorian Treasure-House*, pp. 39–40.

49 On the symbolic contrast between Loamshire and Stonyshire, see George Creeger, "The Interpretation of *Adam Bede*," *Journal of English Literary History*, 23 (1956), 218–38; rpt. *George Eliot: A Collection of Critical Essays*, pp. 86–106.

50 In his picture of *Dinah Morris Preaching on Hayslope Green* (1861), E. H. Corbould neatly solves the problem posed by George Eliot's detailed and richly significant landscape description. He simply turns Dinah around, so that her backdrop is not the panoramic vista, as in the novel, but Hayslope village and a piece of the intervening green, an altogether more manageable subject (fig. 25).

51 Davis, "Pictorialism in George Eliot's Art," p. 115.

52 *Modern Painters,* vol. IV, pt. V, chap. xix, paras. 3, 4, in *Works,* VI, 387–89.

53 John Murdoch, "English Realism," p. 321n., has suggested an analogue for this passage of *Adam Bede* in Caspar David Friedrich's Tetschen Altarpiece, also known as *A Cross in the Mountains* (1808). There is no evidence that Eliot knew or admired the work of Friedrich, but her affinities with him are nonetheless strong.

54 On the recognition scene in *The Ambassadors,* see Garrett, *Scene and Symbol,* pp. 122–23. On James's use of picturesque landscapes in general, see Richards, "Henry James's Use of the Visual Arts," pp. 81–87.

55 Squires, *The Pastoral Novel,* pp. 60–67. The Red Deeps in *The Mill on the Floss* is a vestigial *locus amoenus.* See also Ware Commons in chapter 12 of John Fowles's *The French Lieutenant's Woman* (1969).

56 Murdoch, "English Realism," p. 322, links a different passage of *Adam Bede* with *Waiting.* There is no evidence that George Eliot knew Millais's picture, now in the City Art Gallery at Birmingham.

57 Barbara Hardy, "The Surface of the Novel: Chapter 30," in *Middlemarch: Critical Approaches to the Novel,* p. 165.

58 For Ruskin's attack on aerial perspective, see *The Stones of Venice,* vol. III, chap. ii, paras. 18–22, in *Works,* XI, 57–60.

59 Sterne, parodying the jargon of art critics, speaks of "the corregiescity of Correggio" in *Tristram Shandy* (Bk. III, chap. 12). Hazlitt quotes the phrase in his essay on "English Students at Rome"; see *The Complete Works of William Hazlitt,* ed. P. P. Howe (London: J. M. Dent and Sons, 1933), XVII, 139.

60 Richard S. Lyons, "The Method of *Middlemarch,*" *Nineteenth-Century Fiction,* 21 (1966), 43.

61 E. D. H. Johnson, "The Truer Message: Setting in *Emma, Middlemarch,* and *Howard's End,*" in *Romantic and Modern: Revaluations of Literary Tradition,* ed. George Bornstein (Pittsburgh: University of Pittsburgh Press, 1977), p. 200.

62 "Art and Belles Lettres," *Westminster Review,* 9 (1856), 631.

63 John Stuart Mill, "Tennyson's Poems," *London Review,* I (1835), 404–05.

64 Davis, "Pictorialism in George Eliot's Art," p. 121, and Johnson,

"The Truer Message," p. 202. Gillian Beer, "Myth and the Single Consciousness," p. 103, finds "echoes of Christian mythology" in the scene.

65 *Modern Painters,* vol. IV, pt. V, chap. i, para. 7, in *Works,* VI, 14–15.

66 See J. A. Schmoll gen. Eisenwerth, "Fensterbilder: Motivketten in der europäischen Malerei," in *Studien zur Kunst des 19. Jahrhunderts,* No. VI–*Beiträge zur Motivkunde des 19. Jahrhunderts* (Munich: Prestel Verlag, 1970), pp. 13–165; Rosenblum, *Modern Painting and the Northern Romantic Tradition,* p. 66; and Finke, *German Painting,* pp. 25–26, 87.

67 Henry Auster, "George Eliot and the Modern Temper," in *The Worlds of Victorian Fiction,* ed. Jerome H. Buckley (Cambridge, Mass.: Harvard University Press, 1975), p. 97.

Chapter 9

1 All of these illustrations were reprinted in *The Cornhill Gallery* (London, 1865).

2 See Leonée and Richard Ormond, *Lord Leighton* (New Haven: Yale University Press, 1975), pp. 5–6. Leighton had also studied in Frankfurt with Eduard Steinle, sometimes called "the last of the Nazarenes"; see Andrews, *The Nazarenes,* p. 69.

3 Mrs. Russell Barrington, *The Life, Letters, and Work of Frederic Baron Leighton* (New York: Macmillan, 1906), I, 48.

4 Ibid., I, 186n. Peter Conrad, *The Victorian Treasure-House,* p. 126, compares the conscientious historicism of *Cimabue's Madonna* with that of *Romola.*

5 On Leighton's acquaintance with Vasari subjects in Florentine academic painting, see Leonée and Richard Ormond, *Lord Leighton,* p. 8. On the popularity of such subjects in French salon painting, see Francis Haskell, "The Old Masters in Nineteenth-Century French Painting," *The Art Quarterly,* 34 (1971), 55–85. On the connections between paintings from Vasari and Browning's artist-monologues, see Leonée Ormond, "Browning and Painting," in *Robert Browning,* ed. Isobel Armstrong (London: G. Bell & Sons, 1974), pp. 184–210.

6 Leighton's other pictures in 1862 were *The Star of Bethlehem, Odalisque, Sisters, Duett,* and *Sea Echoes.* No. 229 in the same exhibition was *Alexander VI signing the death-warrant of*

Savonarola by P. Levin. On 4 April 1864 the Leweses visited Leighton's studio for a private view of the pictures he was sending to the academy that year; among them were *Dante at Verona* and *Orpheus and Eurydice* (*Letters,* IV, 143).

7 "Ariadne in Naxos" and "The Great God Pan"; see Leonée and Richard Ormond, *Lord Leighton,* p. 58.

8 See George and Edward Dalziel, *The Brothers Dalziel: A Record of Fifty Years' Work 1840-1890* (London: Methuen, 1901), pp. 237–44, and T. S. R. Boase, "Biblical Illustration in Nineteenth-Century English Art," *Journal of the Warburg and Courtauld Institutes,* 29 (1966), 363.

9 Barrington, *Life,* II, 95.

10 See Leonée and Richard Ormond, *Lord Leighton,* p. 58. I am indebted to the Ormonds and to Gordon S. Haight for helping me to identify the stages through which Leighton's work passed.

11 See Percy Muir, *Victorian Illustrated Books* (London: B. T. Batsford, 1971), pp. 6–7.

12 On the Sixties school, see Gleeson White, *English Illustration: 'The Sixties'* (1897; rpt. Bath: Kingsmead Reprints, 1970); Joseph Pennell, *Modern Illustration* (London: George Bell, 1895); George and Edward Dalziel, *The Brothers Dalziel*; Forrest Reid, *Illustrators of the Sixties* (1928; rpt. New York: Dover Publications, 1975); T. S. R. Boase, *English Art 1800–1876* (Oxford: Clarendon Press, 1959), pp. 288–91; and N. John Hall, "Millais's Illustrations for Trollope," *University of Pennsylvania Library Chronicle,* 42 (Spring 1977), 23–45.

13 See John Harvey, *Victorian Novelists and Their Illustrators* (London: Sidgwick and Jackson, 1970), p. 161, and Anthony Burton, "Thackeray's Collaborations with Cruikshank, Doyle, and Walker," *Costerus,* 2 (1974), 174.

14 See Reid, *Illustrators of the Sixties,* p. 207.

15 Fra Bartolommeo's famous portrait of Savonarola is evoked in chapter 15 of *Romola* and was a central inspiration of the novel (*Letters,* III, 295).

16 Leonée and Richard Ormond, *Lord-Leighton,* p. 59.

17 Barrington, *Life,* II, 96–102, and *Letters,* IV, 39–64.

18 In later years George Eliot told P. G. Hamerton that she was pleased with the *Romola* illustrations, especially with "Leighton's conception of Tito"; see Philip Gilbert Hamerton, *Portfolio Papers* (London: Seeley & Co., 1889), p. 317.

19 Eliot did not care for the illustrations in Blackwood's "cheap edition" of her works and personally requested Mrs. William Allingham, whose work she admired, to undertake the illustration of *Romola* for inclusion in that edition (*Letters,* VI, 341). Eliot did, however, like Birket Foster's title-page vignette of the Hall Farm in the 1867 Illustrated Edition of *Adam Bede* (*Letters,* IV, 366).

20 Lewes, "Introduction" to *Female Characters of Goethe, from the Original Drawings of William Kaulbach,* 2d ed. (London: Frederick Bruckmann, 1874).

21 For other statements of this principle, see Hamerton, *Portfolio Papers,* p. 312; Ralph Cohen, *The Art of Discrimination,* pp. 2, 250–54; and Anthony Burton, "Cruikshank as an Illustrator of Fiction," in *George Cruikshank: A Revaluation,* ed. Robert L. Patten, special number of *The Princeton University Library Chronicle,* 35 (1973–74), 93. On the interpretive element in Pre-Raphaelite illustration, see White, *English Illustration,* p. 106, Reid, *Illustrators of the Sixties,* pp. 31–32; Laurence Housman, *Arthur Boyd Houghton* (London: Kegan Paul, Trench, Trubner & Co., 1896), p. 13; and Allan R. Life, "The Periodical Illustrations of John Everett Millais and Their Literary Interpretation," *Victorian Periodicals Newsletter,* 9 (June 1976), 50–68.

22 See J. Hillis Miller and David Borowitz, *Charles Dickens and George Cruikshank* (Los Angeles: William Andrews Clark Memorial Library, 1971), pp. 42–53, and Ronald Paulson, "The Tradition of Comic Illustration from Hogarth to Cruikshank," in Patten, ed., *George Cruikshank: A Revaluation,* pp. 36–37. Despite these reminders, a simplistic criterion of fidelity to the text remains surprisingly tenacious in critical discussions of English and American literary illustration; see, for example, Nevius, *Cooper's Landscapes,* pp. 113–23.

23 Catherine Gordon, "The Illustration of Sir Walter Scott: Nineteenth-Century Enthusiasm and Adaptation," *Journal of the Warburg and Courtauld Institutes,* 34 (1971), 297–317.

24 Miller, *Charles Dickens and George Cruikshank,* p. 52.

25 By this I do not mean what Miller (p. 49) calls the artist's "unique sensibility or angle of vision on the world." I am referring to a property of the artist's pictures, not of his mind.

26 Miller, *Charles Dickens and George Cruikshank,* p. 53.

27 See *Romantic Art in Britain: Paintings and Drawings, 1760–1869* (Philadelphia Museum of Art, 1968), pp. 68–69.

28 For this dating, see *Official Catalogue of the Fine Art Department, International Exhibition 1862*, p. 14, and *Letters*, IV, 50.

29 The lantern is based on one at the Strozzi Palace in Florence which Leighton sketched in 1852; see Leonée and Richard Ormond, *Lord Leighton*, p. 59.

30 On the sources of Wright's painting, see *Romantic Art in Britain*, p. 68, and Benedict Nicolson, "Joseph Wright's Early Subject Pictures," *The Burlington Magazine*, 96 (1954), 72–80.

31 Leonée and Richard Ormond, *Lord Leighton*, pp. 55, 85.

32 See Philip Hook, "The Classical Revival in English Painting," *Connoisseur*, 192 (1976), 124.

33 Leonée and Richard Ormond, *Lord Leighton*, p. 66.

34 Ibid., p. 59.

35 Ibid., p. 77, pl. 166.

36 Ibid., p. 89, pl. 102.

37 Ibid., p. 89.

38 Burton, "Cruikshank as an Illustrator of Fiction," p. 94.

39 See Cohen, *The Art of Discrimination*, p. 257, and Michael Steig, "The Iconography of *David Copperfield*," *Hartford Studies in Literature*, 2 (1970), 1–18.

40 His uncertainty about Piero prompted Leighton to ask George Eliot whether she knew of any extant portraits of the artist (*Letters*, IV, 55).

41 On the tradition of "la représentation des cabinets d'amateurs," see Legrand, *Les peintres flamands de genre*, pp. 14–15. On the most famous English painting in this mode, see Mary Webster Lightbown, "Zoffany's Painting of Charles Towneley's Library in Park Street," *The Burlington Magazine*, 106 (1964), 316–23. Leighton's illustration follows the convention, noted by Paulson (*Emblem and Expression*, pp. 153–54), of creating significant visual relationships between the collector and his artifacts; thus Bardo is associated with the marble-eyed Roman bust, whereas Romola is linked with the beautiful feminine torso at the foot of the reading-desk.

42 See *Letters*, IV, 40, and Sybille Pantazzi, "Author and Illustrator: Images in Confrontation," *Victorian Periodicals Newsletter*, 9 (June 1976), 47.

43 See Leonée and Richard Ormond, *Lord Leighton*, plate 16.

44 See especially E. H. Gombrich, *Art and Illusion: A Study in the Psychology of Pictorial Representation* (Princeton: Princeton University Press, 1972).

Chapter 10

1 Barrington, *Life,* I, 2.
2 DeLaura, "*Romola* and the Origin of the Paterian View of Life," pp. 225–26.
3 Beer, "Music and the Visual Arts in the Novels of George Eliot," p. 18.
4 Eliot, "Art and Belles Lettres," *Westminster Review,* 65 (1856), 626.
5 Richard L. Stein, *The Ritual of Interpretation: The Fine Arts as Literature in Ruskin, Rossetti, and Pater* (Cambridge, Mass.: Harvard University Press, 1975), p. 38.

Index